The Holocaust

PROBLEMS IN EUROPEAN
CIVILIZATION SERIES

The Holocaust

PROBLEMS AND PERSPECTIVES OF INTERPRETATION

Edited by

Donald L. Niewyk

Southern Methodist University

Houghton Mifflin Company   Boston New York

Editor-in-Chief: Jean Woy
Assistant Editor: Keith Mahoney
Associate Project Editor: Gabrielle Stone
Senior Production/Design Coordinator: Sarah Ambrose
Manufacturing Coordinator: Michael O'Dea
Marketing Manager: Clint Crockett

Senior Designer: Henry Rachlin
Cover Image: *The Deportation of a Jewish Family* by Chris
Baeckman, Holland 1944.
Cover Design: Alwin Velásquez

Printed in the U.S.A.

Library of Congress Catalog Number: 96-76939

ISBN: 0–669–41700–9

00 01-DH-10 9 8 7

Preface

A vast literature on the Holocaust has appeared during the last three decades. Growing interest in the subject has been accompanied by impatience with earlier views of the mass murder of Europe's Jews as either unworthy of special attention — "just another Nazi atrocity" — or else too horrible to be understood or even imagined by those who were not there. If the former view belittled the genocide conducted by the Nazis, the latter led to its mystification. But today, more than ever before, scholars, students, and the public at large sense that much depends on coming to terms with the Holocaust. For who can say who the victims might be next time?

This volume brings together some of the most important and stimulating contributions to our understanding of the genocide of the Jews. These readings have been selected for the purpose of acquainting students with a variety of views, including those of the victims themselves. After an introduction that contains a brief summary of the history of the Holocaust, Part I explores its origins and the roles played by Hitler and the Nazi hierarchy in setting the murder machinery in motion. Part II compares two conflicting views of Jewish behavior during the Holocaust and invites readers to evaluate them on the basis of selected survivors' memoirs. Part III examines charges that the Jews failed to put up any significant resistance to their tormentors. Part IV, new to this edition, looks at the motivations of Holocaust perpetrators. Part V inquires into the attitudes and actions of bystanders — Germans, western Europeans, and especially, Poles — while the Jews were being murdered. Finally, Part VI considers the possibilities that some Jews might have been saved from the gas chambers through negotiation, military action, or diplomatic intercession by outside forces.

I am grateful to Professors Richard S. Levy, Michael Stanislawski, Steven Zipperstein, Celia Applegate, Lorenz J. Firsching, Sybil Milton, Marc Saperstein, Christopher Browning, and Daniel Goldhagen for their valuable advice in selecting the contents of this book. Naturally no two scholars would be likely to choose exactly the same readings on any complex topic such as this one, and any failings with regard to the selections included in this volume must be attributed to me.

For their expert editorial assistance in assembling this anthology, I want to thank James Miller and Lauren Johnson. In addition, I'd like to thank the staff at Houghton Mifflin, including Jean Woy, Keith Mahoney, Gabrielle Stone, and Irene Cinelli.

Donald L. Niewyk

Contents

Chronology of Events

1939	September 1	Nazi Germany attacks Poland, beginning World War II.
	September–December	Polish Jews from areas annexed to Germany expelled to central Poland.
	October–November	First ghettos established in Poland.
1940	January	Start of "Euthanasia Program" — mental patients gassed in Germany.
	April 27	Himmler orders creation of Auschwitz concentration camp.
	October	Warsaw ghetto established.
1941	June 22	Nazi Germany invades the Soviet Union, unleashing mobile killing units in the process.
	July 31	Göring orders Heydrich to formulate a "comprehensive solution to the Jewish problem."
	September 3	First experimental gassings of Soviet POWs at Auschwitz.
	September 29–30	Mass murder of Jews at Babi Yar, near Kiev.
	December 8	Gassing of Jews begins at Chelmno.
1942	January 20	Wannsee Conference outlines measures to exterminate Jews.
	March–July	Exterminations begin at "Operation Reinhard" camps: Belzec, Sobibor, and Treblinka.
	May 4	Start of mass gassings at Auschwitz.
	July	Start of deportations of Dutch and French Jews to Auschwitz and of Warsaw Jews to Treblinka.

	September	Start of mass gassings at Maidanek.
	December 16	Gypsies ordered sent to Auschwitz.
1943	March 15	Start of deportations of Greek Jews to Auschwitz.
	April 19– May 16	Warsaw ghetto uprising.
	June	Himmler orders liquidation of Polish and Russian ghettos.
	August 2	Revolt at Treblinka.
	September	7,500 Danish Jews rescued.
	October 14	Revolt at Sobibor.
	October 19	Operation Reinhard declared complete; Belzec, Sobibor, and Treblinka cease functioning.
1944	April 27	Start of deportations of Hungarian Jews to Auschwitz.
	July 24	Soviet troops liberate Maidanek.
	August	The last ghetto, Lodz, liquidated.
	October 7	Revolt by Jewish *Sonderkommando* at Auschwitz.
	November 27	Himmler orders end of gassings.
1945	January 27	Soviet troops liberate Auschwitz.
	April 11	Buchenwald is first concentration camp in Germany to be liberated by the Allies.
	May 7	Nazi Germany surrenders.

Glossary

AK	"Home Army," the main Polish underground army.
Barbarossa	The German plan to attack the USSR in 1941.
Einsatzgruppen	"Emergency Squads," mobile killing units of the SS.
General Government	Nazi-occupied central Poland during World War II.
Judenrat	Jewish Council.
Kapos	Prisoner foremen.
Katyn Forest	Site of Soviet massacre of Polish officers, 1941.
NSDAP	The Nazi Party.
RSHA	"Reich Security Main Office," the central coordinating agency of the SS.
SD	"Security Service," the SS intelligence agency.
Sonderkommando	"Special Detail" of prisoners or of Nazi units.
Waffen SS	"Armed SS," military units of the SS.
Wehrmacht	The German armed services.
ZOB	"Jewish Fighting Organization" in Poland.

Poland, 1939–1945, with Locations of Concentration and Extermination Camps

■ Concentration camp

☠ Extermination camp

☠■ Concentration and extermination camp

▨ Annexed by Germany, 1939

▨ General Government—occupied by Germany, 1939

▨ Territory occupied by USSR, 1939, and Germany, 1941

Note: In addition to the concentration and extermination camps shown here, there were hundreds of forced labor camps for Jews, Poles, Gypsies, Russians, and other victims of the Nazis.

Estimated Jewish Deaths in the Holocaust

Country	Pre-Holocaust Jewish Population	Minimum Loss	Maximum Loss
Austria	185,000	50,000	65,000
Belgium	66,000	24,000	29,000
Czechoslovakia	357,000	260,000	277,000
Denmark	8,000	60	100
Estonia	4,500	1,500	2,000
France	350,000	77,000	83,000
Germany	566,000	125,000	142,000
Greece	77,000	60,000	67,000
Hungary	825,000	402,000	569,000
Italy	45,000	7,500	9,000
Latvia	92,000	70,000	72,000
Lithuania	168,000	130,000	143,000
Luxembourg	3,500	1,000	2,000
Netherlands	140,000	100,000	106,000
Norway	1,700	800	800
Poland	3,300,000	2,900,000	3,000,000
Roumania	760,000	270,000	287,000
Soviet Union	3,000,000	700,000	1,100,000
Yugoslavia	70,000	56,000	63,000
TOTAL	10,018,700	5,234,860	6,016,900

Note: There is uncertainty about these statistics because they must be drawn from fragmentary and sometimes inaccurate German records, Jewish sources, and various prewar and postwar census data. Border changes and diverse ways of defining Jews further complicate the estimates. Two somewhat different approaches to figuring Jewish losses may be found in Raul Hilberg, *The Destruction of the European Jews*, rev. ed. (New York: Holmes and Meier, 1985), pp. 1201–1220; and Israel Gutman and Robert Rozett, "Estimated Jewish Losses in the Holocaust," in *Encyclopedia of the Holocaust*, ed. Israel Gutman, vol. IV (New York: Macmillan, 1990), pp. 1797–1802.

Introduction

The Nazi slaughter of European Jewry during World War II, commonly referred to as the Holocaust,[1] occupies a special place in recent history. The genocide of innocents by one of the world's most advanced nations mocks our optimism about human reason and progress. It raises doubts about our ability to live together on the same planet with people of other cultures and persuasions.

Before it happened, virtually no one thought such a slaughter likely or even possible. To be sure, for many centuries antisemitism had been widespread throughout Europe. Devout Christians had viewed the Jews as Christ killers and deliberate misbelievers, but conversion was considered the inevitable cure, however long it might be delayed. Following the Jews' emancipation from discriminatory laws in the nineteenth century, the old religious antisemitism was joined by secular nationalisms that challenged the Jews' qualifications for membership in the nations in which they lived. Secular antisemites objected when the Jews, newly freed from persecution, often tied their destinies to growing capitalist economies, to liberal and socialist political movements, and to modernist trends in music, literature, architecture, and the theater. Success in banking, business, politics, and culture rendered the Jews far more visible than their small numbers ordinarily would have warranted. Europeans who felt threatened by modernity, and especially those who lost status as the result of economic changes and the spread of democracy, sometimes blamed the Jews for their plight.

Political parties that advocated antisemitism rarely won victories before 1914, but anti-Jewish attitudes became fairly commonplace in many European countries and in North America. If the "good" German (or Frenchman, or Russian) was viewed as pious, conservative, patriotic, and trusting, "the Jew" was stereotyped as materialistic, left-leaning, cosmopolitan, and manipulative. Antisemitism before World War I was more a war of words and a way to define one's own national identity ("we are the opposite of everything the Jews are") than a program for radical action. Antisemitic minorities that took the "Jewish problem" seriously advocated solving it by

---

[1]The word "Holocaust," first used in the late 1950s to refer to the Jewish tragedy during World War II, means "a burnt sacrifice offered solely to God." The problems with that meaning are obvious, but no other term has succeeded in taking its place. It has become a convention, and we will have to make do with it.

assimilating the Jews into the larger population or else repealing their emancipation and restoring the old discriminatory laws. Even the most inveterate antisemites, those who postulated a Jewish conspiracy to dominate the Western economy, recommended expulsion as a remedy of last resort. Only a few marginal figures hinted darkly at the need for still more radical policies. Hence antisemitism was a necessary precondition for the Holocaust but did not make it inevitable.

An ominous development of the late nineteenth century was the rise of modern biological racial "science." This now discredited offshoot of Darwinism assumed the primacy and permanence of inherited racial characteristics. Married to antisemitism, it could lead to the view that Jews were irredeemably depraved. But even those who played dangerously with racist ideas probably had no thought of racial annihilation, of genocide. When it became known that the Turks had committed genocide against the Armenians during World War I, Europeans dismissed it as the act of non-Christian barbarians acting in the fury of war. Western civilization, they supposed, had risen above such savagery.

After World War I, Europe experienced severe economic and political upheavals that intensified antisemitism almost everywhere. Added to the old charges that Jews were unpatriotic and greedy was the accusation that they were behind the spread of Communism. The participation of a few Jewish intellectuals and politicians in the Bolshevik Revolution in Russia and in Communist revolts elsewhere in Europe rendered this plausible. In Germany, Adolf Hitler, who had become a racial antisemite as a youth in his native Austria, made attacks on the Jews from the beginning of his career in the Nazi party in postwar Munich. Such attacks became staples of Nazi propaganda throughout his rise to power, but they were not employed consistently. In their efforts to be all things to all Germans, Hitler and his followers played up opposition to the Jews when it helped them, and played it down when it did not. As a result, no one could be sure what, if anything, the Nazis would do to the Jews in a future Third Reich. Germans who supported Hitler did so less because he was an antisemite than because he seemed to provide a clear alternative to the failed German republic and a means of defense against a threatening Communist movement. And yet, antisemitism was sufficiently commonplace in Germany to be at least acceptable to the 44 percent of Germans who voted for the Nazis in the last elections held before Hitler became dictator in 1933.

Once in power, the Nazis showed that they were sincere antisemites from the start. Jews were fired from government jobs, and were subjected to discriminatory laws, sporadic economic boycotts, and physical violence, all designed to make them despair of a future in Germany and leave the country. In 1935 the infamous Nuremberg Laws deprived Jews of their German citizenship and outlawed sexual relations between Jews and "Aryans." The Nazis did not, however, press too hard against the Jews at first, fearing to upset the German economy, which was still recovering from the Great Depression, and worrying that fierce antisemitism would spawn costly foreign boycotts of German goods. Jews were sent to concentration camps only if they had been active in anti-Nazi political parties. As they moved toward the 1936 Berlin Olympics, Hitler and his lackeys were on their best behavior in order to make a positive impression on the world.

After 1936 the ever more self-confident Nazis increasingly cracked down on what was left of the Jewish community in Germany. The Third Reich was moving toward war and wanted to rid itself of its Jewish "fifth column" as soon as possible. More and more Jewish firms were "Aryanized," that is, expropriated by the state at a fraction of their value, and Jews were banned from most occupations. On the night of November 9–10, 1938, the Nazis used the excuse of a revenge attack by a Jewish teenager on a German diplomat in Paris to unleash a nationwide pogrom against the Jews. Named the "Crystal Night" for the broken windowglass that littered the streets and sidewalks in Jewish neighborhoods, it resulted in the burning of hundreds of synagogues and the beatings and arrests of thousands of Jews, several of whom were murdered. For the first time large numbers of Jews were sent indiscriminately to concentration camps and released only if they promised to leave Germany promptly. Most wanted desperately to go. The problem was finding countries that would admit them. Nazi confiscation of Jewish wealth meant that they would be penniless refugees seeking shelter in a world still sunk in depression. The democracies, preoccupied with their own problems, showed only limited understanding of the plight of the German Jews. Palestine was then a British mandate with an Arab majority that fiercely resisted any increase in the Jewish presence there. Never very particular about legalities, the Nazis resorted to "dumping" groups of Jews without papers across borders or aboard outward-bound ships. By the outbreak of the Second World War in September 1939, only just over half of the approximately 780,000 German and Austrian Jews had managed to emigrate from Hitler's expanding empire.

Emigration or else deportation remained the Nazi solutions to the "Jewish problem" throughout the first year of the War. Nazi officials discussed sending all of Europe's Jews to the French-held island of Madagascar in the Indian Ocean or else to Siberia as soon as victory was won. Hence the large numbers of Polish Jews who had come under Nazi control were concentrated in cities and large towns, and subjected to brutal forced labor, but rarely anything worse. Jews in Hitler's enlarged "Greater Germany" began to be deported to ghettos in the part of occupied Poland not annexed to Germany or, in smaller numbers, to France for eventual deportation to distant dumping grounds. What ultimately made such deportations impossible was Hitler's failure to bring his war to a successful conclusion. Unable to defeat or reach a negotiated settlement with Great Britain, Hitler turned his armies against the Soviet Union in June 1941. At the same time the mass murder of Soviet Jews began.

As German forces swept across eastern Poland and into the USSR in the summer and fall of 1941, they were followed immediately by the mobile killing units called *Einsatzgruppen* (literally "emergency squads") under the command of the SS, which was the chief agency of terror throughout Nazi-dominated Europe. These units were assigned the task of liquidating all known or potential enemies of the Third Reich, especially political officials, Communist party functionaries, and Jews. Typically the *Einsatzgruppen* herded their victims into fields to be shot and buried in mass graves, as happened to 33,000, most of them Jews, at Babi Yar just outside Kiev on September 29–30, 1941. Occasionally the killers enlisted local antisemites to help do their work for them. Altogether the 3,000 members of the *Einsatzgruppen* were responsible for the deaths of between one and two million Jews.

Although the *Einsatzgruppen* continued their murderous sweeps on the eastern front into the later war years, they were never adequate to cope with all of the eleven million European Jews. As early as July 1941 Hermann Göring ordered Reinhard Heydrich, after Heinrich Himmler the most powerful SS leader, to formulate a "comprehensive solution to the Jewish problem." Heydrich's plan, approved in secrecy at a conference of top Nazi officials held in the Berlin suburb of Wannsee in January 1942, called for the SS to exterminate some Jews slowly, through forced labor, and the rest quickly in gas chambers. Under its terms, Jews from all over Nazi-occupied Europe continued to be concentrated in Eastern European cities where they were forced to work for the Germans in closed ghettos or at nearby labor camps. Those who were too young, too old, too weak, or simply not needed for work were sent to newly constructed extermination centers according to carefully calculated timetables corresponding to the camps' capacities.

The Jewish ghettos of such cities as Warsaw, Lodz, Vilna, and Minsk were hideously overcrowded places of starvation, backbreaking labor, disease, and death. Because they were imperfectly sealed off from the rest of the cities, smuggling alone made it possible for the inhabitants to survive. The exception, and then only in relative terms, was the Theresienstadt ghetto in Czechoslovakia, where prominent prisoners were held under model conditions to fool the International Red Cross and other inquisitive foreigners. The Nazis assigned control of the ghettos to Jewish Councils that governed with the aid of Jewish police. The Germans maintained overall control by executing uncooperative Jewish leaders and by holding the ghetto residents to "collective responsibility," shooting the family and friends of those who resisted or escaped. Only rarely did the Jewish Councils themselves resist, preferring to buy time by producing goods that were badly needed by the Nazi war machine. The one major ghetto uprising, that in Warsaw in April and May 1943, came only after most of its occupants had been transported to death camps. Hopes of saving at least a remnant of the Jewish communities were dashed when the last of the ghettos were liquidated in the summer of 1944, shortly before the arrival of the Red Army. Their pitiful remnants were sent to labor and extermination camps closer to Germany.

The extermination centers, all located in territory conquered from Poland, were of two kinds. Chelmno and the "Operation Reinhard" camps[2] of Treblinka, Belzec, and Sobibor were strictly death camps. Except for small crews of slave laborers who disposed of the corpses, the victims were gassed immediately on their arrival. The Nazis were already experienced in the use of poison gas. It had been

---

[2]They came to be so-named for Reinhard Heydrich after his assassination by Czech patriots in Prague in May 1942.

employed in their secret "euthanasia" program in which more than 70,000 incurably ill Germans, most of them mental patients, had been murdered in gas chambers. Experimental gassings of Soviet POWs at Auschwitz and of Jews at Chelmno had occurred late in 1941. By the time all four death camps were shut down late in 1943, they had claimed approximately 1,600,000 lives. Almost all of the victims were Jews.

Unlike the four camps dedicated exclusively to extermination, Auschwitz and Maidanek were both killing and slave labor centers. New arrivals were selected for work or immediate death. Auschwitz, by far the larger of the two, had been founded in 1940 as a concentration camp for first Polish and then Soviet POWs. During the Holocaust it grew to occupy several square miles covered by huge synthetic rubber and oil factories, various smaller military industries, administration buildings, and barracks for more than 70,000 prisoners. For the prisoners, labor in the factories and the outlying coal mines was hell. Tens of thousands of them were literally worked to death, to be replaced from the constant inflow of new slaves. Some were resourceful enough, or lucky enough, to land desirable positions in the camp kitchens, offices, or medical wards. Others were chosen by SS doctors for hideous medical experiments that resulted in painful deaths and permanent mutilations. All were deprived of adequate food, clothing, rest, privacy, and human dignity. In addition, at Auschwitz-Birkenau, gas chambers and crematoria disposed of at least a million victims, most of them Jewish, before they ceased to function in November 1944.

As Hitler's empire crumbled, the pathetic survivors of the camps were force-marched to concentration and slave-labor facilities in Germany itself. There, in the final frantic days of the war their food was cut off and many died of starvation and disease. When British and American forces liberated camps such as Bergen-Belsen, Dachau, and Buchenwald, the grounds were strewn with the dead and dying. Estimates of the Jewish dead from all causes — shootings, gassings, hyperexploitation, and general privation — range from just over five million to more than six million. These were not the only innocent victims of Nazi racial madness. Hundreds of thousands of Gypsies and millions of Polish slave laborers and Soviet prisoners of war died at German hands. With the possible exception of the Gypsies, however, only the Jews had been targeted for total annihilation for purely racial reasons, making the Holocaust unique in world history.

The enormity of the Holocaust was not fully apparent to the world in the immediate postwar years. At the Nuremberg trials of the major German war criminals it was treated as part of Nazi crimes against humanity in general. Survivors set down their experiences in memoirs, and the Yad Vashem research institute established in Jerusalem in 1954 painstakingly assembled documentary evidnce of Nazi efforts to eradicate the Jews. But not until the 1960's did the Holocaust become genuinely visible to scholars, students, and the general public.

The trial of Adolf Eichmann in 1961 is usually regarded as the turning point. Eichmann, the SS expert on Jewish affairs who had organized the transportation of Jews from all over Europe to the death camps, escaped to Argentina after the war. Discovered and kidnapped by Israeli agents, his trial in Jerusalem created a sensation. Also in the year of the Eichmann trial Raul Hilberg's *The Destruction of the European Jews* made its appearance. The first massively documented history of the Holocaust, it remains today in a revised version one of the standard works on the subject. Since then thousands of books and articles on the Holocaust have appeared, making it one of the best-documented events in recent history. Efforts to deny that it ever happened can safely be regarded as the work of malicious zealots.

With the main features of the Holocaust clearly visible to all but the willfully blind, historians have turned their attention to aspects of the story for which the evidence is incomplete or ambiguous. These are not minor matters by any means, but turn on such issues as Hitler's role in the event, Jewish responses to persecution, and reactions by onlookers both inside and outside Nazi-controlled Europe. This anthology presents selected points of view on these issues with the goal of sketching the broad outlines of the debates and the trends in historiography. Readers are urged to suppress the perhaps natural inclination to suppose that all of these well-crafted arguments are equally valid, since, as we shall see, historians sometimes evaluate the evidence in very different ways. Nor should anyone feel compelled arbitrarily to adopt one position or another. Comparing historical interpretations sheds light on the process by which we come closer to the truth through inquiry and debate. If it stimulates thought and curiosity about the Holocaust, useful titles are given in the "Suggestions for Additional Reading" at the end of this volume.

A shop in Vienna marked "Jew" and defaced with a swastika shortly after the German seizure of Austria in 1938. (UPI Bettmann Newsphotos)

PART

I

Origins of the Holocaust

Variety of Opinion

We shall begin by focusing on the earliest attestable symptoms in the biographical record of Hitler's personal antisemitism, his congenital hatred for the Jews. For the line that leads from these earliest manifestations to the liquidation orders that Hitler personally issued during the war . . . is a direct one.

Gerald Fleming

Hitler gave no formal order to carry out the Final Solution of the "European Jewish question." . . . It was founded upon improvised measures that were rooted in earlier stages of planning and also escalated them.

Hans Mommsen

It would appear that the euphoria of victory in the summer of 1941 and the intoxicating vision of Europe at their feet, not the dashed expectations and frustrations of the last months of the year, induced the Nazis to set the fateful process in motion.

Christopher R. Browning

9

How did the Nazi "Final Solution" come about? For a significant group of historians the answer is clear: Hitler harbored murderous intentions from a very early date and merely waited for the right moment to act. Once his war provided sufficient cover, he ordered the Holocaust. These historians are now referred to as "intentionalists" for stressing what they view as the Führer's unswerving intention to slaughter the Jews. In recent years various aspects of this view have been challenged by historians known as "functionalists." Finding no convincing evidence of a Hitlerian master plan to exterminate the Jews, they see instead a series of decentralized anti-Jewish measures, functionally related to one another, that culminated in genocide. The debate between the two schools raises serious questions about how much of the Holocaust can be explained purely in terms of Hitler's hatred for the Jews.

Gerald Fleming draws a direct line from Hitler's early anti-semitism to the Holocaust in one of the most powerful statements of the intentionalist viewpoint. Central to this argument are Hitler's absolute hatred of the Jews and his absolute control over the Third Reich; he awaited only the opportunity afforded in 1941 by his invasion of the Soviet Union. Although other intentionalists interpret the increasingly severe persecution of the Jews in prewar Nazi Germany as part of a systematic program leading to annihilation, Fleming concentrates on concrete plans for murder. The euthanasia of mental patients in Germany was, in his view, deliberate technical preparation for genocide. The reason why no written order by Hitler commanding the killing of the Jews has ever been found, Fleming argues, is that Hitler, a master dissembler, knew how to keep his responsibility for atrocities secret by using code words and giving verbal orders. But no one who actually carried out the murderous orders passed on by others ever doubted that "it is the Führer's wish." And, says Fleming, they were right.

Hans Mommsen doubts that there was any such Führer order or any long-standing intention on Hitler's part to annihilate the Jews. Together with other historians of the functionalist school, he sees the Holocaust emerging from improvisation, not plan. The functionalists have argued that before the war Hitler showed little interest in anti-Jewish policies, which evolved as the result of pressures from radical antisemites at lower levels of the Nazi party or else from initiatives by other Nazi leaders, such as economic boss Hermann Göring and propaganda minister Joseph Goebbels. Mommsen here presents his reconstruction of events following the German invasion of the USSR in June 1941. Nazi rulers in occupied Eastern Europe, faced with additional millions of unwanted Jews and eager to solve this problem in ways they thought Hitler would approve, adopted increasingly barbarous methods. This process of "cumulative radicalization" of Nazi policies obviously was made possible by Hitler's fierce antisemitism, but the decisions themselves did not come directly from the dictator; he merely was informed of the steps that led to genocide sometime after they were taken, and did not disapprove. Mommsen's interpretation is part of a broader analysis of the Nazi regime as a chaotic assemblage of rival party and state institutions that constantly fought one another for power and influence. In this controversial view, Hitler, far from being absolute master of the Third Reich, was in some ways a "weak dictator" in that he was lazy, indecisive, and preoccupied with foreign policy and military concerns. He preferred to leave most other matters to his subordinates. The reader should ponder whether that was likely to be true in the particular case of the Holocaust.

Christopher R. Browning takes a middle position. Calling himself a "moderate functionalist," he, too, sees no clear evidence that Hitler was planning genocide all along. But he also assembles suggestive evidence that the dictator gave a "nod" that his minions enthusiastically interpreted as a green light to plan and prepare genocide. This happened during the summer of 1941, when the Nazis were so jubilant over their victories in Russia that they thought anything, even genocide, was possible. Browning accepts the postwar testimony of Adolf Eichmann and of Auschwitz commander Rudolf Höss that they learned of plans to murder the European Jews during those summer months. In the passage reproduced here, Browning argues that the timing of the construction of the first death camps similarly points to a decision made at that time. Not everyone in the Nazi hierarchy learned about it right away, which gave the impression of incoherence to Nazi

Jewish policy as other departments of party and state pursued the old deportation plans. But by October, Hitler's order was firmly taking hold.

It should already be apparent that different historians have used the same body of evidence to reach widely conflicting interpretations. Here, as is not infrequently true in historical research, the sources are incomplete. Maybe one day some resourceful scholar will uncover direct evidence, perhaps something like a signed and dated Führer order for the Holocaust. Until then, we will have to make up our minds how to reconstruct the circumstantial evidence in the most sensible way.

Gerald Fleming

"It Is the Führer's Wish"

We shall begin by focusing on the earliest attestable symptoms in the biographical record of Hitler's personal anti-Semitism, his congenital hatred for the Jews. For the line that leads from these early manifestations to the liquidation orders that Hitler personally issued during the war — the actual target of this investigation — is a direct one. A sample taken from Hitler's utterances over the years reveals this striking continuity: Hitler's remark to his childhood friend, August Kubizek, as the two passed the small synagogue in the Bethlehemstrasse in Linz, "That does not belong here in Linz"; Hitler's unshakable conviction that "the Jews had continued to perform ritual murders" up to the most recent past; the Führer's statement on 21 October 1941, at noon in the Führer's Headquarters, preserved in a memorandum signed by Martin Bormann:[1] "When we finally stamp out this plague, we shall have accomplished for mankind a deed whose significance our men out there on the battlefield cannot

[1]Bormann was head of the Nazi Party Chancellory. — Ed.

even imagine yet"; and Hitler's assertion four days later, in the presence of Himmler and Heydrich: "It is good that we are preceded by an aura of terror for our plans to exterminate Jewry." This unbroken continuity of explicit utterances was reflected in a more or less tacit continuity of deeds. Hitler's anti-Semitism in his Linz years (1904–1907) was followed by his introduction into the Viennese "Antisemitenbund" (Anti-Semite Association) in April 1908. Much later, but still to be ranged along the same continuum, were the first shootings of German Jews in Fort IX in Kovno on 25 November 1941 and in the Rumbuli Forest outside Riga on 30 November 1941 at 8:15 A.M. And in the following year report number 51, addressed "to the Führer, re: campaign against gangs," inventories 362,211 Jews executed for the period from 1 September to 1 December 1942. This report from the Reichsführer-SS Heinrich Himmler was submitted to Hitler on 31 December 1942 by Hitler's personal adjutant, Hauptsturmführer Pfeiffer, as indicated in Pfeiffer's hand on page one of the report.

Hitler's objection at fifteen or sixteen to the synagogue in Linz raises the question whether the young Hitler might have been influenced by remarks at home or by his classmates, and perhaps also his teachers, at the Realschule in Linz, and had thereby learned to understand the word "Jew" in an increasingly pejorative sense. Hitler had the following to say about his attitude in Linz to the Jewish problem: "It is difficult if not impossible for me to say today when the word 'Jew' first gave me pause for serious reflection. I cannot recall ever having even heard the word in my father's house while he was still alive. I believe that the old gentleman would have regarded as culturally backward a particular emphasis given to this word. . . . At school I found no reason to question the picture I received from home, either. . . . It was not until I was fourteen or fifteen that I came across the word 'Jew' more frequently, partly in connection with political discussions."

According to Hitler's childhood friend, August Kubizek, nicknamed "Gustl" by Hitler (the two youths were very close from 1904 to 1908, chiefly because of their mutual love of Wagner's music), Hitler "touched up" the portrait of his father in *Mein Kampf* to give it a more "liberal tint." The customs inspector Alois Hitler was, again according to Kubizek, a regular at the local worthies' lunch table in his Leonding pub, where many believed in the ideas of the anti-Semitic politician August Georg von Schönerer. Clearly, even Hitler's father had wanted "nothing to do with the Jews." Hitler's account of his schooldays in Linz further conceals the fact that certain teachers at the Realschule in Linz were unequivocal anti-Semites and had "openly professed their anti-Semitism," and that Hitler himself was, already in 1904 at the tender age of fifteen, "a pronounced anti-Semite. " According to Werner Maser, schoolmates of Hitler from his Linz period independently concur on the fact that as early as his schooldays of 1904–1905, Hitler was a "biological anti-Semite," and that this biological anti-Semitism of the young Hitler can be traced back to a programmatic pamphlet of the "Alldeutsche Verband" (Pan-German League), published in 1904, which Hitler had read and which he had openly talked about during recesses at the Realschule in Linz. This pamphlet, they allege, was studded with references to biological anti-Semitism. In the 1890s the Alldeutsche Verband had indeed issued warnings against the "Jewish peril," demanding that rigorous restrictions be imposed on the "Jewish press" — which included the *Berliner Tageblatt* and the *Frankfurter Zeitung* — and advocating that the Jews be treated as "foreigners." Yet in the registered publications of the Alldeutsche Verband from the years 1891–1901, there is no trace of a discussion of biological anti-Semitism. Since, according to Kubizek's fully credible recollection, Adolf Hitler went off to Vienna already "a pronounced anti-Semite," we cannot rule out the possibility that he had been influenced by individual teachers at the Realschule in Linz. . . .

The friendship between Hitler and his childhood companion Kubizek was cemented by their mutual passion for the music of Richard Wagner. Wagner's tracts and essays were readily available in lending libraries in Linz, and the sixteen- or seventeen-year-old Hitler absorbed the works and life of Wagner with systematic diligence. Today it seems clear that the genius of this artist, unfortunately for the German people, contributed to the creation of a political monster, for the collected works of Wagner exerted a decisive influence on Hitler's development and consequently on National Socialism. To quote Hitler's own words, "Whoever wishes to comprehend National Socialism must first know Richard Wagner." And with good reason. In his *Bayreuther Blätter* Wagner gave expression to a synoptic view of history and of the world, to a *Weltanschauung* that was founded on a racial theory. Transmitted through the writings and pamphlets of Georg von Lanz-Liebenfels and Theodor Fritsch, which Hitler read and reread in his first years in Vienna, the substance of Wagner's thought found its way into the heart of the National Socialist *Weltanschauung* — the National Socialist racial doctrine.

This racial doctrine rested on the following axioms: (1) The fundamental inequality of mankind, determined by genetic traits; (2) the existence of different human types (races); (3) the existence of an irrevocably inferior race, a kind of anti-race: the Jews. From these postulates the Nazis deduced that the best and purest race (the Aryan-Germanic race) has a preordained title to rule and to prevail; and that therefore, the races of inferior status — the less significant, culturally impoverished races — exist to serve the master race. Finally, at the bottom end of the scale, the anti-race (the Jewish race) represents "worthless life" (*unwertes Leben*).

Like Hitler, Wagner looked forward to a time when there would be "no more Jews." Like Hitler, he yearned for "the emancipation from the yoke of Judaism" and spoke urgently of "this war of liberation." Whether Wagner would have assented to the nucleus of Hitler's *Weltanschauung* — to the "elimination," "ridding," "evacuation," "reduction," (read: "extermination") of the Jews — is another question.

Feeling himself to be misunderstood and thwarted by his surroundings, the young Hitler lost himself in Wagner's world. There he could find consolation, understanding, and the welcome affirmation of his personal prejudices — an afffirmation he later repeatedly sought and would later also admit had provided the major impetus for his reading. It is no accident that Hitler was especially fond of quoting from act 2, scene 3 of the *Meistersinger:*

> *Und doch's will halt nicht gehen:* —
> *Ich fühl's and kann's nicht verstehen,* —
> *kann's nicht behalten, doch auch nicht vergessen:*
> *und fass ich es ganz, kann ich's nicht ermessen!* —

> *And yet, it just won't go* —
> *I feel it, and cannot understand it* —
> *I cannot hold on to it, nor yet forget it;*
> *and if I grasp it wholly, I cannot measure it!* —

For Hitler in his Vienna years these lines were an ever-potent spell by which his hero Wagner had lashed out at his contemporaries' lack of understanding. Shortly before the war broke out in 1939, the Reich Chancellor revealed to Winifred Wagner in Bayreuth that it was the production of the *Rienzi* in Linz, when he was seventeen, which first incited him to become a politician. "That was the hour when it all began," by which Hitler meant that his experience of the Wagner opera had opened his eyes to his mission in life: to elevate his nation to greatness and power.

Hitler's definitive decision to pursue a political career came, according to him, when he discovered that he was a uniquely gifted public speaker. In other words, Hitler saw, with increasing certainty, that he could convince the German masses of his entitlement to power and leadership. But the real mission that lay behind this claim to power was formulated in his maxim: "Indem ich mich des Juden erwehre, kämpfe ich für das Werk des Herrn" (By keeping the Jews at bay, I fight for the good Lord's way). With this slogan Hitler, the anti-Semitic nationalist, sought to present himself as a new *Christus militans*. With his linguistic shrewdness he had wisely come up with a formula that the National Socialist propagandists would inevitably make use of. Its overtones of traditional Christian anti-Semitism were easy enough to link up with the Nazi brand of biological anti-Semitism; the move from the one form of anti-Semitism to the other constituted a big step, but nonetheless, no more than a step.

Hitler's frustration in his youth with a world that he felt misunderstood him reached crisis proportions when, as an art student at eighteen and nineteen, he failed the examination that would have gained him entry to the art academy of Vienna. His unsatisfactory portfolio was the official reason for his failure; but Hitler placed the blame for this great disappointment on the Jews. Many years later he recounted to friends that he had learned, after the exams were over, that four of the seven members of the examination committee were Jews; whereupon he had sent the director of the academy a letter of protest that closed with the threat, "The Jews will pay for this." The incident was a total confabulation. And yet, this retrospective explanation for his failure of the entrance exams indicates the degree to which Hitler was gripped by a pathological hatred for the Jews. The personal component of this hatred combined with Hitler's repeatedly articulated delusion of a global Jewish conspiracy to serve as a safety valve that, ironically, protected him from a future, subjectively insurmountable mental illness. . . .

In retrospect, we can say that Hitler's political career was directly shaped by two experiences, which in their combined impact dictated both his political goal and the means by which to achieve it. The first experience was his service on the front and the shock of defeat; the second was his growing awareness that he could mobilize the masses, that he could virtually "conquer" them with his powers of suggestion. Of the two, the first in particular left an indelible imprint on Hitler for life. "A November 1918 shall never repeat itself in German history," Hitler vowed on 1 September 1939, the day on which World War II broke out. His experience of the short-lived November Revolution of 1918, which he regarded as a Jewish-Marxist plot against the German nation, translated over time into the obsessive idea that Providence had elected him to perform an unprecedented feat in the history of the German people. In its radicalization, his hatred for the Jews thus acquired the dimensions of a destiny. Nearly five months after his Reichstag address of 1 September 1939, Hitler prophesied to Czechoslovak Foreign Minister František Chvalkovsky: "The Jews shall be annihilated in our land. They shall not have staged 9 November 1918 with impunity. That day shall be avenged!"

As Kubizek reports, the *Rienzi* production in Linz provoked in Hitler his sense of mission. It was 9 November 1918, however, that gave him his true raison d'être: the unswerving conviction that the antichrist — Jewry — must be exterminated. From his speeches of 1919 and 1920 to his political testament of 29 April 1945, Hitler continuously held this goal up before the German nation. These key experiences prior to his political career thus formed the basis on which, in the early twenties, Hitler developed a strategy that would enable him to realize his goal.

The plan entailed several steps. The first stage in Hitler's political conception was to "uncover the Jewish imperialist designs on world hegemony and parade them before the largest segments of our nation" (27 January 1921), to immunize the masses against the "Jewish-Marxist poison" of internationalism and class struggle. Already at this rudimentary stage the masses were to be roused and made ready for the day when they would put an end — by violence, if necessary — to the "Jewish dominion" that had afflicted the nation since 1918.

"Hatred, burning hatred — this is what we want to pour into the souls of our millions of fellow Germans, until the flame of rage ignites in Germany and avenges the corrupters of our nation," wrote Hitler on 8 February 1921, in *Der Völkische Beobachter*.[2] The second step in Hitler's strategy was to translate agitation into an effective mass movement. Propaganda and organizing would be crucial in the third step, which would establish the prerequisites for victory in the final phase of the struggle against the domestic political enemy. Step four would definitively grant domestic peace through the founding of a "genuinely National Socialist Grossdeutschland [German and Austrian nation]" to be headed by a national "government invested with power and authority." The military and economic power of Grossdeutschland would, in step five, assure the permanent establishment, for Führer and country, of Germany's proper place in the system of world powers. By "proper place," Hitler had nothing less in mind for his nation than a preeminent, superpower role in a restructured, new Europe. The open enemy of this new Europe, the eternal archenemy to whom the collective guilt for all evil was inexplicably attached, was of course "the Jew." . . .

In his capacity as chief administrator of the Four Year Plan, on 24 January 1939, Göring assigned Reinhard Heydrich, the head of the Security Police, to bring "the Jewish question . . . to as favorable a solution as present circumstances permit," through emigration. At this stage, the objective of the German Jewish policy was still, in general, to remove the Jews from Germany and from the already annexed territories. With this object in view, Göring created a central agency for Jewish emigration in 1939 and then turned it over to Heydrich. In line with this policy, the Foreign Office proposed, after the fall of France in July 1940, that all Jews be removed not simply from the Reich and the annexed territories, but from Europe as a whole. It further recommended that "the island of Madagascar be requested as a resettlement area for the Jews from France."

The Madagascar Plan had not yet been conceived when, in June 1940, Heydrich informed Joachim von Ribbentrop, the Reich Foreign Secretary, that more than 200,000 Jews had "emigrated from the Reich," but the "problem as a whole" — namely, the fact that almost

[2]The main Nazi Party newspaper. — Ed.

three and a quarter million Jews stood under German jurisdiction — could no longer be resolved *"through emigration"* (emphasis in the original). "A territorial Final Solution has thus become necessary," Heydrich wrote to von Ribbentrop; while in a predated memorandum from the summer of 1940, in connection with the "treatment of foreign nationals in the East," Himmler wrote, "I hope to see the concept of Jew completely eradicated, through a large-scale deportation of the entire Jewish population to Africa, or else to some colony." At the same time, "out of inner conviction," he still rejected "the physical extermination of a race through Bolshevik methods as un-Germanic and impracticable."

It was almost a year before the Jewish policy of the Third Reich took its fateful turn, in the summer of 1941. On 10–11 November 1941, the Higher SS and Police Leader Ostland, Friedrich Jeckeln, received precise liquidation instructions in the Prinz Albrechtstrasse headquarters from the Reichsführer-SS Himmler, in which we find — as transmitted by Jeckeln — the formula, "the Führer's wish" (*des Führers Wunsch*). In place of emigration from Europe, the solution was now couched in terms of an "evacuation to the East." This formula stood for the physical liquidation, and the liquidation through labor, of the Jewish deportees.

On 20 May 1941, Walter Schellenberg, acting for Heydrich, notified the departments of the Security Police by circular that "in view of the undoubtedly imminent Final Solution of the Jewish question," the emigration of Jews from France and Belgium was to be forbidden. This decree was issued two months after Hitler had addressed the assembled generals and disclosed his views on the conduct of the war in the East that "deviated from the normal rules." On 1 October, Heydrich's Adviser on Jewish Affairs in the Reich Main Security Office, Adolf Eichmann, broke the news to the German Jews. On 23 October, five days after the departure of the first RSHA convoy of Jews out of Berlin, Eichmann's immediate superior, SS-Brigadeführer Heinrich Müller of the Gestapo, issued a related set of instructions to the offices of the Sipo (*Sicherheitspolizei* or Security Police) and the SD (*Sicherheitsdienst*, or Security Service). This same Gestapo chief, on 1 August 1941, had wired coded instructions to the commanders of the four Einsatzgruppen (operational task forces) to the effect that "the Führer is to be kept informed continually from here about the work of the Einsatzgruppen in the East." It was doubtless "the Führer's wish" to be continually updated on the mass shootings conducted by Einsatzgruppen A, B, C, and D. Since we find that this expression of Hitler's will, equivalent in force to a command, was closely connected with the mass shootings that occurred outside Riga in November and December of 1941, the following comments are worth quoting. Dr. Werner Best[3] has said: "I can attest that, seen 'from below,' that is, from the perspective of those who received the orders, the formulas 'der Führer wunscht' [the Führer wishes] and 'der Führer hat befohlen' [the Führer has ordered] were perfectly synonymous. . . . At the receiving end as well . . . the word 'wish' was used as an equivalent to 'order.'" And according to Richard Schulze-Kossens: "The verbal expressions 'der Führer wünscht,' 'es ist des Führers Wunsch' [it is the Führer's wish], and 'was des Führers Wunsch ist' [which is the Führer's wish] . . . are identical in meaning. Although these are not direct orders, they are, nonetheless, to be interpreted as such. If, therefore, he were to tell me to signal to the Leibstandarte [Hitler's bodyguard] . . . 'it is my wish that they do this and that immediately,' then the commander of the Leibstandarte naturally would view this as an order. The 'wish' is always communicated by a third party and is not explicitly passed on as a Führer-order. But it does indeed have the force of an order."

The planned killing of all Jews that could be seized was a comprehensive task. To synchronize the simultaneous liquidations of great masses at the appropriate sites required a procedure thought out with absolute precision down to the smallest detail. Also needed was an organization that would ensure the swift and regular flow of Jews to be delivered to the extermination camps. In the summer of 1941, in line with directives issued by the Führer, three commissions were handed out: one from the Reichsführer-SS Heinrich Himmler to the Commandant of Auschwitz, Rudolf Höss, another, likewise from Himmler, to Christian Wirth, and a third, dated 31 July 1941, passed on by Göring to Heydrich. Himmler's assignment to Höss was issued verbally, as were those to the killing specialist of the euthanasia program, Christian Wirth. Göring's written commission resulted in the postponed Wannsee Conference of 20 January 1942.

---

[3] The leading Gestapo lawyer and legal advisor to Hitler. — Ed.

Since 1936 it had become common practice to pass on the powers that Göring had received by the ordinance of 18 October 1936 to special deputies whose spheres of jurisdiction overlapped the normal departmental competence. Fritz Sauckel, authorized personally by Hitler to supervise the deployment of labor forces, likewise derived his powers via Göring from the ordinance of 18 October 1936. But apart from direct assignments from Hitler, Sauckel operated independently. When conflicts arose with Albert Speer, the Reich Minister for Armament and Production, Sauckel looked not to Göring for assistance, but to Hitler. Göring was only the formal middleman; he transferred "his competencies for directing the highest Reich officials" onto others, as Hitler authorized him to do. By the same token, it was Himmler, rather than Göring, who was Heydrich's actual superior in the latter's function as "the deputy for the preparation of the Final Solution of the European Jewish question." It was from Reichsführer-SS Himmler that Heydrich received the order to proceed with the execution of the Final Solution of the Jewish question.

In the summer of 1941, Himmler disclosed to Rudolf Höss, "without the presence of an adjutant," that the Führer had ordered "the Final Solution of the Jewish question" and that now "whatever Jews we can reach" were to be eliminated "without exception" during the war. Höss would receive further details from Adolf Eichmann, who would see him. Eichmann did contact Höss shortly afterward, in Auschwitz, where the large-scale operations were to be "forced through." Eichmann further initiated Höss into the plans for the liquidation actions that had been envisaged for the individual countries.

First destined for Auschwitz were the Jews in Upper East Silesia and the adjacent parts of occupied Poland; simultaneously at first, and thereafter depending upon their location, the Jews from Germany and Czechoslovakia; finally, those from the West — France, Belgium, and Holland. The logistics of the liquidations were discussed: "Only gas could be considered." To eliminate the anticipated masses by shootings alone would have been physically impossible, and also too great a strain on the SS men who would have to perform this assignment — especially "in view of the women and children."

At the time of their discussion in Auschwitz, neither of the two men knew yet which gas would be considered for the mass liquidations. In any case, Eichmann ruled out "the use of carbon-monoxide gas through nozzles in shower facilities, a method that had been applied in the elimination of mental patients at a few locations in the Reich," because it would require "too many new buildings," and because "the procurement of sufficient quantities of gas for such great numbers [would be] very problematic." But after Zyklon B had been tested on Russian prisoners of war in Auschwitz in autumn 1941 and had proven its effectiveness in "bringing about instantaneous death," Höss passed the news on to Eichmann during the latter's next visit to Auschwitz, "and we decided," Höss writes, "to employ this gas in future mass exterminations."

Before Rudolf Höss and Adolf Eichmann determined which gas would be used in the mass liquidations of European Jews at Auschwitz, the RFSS Himmler had witnessed the shooting, which he personally initiated, of between 120 and 180 Jewish men and women — Russian civilians from Minsk who had not been active as partisans. On the basis of this gruesome personal experience, he ordered that a better means of killing be found; this did not, however, prevent the Einsatzgruppen from following through the orders they had received at the beginning of the Russian military campaign. By the end of 1941 they had shot approximately one million people to death.

Did individual leaders of the Einsatzkommandos ask Himmler who it was that bore the responsibility for the mass exterminations of the Jews? One of these Einsatz leaders, at any rate, did venture to ask. In the middle of August 1941, in Minsk, on the very day when the 120 to 180 Jewish civilians were shot, the head of Einsatzkommando unit 8, Obersturmbannführer (Lieutenant Colonel) Dr. Otto Bradfisch, put the key question to Himmler. As Bradfisch recalls: "As soon as Himmler arrived in Minsk, I turned to him and asked him who was taking responsibility for the mass extermination of the Jews. Himmler made this conversation the occasion for a speech, in which he told the members of Einsatzkommando 8, as well as those members of the Security Police who were present, not to worry — the orders had been personally given by Hitler. It was a question, then, of a Führer-order, which had the force of law, and he and Hitler alone bore the responsibility for these orders." Himmler's private reply to Bradfisch before the execution had been no different:

"Himmler answered me in a fairly sharp tone that these orders had come from Hitler as the supreme Führer of the German government, and that they had the force of law."

The question of responsibility was raised again during this same period of time, by the director of department III in Himmler's command staff, the SS and Police Judge Horst Bender. "Himmler categorically stated that this measure had been personally ordered by Hitler, out of political and military considerations, and it therefore stood above all jurisdiction, including the SS and police jurisdiction."

It should also be noted here that of the 6,500 German Jews who were deported to Minsk, only 11 survived the action.

Bruno Streckenbach, a department head of the Reich Main Security Office, who was entrusted with selecting the personnel of the Einsatzgruppen, also brought up the subject of the mass exterminations before Heydrich and Himmler. Heydrich's response, in September 1941, was "that it was pointless to criticize this operation or to oppose it. This was strictly a matter of a Führer-order; for in connection with this war, which represented the final, violent clash of two irreconcilably opposed *Weltanschauungen*, the Führer had expressed his resolve to find simultaneously a solution to the Jewish problem." Himmler's comments struck a similar, "though much sharper note" when, following Heydrich's death, Streckenbach again raised the issue: "Himmler vehemently forbade any criticism. Further, he stressed that this was a matter of a 'Führer-order,' and that he considered it his historical obligation to carry out the order, which affected the police and the Wehrmacht equally, with whatever means he had at his disposal."

Gottlob Berger, Chief of the SS Main Administrative Office, also broached the subject of the mass liquidations with Himmler, once prior to, and a second time following, Heydrich's death. On the first occasion, Himmler "was visibly pained, and he cited as authority orders from Hitler." On the next occasion, Himmler indicated that he shared Berger's view "that it would have been better not to have created the so-called Einsatzgruppen."

Now what did the Reichsführer SS have to say about the responsibility and authorizations for the mass exterminations of the Jews in his secret speeches? Four crucial excerpts will clarify this point:

1. Himmler's secret address of 26 January 1944 before an audience of generals who had gathered in the municipal theater in Posen is described at length in a statutory declaration made by Freiherr von Gersdorff:

   At the end of January 1944 I had to attend a meeting that was held in connection with a training course for commanding generals and commanding officers of army corps. The meeting was convened by the highest-ranking National Socialist political officer, General Reineke, and was held in the municipal theater of Posen, the former capital of the so-called Warthegau. Three hundred generals, admirals, and general staff offficers from the German Wehrmacht were present.

   On 26 January 1944, the Reichsführer SS and Chief of Police Heinrich Himmler gave a briefing on the domestic and foreign security situation. In this context, he also dealt with the Jewish question. Naturally I can no longer recall the exact wording of his remarks. But I can assure you that the following represents, if not the very words he spoke, then at least the gist of these: "When the Führer gave me the order to carry out the total solution of the Jewish question, I at first hesitated, uncertain whether I could demand of my worthy SS men the execution of such a horrid assignment. . . . But this was ultimately a matter of a Führer-order, and therefore I could have no misgivings. In the meantime, the assignment has been carried out, and there is no longer a Jewish question."

2. On 5 May 1944 in Sonthofen, the Reichsführer-SS Himmler had the following to say on this same complex of issues: "Please understand how difficult it was for me to perform this soldierly command, which I followed and performed out of obedience and the fullest conviction."

3. On 24 May 1944, Himmler's words on the ordered Final Solution were as follows: "Another question that was of decisive importance for the internal security of the Reich and of Europe as a whole was the Jewish question. It was resolved uncompromisingly as ordered and with complete understanding."

4. And on 21 June 1944: "It was the most dreadful assignment and the most awful commission that an organization could ever receive: the commission to solve the Jewish question."

These remarks by Himmler, the authenticity of which is beyond all doubt, need only the following commentary: This dreadful assignment, this most awful commission, this soldierly order can only have been given to the Reichsführer SS by Adolf Hitler; no one else stood between them in the chain of command. Since Himmler had received this liquidation order from his Führer, the Reichsführer SS wished to make it clear to his listeners that, for all his obedience, had the commission not come from "the highest level" he could *never* have given the command on his *own* initiative. . . .

On the night of 28 to 29 April [1945], after Hitler had finally granted his faithful mistress, Eva Braun, her long-cherished wish for marriage, he called in his secretary to dictate his personal and political testament, to be typed in three copies.

This testament is the last venomous word of the demagogic orator, the obsessed zealot, the battling, and now fallen, prophet. Beyond the collapse of the Third Reich, Hitler sought once again to bind the German nation to an eternal, wretched hatred for the Jews: "Centuries may lapse, but from the ruins of our cities and monuments will rise anew the hatred for that people to whom we owe all this, they who are ultimately responsible: international Jewry and its acolytes!"

What, after all, had Hitler announced before members of the press on 10 November 1938? "Circumstances have forced me to talk for decades practically only of peace. . . . This constraint was the reason why I only talked peace over the years. Then it became necessary to realign gradually the psychological bearings of the German people and to make it slowly clear to them that there are things which must be accomplished by means of violence if they cannot be accomplished by peaceful means." Hitler's meaning was clearer still on 25 January 1939, when he addressed the officer training class of 1938: "Only the most recent periods have managed to show a dichotomy, so to speak, between war and politics; of course, such irreconcilability could not objectively and actually exist. . . . During the great periods that shape history, that is, in the formation of the state, politics is in effect the art of the possible; which is to say, attaining an objective by using every conceivable means: persuasion, obligation, intelligence, determination, kindness, shrewdness, even brutality — that is, even the sword, when other means fail."

He had not left "a shred of doubt," Hitler resumed in his political testament some six years later, that "the real culprit in this murderous contest," Judaism, would be "called to account." "Further, I have made it quite clear that this time, . . . the real culprit must expiate his guilt, though by more humane means." . . .

Hitler's self-justifying remarks about the expiation of Jewish guilt through "more humane means" wore this face in sordid practice, stripped of their incidental components of opportunism, servility, weakness, and petty-bourgeois obsequiousness of a following whose idealism he abused. Shortly before 4:00 A.M. on 29 April 1945, Hitler dictated the final sentence of his political testament: "Above all, I obligate the leaders of the nation and their following to a strict observance of the racial laws, and to a merciless resistance to the poisoners of all peoples, international Jewry."

As he had done earlier in the pages of *Mein Kampf,* Hitler again attributed to the Jews "a unificatory devil-function," to justify this hatred.

Adolf Hitler's Final Solution ideology represented in stark reality a cult of the irrational bordering on lunacy yet advanced under the guise of ice-cold reason, a cult whose founder saw himself as the benefactor and savior of his Greater German Reich.

Now that the huge surge of power had ebbed away and the great gamble had failed, the only remaining course for Hitler, given his painful realization of all that had happened, was suicide. On 30 April 1945, between 2:00 and 3:00 p.m., Adolf Hitler, the most notorious anti-Semite of all time, put his Walther pistol against his right temple, bit into a cyanide capsule, and pulled the trigger.

Hans Mommsen

There Was No Führer Order

Hitler gave no formal order to carry out the Final Solution of the "European Jewish question." . . . Preparations for the systematic implementation of the Final Solution were begun only in late autumn of 1941 and were not based on a written order. There are also many internal reasons for believing that Hitler never gave such an order orally, either.

The exclusively metaphoric language in which the *Führer* discussed the "Jewish problem," as well as his general reluctance to take decisions that might have caused public opposition and perhaps have had to be withdrawn, make it unlikely that he would have come to a binding decision. Remarkably, even in early 1942 Hitler considered reactivating the abandoned Madagascar Plan. If one attributes such behaviour to a desire to dissemble even among his closest friends, then it would simply be evidence of the extent to which he shrank from referring openly to the factory-style destruction of human life. His conduct in this and other matters, however, appears to be due less to an extreme intellectual cynicism than to an ability to dissociate himself completely from reality.

Hitler's speech to the *Reichstag* on 30 January 1939 is cited more than any other as evidence of his early intention to destroy the Jews systematically:

> *Today I shall once more be a prophet. If the international Jewish financiers inside and outside Europe should again succeed in plunging the nations into another world war, then the result will not be the Bolshevization of the world and thus a victory for Jewry, but the annihilation of the Jewish Race in Europe. . . .*

Although at first sight the connection with the subsequent genocide policy may appear to be evident, the political motive behind this statement is in fact ambivalent. Such threats were intended primarily

Text by Hans Mommsen, "The Realization of the Unthinkable" in Gerhard Hirschfeld (ed.), *The Policies of Genocide*, 1986. Reprinted by permission of Unwin Hyman, HarperCollins Publishers Ltd.

to exert pressure on the Western nations, particularly Britain and the United States. They are thus connected with the hostage argument, which had surfaced as early as 1923: in that year the radical anti-semite Hermann Esser had argued that, in the event of a French invasion, one German Jew should be shot for every French soldier who stepped onto German soil. . . .

Hitler considered the "Jewish question" from a visionary political perspective that did not reflect the real situation. The struggle against Jewry was for him an almost metaphysical objective; as his "Political Testament" reveals, it eventually took on a chiliastic dimension. Hitler had always sympathized with "spontaneous" attacks on Jews. They reflected his belief that anti-semitic opinions could be used both for mass mobilization and for the integration of the party's supporters. A campaign of extermination, implemented with extreme secrecy and with an increasingly bad conscience (as in the case of Himmler), was not completely compatible with this concept. . . .

The realization of the Final Solution became psychologically possible because Hitler's phrase concerning the "destruction of the Jewish race in Europe" was adopted as a direct maxim for action, particularly by Himmler. Hitler, it must be conceded, was the ideological and political author of the Final Solution. However, it was translated from an apparently utopian programme into a concrete strategy partly because of the problems he created for himself, and partly because of the ambitions of Heinrich Himmler and his SS to achieve the millennium in the *Führer's* own lifetime and thus to provide special proof of the indispensability of the SS within the National Socialist power structure. Himmler's statements indicate that he intended to fulfil in one single, "masterful," self-sacrificial act something that had actually been intended as a timeless programme. He thus directed a large part of his energies towards a programme that, for Hitler, had only a low priority in comparison with the conduct of the war.

Himmler and Heydrich thus played a decisive role in implementing the Final Solution. Nevertheless, it must be stressed that a purely personalized interpretation would prevent full understanding of the issue. The eventual step towards mass destruction occurred at the end of a complex political process. During this process, internal antagonisms within the system gradually blocked all

alternative options, so that the physical liquidation of the Jews ultimately appeared to be the only way out. . . .

The attack on the Soviet Union on 22 June 1941, and the daz-
zling early successes of the German armies, influenced the planning
process in the RSHA. The Commissar Order,[1] and the deliberate use
of the *Einsatzgruppen* to liquidate Jewish population groups in the
occupied areas, signalled the start of a new phase. Initially, however,
the belief that a "solution" of the "Jewish question" could be implemented only after the war was retained. In summer 1941 the Nazi
leadership expected the Soviet Union to be defeated in a matter of
weeks, and at latest by autumn of that year, although they accepted
that skirmishes might continue in the Asiatic regions of the Soviet
Union. It was taken for granted that Britain would have been forced
to yield by this time.

Only against this background is a correct interpretation possible
of the authorization given by Goering to Heydrich on 31 July 1941 in
which Heydrich was instructed "to present for my early consideration
an overall draft plan describing the organizational, technical and
material requirements for carrying out the Final Solution which we
seek." The authorization, drafted by Eichmann and submitted to
Goering for his signature, is not connected with any preceding order
from Hitler, although the existence of such an order has often been
suspected. Its context is clearly that of the strategy pursued until that
point, which was not yet directed towards systematic extermination.
Its aim was a "solution" that would no longer be implemented under
the cover of war in the East.

At the same time, the *Einsatzgruppen* were carrying out their
massacres. These were based on the Commissar Order, unlike the
systematic policy of the Final Solution that followed. There can be
no doubt that Hitler approved and supported these measures,
although it is a matter for conjecture how far he took notice of actual
events. Approximately 1.4 million Jews were murdered in these
extensive operations, which were carried out on the pretext of secur-
ing the rear area of the battle zone; Hitler had from the outset
declared the campaign against the Soviet Union to be a war of anni-

---

[1] Hitler's order of May 1941 for the execution of all captured Soviet political officials.
— Ed.

hilation. Nevertheless, it is almost inexplicable that the leaders and members of the *Einsatzgruppen* lent themselves to this unimaginably barbarous slaughter and that the Army — with few exceptions — either stood by, weapons at the ready, or in many cases gave active support to the *Einsatzgruppen*. In the framework of National Socialist propaganda against "subhumanity," the Russian Jews, like the Polish Jews before them, were classed as the lowest of the low. The massacres also provided an opportunity to rid the German-occupied territories of a part of the Jewish population, which had by then increased beyond any "manageable" size. The fact that the killings were carried out on oral orders only, and that the *Einsatzgruppen* were careful to avoid giving only racial reasons for them in their reports, indicates that the decision to liquidate the entire Jewish population had not yet fully matured.

A decisive turning-point was necessary before leading offficials would adopt a course of action that had been unthinkable only a short time before. Certainly, everything was propelling events towards a violent "solution" of the "Jewish problem" which the Nazis had created for themselves. The logistic prerequisites for the mass movement of populations were completely lacking. Conditions in the improvised ghettos were appalling, and appeared completely unacceptable to the German sense of order. In summer 1940 Greiser[2] had already described conditions in the Lodz ghetto as untenable from the "point of view of nutrition and the control of epidemics." On 16 July 1941, SS-*Sturmbannführer* Höppner drew attention to the catastrophic conditions in the ghetto which, as a transit camp for the Jews transported from the Old Reich, was permanently overcrowded. Besides, it was the only ghetto within the Reich and was regarded by Greiser as an intolerable burden. Höppner added in his letter to Eichmann that "it should be seriously considered whether it might not be the most humane solution to dispose of those Jews who are unfit for work by some quick-acting means. At any rate this would be more agreeable than letting them starve."

Martin Broszat has emphasized the symptomatic significance of this reaction. It is not an isolated one. The idea that it would ultimately be more "humane" to finish off the victims quickly had

---

[2] SS General Arthur Greiser, Gauleiter and Reich Governor of the Warthegau, an area annexed to Germany from Poland in 1939. — Ed.

already emerged in 1940; it was frequently prompted by the sight of countless trains standing at stations in the biting cold, with their captive Jewish passengers deprived even of drinking water during the dreadful journey to the *Generalgouvernement*. The war in the East provided even more reasons for such arguments. The indescribably cruel treatment of the civilian population caused few protests and produced instead a fatal blunting of moral feeling among the Germans. The partial liquidation of transports of Jews from the Old Reich and the annexed territories was a desperate new step. It could not be justified as part of the destruction of Bolshevik resistance cells. A pseudo-moral justification was needed as a precondition for the systematic implementation of the Final Solution. Inhumanity had first to be declared as "humanity" before it could be put into technocratic practice, with moral inhibitions thereafter reduced to a minimum. Then, once the necessary bureaucratic apparatus had been created, a programme could be set in motion that was applicable to all deportees, including women and children.

The operations of the *Einsatzgruppen* served as the link that enabled the exception — premeditated liquidation — to become the general rule. The immediate liquidation of groups of German Jews deported to the *Reichskommissariat Ostland*, to Riga, Kovno and Minsk, did not proceed smoothly. Moreover, like the killings begun with the assistance of the "euthanasia" experts in Chelmno in December 1941, they also encountered opposition, which led to the suspension of further transports. Even if only for this reason, the change in the Jewish policy of the RSHA was by no means abrupt. One indication of such a change was that Jewish emigration from German-occupied areas of continental Europe was halted, although it had previously been explicitly supported. The head of the *Gestapo*, Müller, announced the prohibition of further Jewish emigration on 23 October 1941. Only ten days previously, Heydrich had actually approved a proposal by the Under-Secretary of State, Martin Luther, that Spanish Jews resident in France should be included in the Spanish Cabinet's plan to send "their" Jews to Spanish Morocco. A few days later his decision was revoked on the grounds that these Jews would then be too far outside the German sphere of influence to be included in the Final Solution to be implemented after the war.

The reference to a "post-war solution" reveals that at this point the decision for systematic genocide had not yet been reached. On

16 December 1941, Frank stated that 3.5 million Jews in the *Generalgouvernement* could not be liquidated, but that "action will have to be taken that will lead to successful destruction, in connection with the major measures which are to be discussed at Reich level." This was a reference to the impending Wannsee Conference, which is usually equated with the immediate launch of the genocide campaign throughout Europe. However, the "operations" mentioned by Heydrich in connection with the "evacuation of the Jews to the East" were presented simply as opportunities to gain practical experience "in view of the coming Final Solution of the Jewish question." The liquidation of those Jews who were deemed unfit for work was implied, and the subsequent destruction of the "remaining stock" explicitly disclosed. The psychological bridge between the emigration and reservation "solutions" and the Holocaust itself was created by the fiction of *Arbeitseinsatz* ("labour mobilization"); reference was also still made to the chimerical "territorial final solution," which was now to be achieved east of the Urals. On the other hand, the formulation that "certain preparatory work for the Final Solution" should be carried out "in the areas concerned," i.e., the *Generalgouvernement*, signified the beginning of selective liquidations. These started early in 1942 and from spring onwards acquired the character of a planned and systematic programme. Even then, however, it was implemented with varying degrees of intensity; initially the measures were mainly improvised and some operations had to be countermanded. It is important to note that the programme of annihilation thus retained its character as a temporary measure taken during the wartime state of emergency. The inclusion in the programme of the Jews in the occupied countries and satellite states originally occurred within the framework of a long-term "labour mobilization" programme; however, even the most elementary requirements for the fulfillment of such a scheme were lacking.

One further development was important for the implementation of the Final Solution. Since autumn 1941, Auschwitz-Birkenau had been expanded into an enormous "prisoner and munitions centre," mainly for the "utilization" of Soviet prisoners of war. The selection of Soviet prisoners, and the brutal treatment inflicted upon them, reflected Himmler's own belief that there were unlimited human reserves in the East. However, the turn of the tide in the war, and the appalling death-rate among the prisoners, meant that fewer human reserves than anticipated were available and that they were urgently needed to fill gaps in the labour market in the Reich itself. Scarcely a week after the Wannsee Conference, Himmler issued his instruction to "equip" the SS concentration camps primarily with German Jews. Birkenau camp, where the technology of gassing had been developed with Soviet prisoners of war as the victims, was now to be part of a comprehensive programme for genocide. *The Generalplan Ost* stood in the background, preventing any attempt to fall back on interim territorial "solutions" to the "Jewish question" in the occupied territory of the Soviet Union. The programme of annihilation was now implemented with astonishing speed and in several waves. This operation (later named "Reinhard" after Reinhard Heydrich, assassinated in Prague in May 1942) formed the direct link between the *Einsatzgruppen* and the factory techniques of the Final Solution. The systematic destruction of the ghettos was followed by the withdrawal of Jewish labour from war industries; Jewish workers were also removed from the SS enterprises in the Lublin region, which then collapsed.

The use of gas vans as a transitional stage in the development of factory methods to destroy human life had begun because of a desire to prevent undesirable side-effects on the SS men caused by the semi-public shootings at Vilna and elsewhere. The fiction that only those Jews who were unfit for work were to be killed remained psychologically important. The selection process on the ramp at Birkenau helped Himmler's thugs to preserve this fiction. It was only a short step from this way of thinking to "orderly" destruction, which could be justified on the grounds that organized killing was more practical and "humane" than death from starvation or epidemics in the ghettos and camps. The horrific conditions produced by the brutal and inhumane treatment of the deported Jews were actually exploited by Goebbels to justify the deadly theory of "subhumanity." More importantly, people who under normal circumstances would have been roused to anger by the treatment of the Jews became indifferent, and their feelings of compassion were dulled. How many had the personal courage to see the whole truth behind the chain of cruelties, rather than putting the blame on occasional abuses?

After all, work camps of all kinds — voluntary Labour service, compulsory labour and ultimately the practice of working people to death — were the civilian counterpart of military service, which sent millions to the slaughter. Everywhere in occupied Europe, even in the Reich itself, the labour camp became part of ordinary life. The atomization of the family, the destruction of traditional social structures, the sending of all age groups and professions to labour camps, training camps, education camps — these were everyday features of the Third Reich. The network of concentration camps and prisoner-of-war camps appeared to be part of this second civilization, offering an extreme example of the exercise of power over human beings.

The transfer of people within this labyrinthine network of camps was nothing unusual. However, the concentration of Jewish citizens in labour camps became an increasingly important transitional stage on the path to the Final Solution. The circumstances in which deportations occurred sometimes excited public criticism, but in general people chose to believe the fiction of the "mobilization of labour"; moreover, the removal of Jews to transit camps ensured that their fate was decided out of sight of their fellow citizens. Even in the occupied areas, resistance to the "mobilization" of Jewish labour occurred only rarely. Within the concentration camps, it had long been the practice to work people literally to death. The concept that arose as a result — that of "destruction by labour" — was one of the most effective pieces of cynicism in National Socialist ideology. The inscription on the gates of Auschwitz — *"Arbeit macht frei"* ("freedom through work") — reveals that cynicism; it illuminates the entire master-race mentality, which degraded human beings into mere numbers and had no respect even for the dead. This attitude first manifested itself in the "euthanasia" programme.

The fiction of mobilizing Jewish labour was used by the perpetrators of the Final Solution as a psychological justification for their actions. It is symptomatic that fanatical anti-semites such as Hans Frank and Wilhelm Kube began to protest against the systematic implementation of the extermination programme when it was turned against the reserves of indispensable Jewish labour in the Eastern regions. When the liquidations were not justified by the pretence that they were measures to combat partisans and to weaken "Jewish-Bolshevik" potential, as was the case with the *Einsatzgruppen*, then they were frequently accounted for by the need to make space for fresh transports. There were phases during which the pace of the extermination programme was slowed, to permit the temporary exploitation of the prisoners by means of forced labour. Many Jews saw this as their only chance of survival.

The use of bureaucratic and technocratic methods to destroy human life also served to suppress quasi-moral inhibitions. The original motive behind the development of technical methods of killing such as carbon monoxide and *Zyklon B* had been to avoid unrest among the general public. However, it was rapidly transformed into a problem of killing-capacity. The decisive preliminary stages of the systematic policy of the Final Solution were thus accompanied by the efforts of the RSHA to learn about these technical possibilities; the instructions given to Eichmann and Höss in autumn 1941 were of this nature.

The Holocaust was not based upon a programme that had been developed over a long period. It was founded upon improvised measures that were rooted in earlier stages of planning and also escalated them. Once it had been set in motion, the extermination of those people who were deemed unfit for work developed a dynamic of its own. The bureaucratic machinery created by Eichmann and Heydrich functioned more or less automatically; it was thus symptomatic that Eichmann consciously circumvented Himmler's order, at the end of 1944, to stop the Final Solution. There was no need for external ideological impulses to keep the process of extermination going. Protests from those parties interested in saving the Jewish workforce — the *Wehrmacht*, the armaments industry, SS-owned factories in the concentration camps, and the administration of the *Generalgouvernement* — proved largely ineffective.

The widespread assumption that the systematic policy of genocide rested on a clear directive from Hitler is based on a misunderstanding of the decision-making process in the *Führer's* headquarters. If such an order had been given, even if only orally, then those in high office around Hitler must have known about it; they had no motive to deny the existence of such a directive in their personal records and testimonies after 1945. Gerald Fleming has made a comprehensive search for traces of such an order from the *Führer*. All he can prove is that at the middle level of command there was talk of it in one form or another; however, Hitler's express approval of criminal orders and his intensification of the fight against partisans seem to be the only concrete basis for these opinions.

In fact, the idea that Hitler set the genocide policy in motion by means of a direct instruction can be completely rejected. Such an order would have compromised the fiction of the "mobilization of labour," which included the theory of "destruction by labour." This could not have been in the *Führer's* interests, especially as he would then have had to choose between the destruction of human lives and the mobilization of labour demanded by the war economy. Hitler consistently avoided making such a choice. This situation made it particularly difficult for the parties opposed to the extermination process to marshal their arguments: first, there was no one to whom they could appeal, and secondly, even if there were, they would have had to break through the taboo that surrounded the Final Solution. Thus it was that *Generalgouverneur* Hans Frank saw no possibility of appealing to Hitler over the withdrawal of urgently needed Jewish workers.

The absence of any direct order for extermination also explains how almost all those in an influential position were able to suppress their awareness of the fact of genocide. Albert Speer provides the most striking example of this tendency. Hitler's dominant position at the centre of all the National Socialist elites reinforced such behaviour, because his conduct was exactly the same as theirs: he took care not to allow conversation to turn to events in the concentration camps. This gave rise to the widespread impression that Heinrich Himmler was the driving force. In terms of ideological motivation this was not the case, for Hitler was always the advocate of radicalization.

The utopian dream of exterminating the Jews could become reality only in the half-light of unclear orders and ideological fanaticism. Then, despite all opposing interests, the process developed its own internal dynamic. It is therefore impossible to assign sole responsibility for events to Hitler, Himmler, Heydrich, Bormann, the SS, and the activists in the German Foreign Ministry. Many leading National Socialists tended to stay out of events as much as possible, although they had actively supported the deportation programme. The willingness with which the Ministries of Justice and the Interior gave up to the Security Service (SD) and the *Gestapo* their jurisdiction over the deportations, which they had initially defended strenuously, is a striking example of a general endeavour among officials to divest themselves of any responsibility whilst accepting that the events themselves were inevitable.

Adolf Eichmann offers a spectacular example of the mechanism of compartmentalized responsibility, which in his case was combined with bureaucratic perfectionism and submissiveness to the demands of the authoritarian state. As he testified in Jerusalem, his authority extended only as far as the gates of Auschwitz-Birkenau; he was just responsible for carrying out the deportations. This fragmenting of responsibilities was a typical feature of the regime. It had its roots in the organization of the NSDAP, which had been imposed by Hitler and his followers during the 1920s. The relative efficiency of the National Socialist system was based precisely upon Hitler's principle of conferring unlimited powers for specific tasks and allowing political coordination between institutions only where it was unavoidable. Any institutionalized communication between the lower levels of government was systematically prevented. Responsibilities were thus segmented. In the various war crimes trials, the former satraps of the regime always pleaded that they had merely followed orders and been cogs in the machine. No one was prepared to accept overall responsibility or to consider the political consequences of the individual decisions that they made. Noncommunication and collective suppression of knowledge complemented each other and, when these mechanisms failed, they were replaced by a vague awareness that involvement in the escalation of crime had gone too far for any opposition to be possible.

If these psychological mechanisms prevented the National Socialist elite from facing up to the escalation of criminality and drawing the necessary conclusions, then we can more easily accept that most ordinary Germans were reluctant to believe rumours and incomplete information. It is significant, in this respect, that the truth about the Holocaust was accepted only with hesitation and reluctance even by Western public opinion and Allied governments. In so far as German civilians must bear a share of moral responsibility, this does not lie in the fact that they did not protest against the Holocaust, particularly in view of its all-pervasive activity; instead, it is to be found in the passive acceptance of the exclusion of the Jewish population, which prepared the way for the Final Solution. An awareness of increasing injustice definitely did exist, as can be seen in the reaction of public opinion to the revelations about the Katyn massacre.

Ideological factors — the effects of anti-semitic propaganda and the authoritarian element in traditional German political culture — are not sufficient in themselves to explain how the Holocaust became reality. The political and bureaucratic mechanisms that permitted the idea of mass extermination to be realized could also have occurred under different social conditions. The ultimately atavistic structure of the National Socialist regime, coupled with the effective power of newly established bureaucracies, proved to be the decisive factor in the selection of negative "elements of *Weltanschauung*" and in the overwhelming loss of reality that was epitomized by Hitler's mentality. The genesis of the Holocaust offers a deterrent example of the way in which otherwise normal individuals can be led astray when they live in a permanent state of emergency, when legal and institutional structures collapse, and when criminal deeds are publicly justified as national achievements. The Holocaust is a warning against racial phobias and social resentment of minority groups; but it is also a reminder that the manipulation and deformation of public and private morality are a constant threat even in advanced industrial societies.

Christopher R. Browning

A Product of Euphoria in Victory

Within the broad spectrum of interpretation, my thesis might be termed "moderate functionalist." I do not accept the intentionalists' view that the key decision — the conception of the Final Solution as a fixed goal — had already been taken long before the war and merely awaited the opportune moment for implementation. My position does not deny the significance of Hitler's anti-Semitism, only that the intention to murder the Jews had been consciously derived from it well in advance.

Concerning Hitler's anti-Semitism, historical consensus exists on the following: Psychologically, it was a deeply held obsession. Ideologically, it was the keystone of his *Weltanschauung*. Without his understanding of politics in terms of a Jewish-Bolshevik conspiracy and his understanding of history in terms of a Social-Darwinist struggle of races (in which the Jews played the most diabolical role), the whole edifice would collapse. Finally, Hitler gave expression to this anti-Semitism in violent threats and fantasies of mass murder. Indeed, for a man whose Social Darwinism implied the final resolution of any conflict in terms of the survival of one adversary through the "destruction" of the other, and whose anti-Semitism was understood in terms of race, mass murder of the Jews was a "logical" deduction. Granted all this, the relationship between Hitler's anti-Semitism and the origin of the Final Solution still remains controversial.

Even if the Final Solution can be "logically" deduced from Hitler's *Weltanschauung*, it is improbable that Hitler made that deduction before 1941 and consciously pursued the systematic murder of the European Jews as a long-held goal. The assumption that

From *Fateful Months: Essay on the Emergence of the Final Solution* by Christopher R. Browning (New York: Holmes & Meier, 1985) Copyright © 1985 by Christopher R. Browning. Reproduced by permission of the publisher.

Nazi Jewish policy was the premeditated and logical consequence of Hitler's anti-Semitism cannot be easily reconciled with his actual behavior in the years before 1941. For example, Hitler's view of the Jews as the "November criminals" who caused Germany's defeat in World War I was as fervently held as any of his anti-Jewish allegations. Indeed, the oft-cited passage from *Mein Kampf* lamenting that twelve or fifteen thousand Jews had not been gassed during the war makes far more sense in the context of the stab-in-the-back legend than as a prophecy or intimation of the Final Solution. The "logical" consequence of the thesis of the Jew as wartime traitor should have been a "preventive" massacre of German Jewry before the western offensive or at least before the attack on Russia.

In actual practice Nazi Jewish policy sought a *judenrein* Germany by facilitating and often coercing Jewish emigration. In order to reserve the limited emigration opportunities for German Jews, the Nazis opposed Jewish emigration from elsewhere on the continent. This policy continued until the fall of 1941, when the Nazis prohibited Jewish emigration from Germany and for the first time justified the blocking of Jewish emigration from other countries in terms of preventing their escape from the German grasp. The efforts of the Nazi Jewish experts to facilitate Jewish emigration both before and during the war, as well as their plans for massive expulsions (what the Nazis euphemistically called "resettlement" or *Umsiedlung*) were not merely tolerated but encouraged by Hitler. It is difficult to reconcile the assumption of a long-held intention to murder the Jews of Europe with this behavior. If Hitler knew he was going to murder the Jews, then he was supporting a policy that "favored" German Jews over other European Jews and "rescued" from death many of those he held most responsible for Germany's earlier defeat.

It has been argued that Hitler was merely awaiting the opportune moment to realize his murderous intentions. Not only does that not explain the pursuit of a contradictory policy of emigration in the meantime, it also does not explain the long delay. If Hitler was merely awaiting the outbreak of conflict to pursue his "war against the Jews," why were the millions of Polish Jews in his hands since the fall of 1939 granted a thirty-month "stay of execution"? They were subjected to sporadic massacre and murderous living conditions but not to systematic extermination until 1942. If Hitler could kill at least seventy thousand Germans through the euthanasia program between 1939 and 1941, why was it not "opportune" to murder several hundred thousand German Jews who constituted an "internal menace" in wartime? It certainly would have occasioned far less opposition than euthanasia. Why was this period not used to make preparations and plans for mass extermination, avoiding the clumsy improvisations of 1941? In short, the practice of Nazi Jewish policy until 1941 does not support the thesis of a long-held, fixed intention to murder the European Jews.

Hitler's anti-Semitism is more plausibly seen as the stimulant or spur to a continuous search for an increasingly radical solution to the Jewish question rather than as the source of a logically deduced and long-held "blueprint" for extermination. As the "satanic" figure behind all other problems, the Jew was for Hitler the ultimate problem and required an ultimate or final solution. Hitler's anti-Semitism thus constituted an ideological imperative which, given the competitive nature of the Nazi state, played a central role in the evolution of Nazi Jewish policy. The rival Nazi chieftains constantly sought to expand their private empires and vied for Hitler's favor through anticipating and pursuing Hitler's desires. In his function as arbiter, Hitler in turn sought to avoid totally antagonizing or alienating any of his close followers, even the most incompetent among them such as Rosenberg and Ribbentrop. Thus, when competing Nazis advocated conflicting policies, all plausibly justified in Nazi terminology, Hitler had great difficulty resolving differences. Paralysis and indecision were often the result. When, however, the competition was carried out at the expense of helpless third parties, such as Jews and populations of occupied territories, protected by no countervailing force, radicalization rather than paralysis followed. Hence it was the conjuncture of Hitler's anti-Semitic obsession, the anarchial and competitive nature of the Nazi state, the vulnerable status of the European Jews, and the war that resulted in the Final Solution.

By 1941 Nazi Jewish policy had reached an impasse. Military and diplomatic success had brought millions of Jews into the German sphere, while the already limited possibilities for Jewish emigration were constricted further through the outbreak of war. Germany's self-imposed "Jewish problem" mushroomed while the traditional solution collapsed. Interim solutions of massive "resettlement" — in Lublin and Madagascar — in like manner were not viable. The imminent invasion of Russia posed the same dilemma once again — further territorial conquest meant more Jews. At some point in the spring of 1941, Hitler decided to break this vicious circle.

Overwhelming documentation exists to show that Germany, under Hitler's prodding, planned and prepared for a *Vernichtungskrieg* — a war of destruction, not a conventional war — in Russia. It would be a clash of ideologies and races, not of nation-states. Detailed negotiations between the army and the SS ended in an agreement with the army's promising logistical support and conceding freedom of action to small mobile SS-units — *Einsatzgruppen* — charged with "special tasks" behind German lines. All customs and international law concerning war and occupation were to be disregarded. . . .

With the decision to murder the Russian Jews, Hitler broke out of the vicious circle in which each military success brought more Jews into the German sphere. This did not, however, immediately alter German Jewish policy on the rest of the continent. Emigration, expulsion, and plans for future "resettlement" still held sway. . . . Thus the preparations for the murderous assault upon the Russian Jews did not have immediate repercussions on Nazi Jewish policy elsewhere. The emergence of the Final Solution for the European Jews was a separate process resulting from a separate though certainly not unrelated decision. . . .

On July 31, 1941, Heydrich received Göring's authorization to prepare a "total solution" (*Gesamtlösung*) of the Jewish question in those territories of Europe under German influence and to coordinate the participation of those organizations whose jurisdictions were touched. The significance of this document is open to debate. Most historians have assumed that it refers to an extermination program. In contrast [functionalists] have interpreted it in terms of a "comprehensive program for the deportation of the Jews" to Russia and an attempt by Heydrich to strengthen his jurisdictional position to carry out this task. . . .

However uncertain the origins of the July authorization and however vague the phraseology about the fate intended for the Jews, this much is known. It was signed by Göring, who two weeks later expressed the opinion that "the Jews in the territories dominated by Germany had nothing more to seek." Göring did not spell out their fate further, except to say that where Jews had to be allowed to work, it could only be in closely guarded labor camps, and that he preferred that Jews be hanged rather than shot, as the latter was too honorable a death. An impending mass expulsion of Jews into Russia was neither mentioned nor implied.

The authorization was received by Heydrich, who already had an authorization signed by Göring for coordinating Jewish emigration, dating from January 1939. When Jewish emigration gave way to plans for massive "resettlement," Heydrich had felt no need for a new "charter" and cited the older one when asserting jurisdiction over the emerging Madagascar Plan in 1940. Moreover, Heydrich had just spent the previous months organizing the *Einsatzgruppen* for the extermination of the Russian Jews, and that murder campaign was now in full swing. The historical context would thus suggest that, if indeed Heydrich was the initiator of the July authorization, he did not need it to continue the emigration and expulsion activities over which he had long established unchallenged jurisdiction but rather because he now faced a new and awesome task that dwarfed even the systematic murder program of the *Einsatzgruppen.*

Precisely how and when Heydrich and his immediate superior, Himmler, became aware of their new task is not and probably never will be known. But given the political structure of the Third Reich, in which rival paladins vied for Hitler's favor and were successful to the degree in which they anticipated and realized his desires, and given the extermination program already underway in Russia, Himmler and Heydrich surely needed little more than a nod from Hitler to perceive that the time had come to extend the killing process to the European Jews. That such a Hitlerian incitement lay behind the July authorization cannot be definitely proven. But the testimony of Rudolf Höss and Adolf Eichmann indicates that at some point in the summer of 1941, whether in July or shortly thereafter is unclear, Himmler and Heydrich began to act on the assumption that Hitler had given them the "green light" to prepare an extermination program. . . .

Given the already apparent inadequacies of the *Einsatzgruppen* operations — their inefficiency, the lack of secrecy, and the psychological burden on the executioners — and their even greater unsuitability for use outside Russia, the most important problem Himmler and Heydrich faced was how and where to kill the Jews. Ultimately the Nazi planners solved this problem by merging three already existing programs with which they had prior experience: the concentration camp system, euthanasia gassing, and Eichmann's specialty of forced emigration and population resettlement. Auschwitz, because of its rail connections, was chosen as one site for a killing center. The possibility of other sites in Russia may have been weighed until the military and transportation situation made this unfeasible. The exact type of gas to be used remained undetermined; in the end the Polish camps manned by euthanasia personnel retained carbon monoxide while Auschwitz and Maidanek adopted Cyclon B.

When was this solution — deportation to camps equipped with gassing facilities — finally approved? The answer lies in another question: When did the construction of the first death camps and the initial shifting of euthanasia personnel begin? The course of events at Auschwitz is not helpful in validating the date, for Auschwitz was already a labor camp at which many Russian prisoners of war were being systematically killed. The gassing of some of these Russian prisoners in September 1941 with Cyclon B in Bunker 11 at the *Stammlager* was followed by at least several gassings of small contingents of local Jews in the "old crematory." However, the gassing of large transports of Jews in the converted farm house at Birkenau did not begin until late January 1942. This sequence provides no clear indication as to when Höss was first aware of this new killing task. Belzec and Chelmno, however, provide a better check, for neither was then in existence as an operating labor camp and both were constructed solely to kill Jews. The date when construction on these camps began can thus provide a crucial check as to when a significant number of Germans knew what they were about in preparing for the Final Solution. Most of the German defendants in the Belzec and Chelmno trials were not at those camps at the beginning and could provide no relevant testimony. However, the testimony of two German defendants in this regard, corroborated by the testimony of local inhabitants in those areas taken by the Poles immediately after the war, clearly points once again to October 1941.

Let us examine the Chelmno evidence first. Since early 1940 a *Sonderkommando* under Herbert Lange, headquartered in Posen, had been carrying out euthanasia operations in East Prussia and the incorporated territories. According to Lange's chauffeur, he drove the *Sonderkommando* chief around the Warthegau in the fall of 1941 searching for a suitable location for a death camp. He then drove Lange to Berlin and back, arriving in Chelmno in late October or early November. Thereafter a team of SS men was assembled from Posen and Lodz, followed by a guard detachment of Order Police. A work force of Polish prisoners from Lodz together with local inhabitants was put to work renovating and fencing the old villa or *Schloss*, where the Jews would be undressed and loaded into the waiting gas vans. After preparations were complete, the gassing began on December 8.

Polish postwar interrogations of the *Volksdeutsche* (ethnic German) inhabitants of the village provide the same sequence. According to the *Amtskommissar* of Chelmno, he was away from town toward the end of 1941 when some SS men arrived and investigated the *Schloss* and other buildings. Some days later, after his return, Lange appeared and confiscated various buildings. Lange returned still later with a team of SS men, followed by police. Some weeks after the arrival of the SS unit, work on the *Schloss* was complete and the first truckloads of Jews arrived. Such a sequence of events would necessitate Lange's having received his initial instructions to establish a death camp at Chelmno no later than mid- or late October but more likely toward the beginning of the month.

The sequence of events at Belzec leads to much the same conclusion. Again we have the testimony of only one German defendant, Josef Oberhauser, initially an employee of the euthanasia program and subsequently adjutant to Christian Wirth, the inspector of the Polish death camps of Operation Reinhard. Oberhauser was assigned to Globocnik[1] in Lublin in October and arrived there in November 1941. His first job consisted of bringing to Belzec building materials as well as Ukrainian guardsmen from their training

[1] SS General Odilo Globocnik, responsible for Belzec, Treblinka, Sobibor, and Maidanek. — Ed.

camp at Trawniki. He was in no doubt as to what was intended in Belzec, as the construction supervisor showed him the plans for the gas chamber. By Christmas the initial construction was finished, and Oberhauser became Wirth's liaison to Globocnik. After the first gassing test killed fifty Jewish workers, Wirth went to Berlin for six weeks. Upon his return in March, the first transports began to arrive.

According to local inhabitants, three SS men came to Belzec in October 1941 and demanded a draft of twenty Polish workers. Work began on November 1 under the direction of a young ethnic German *Baumeister* from Kattowitz, who supervised the construction according to a set of plans. After putting up two barracks and the future gas chamber near the railway siding, the Polish workers were dismissed on December 23. By then black-uniformed former Russian prisoners of war had arrived to carry on the work and guard seventy Jewish laborers. After more barracks, guard towers, and fencing were completed, the Jewish workers were killed in the first test of the gassing facilities in February 1942. Full-time operations then began in March. Thus not only is the Oberhauser testimony confirmed, but an Eichmann visit to an empty camp at Belzec in October 1941 and his reception by a lone police captain fits this sequence of events precisely. The few wooden buildings he saw must have dated from the former Jewish labor camp at Belzec.

While many euthanasia personnel were sent from Germany to Russia in the winter of 1941–1942 and were not reassigned to the death camps until the spring of 1942, some key personnel were already involved earlier. Not only had Wirth and Oberhauser been sent from Berlin in the fall of 1941, but Brack also dispatched to Lublin his chemist, Dr. Helmut Kallmeyer, the man he had unsuccessfully tried to send to Riga in late October. Kallmeyer admitted being sent to Lublin after Christmas, but said no one had had any use for him and he had been quickly sent back. SS-*Untersturmführer* Dr. August Becker, on loan from the SS to the euthanasia program since January 1940 for the purpose of delivering bottled carbon monoxide to the euthanasia institutes, testified frankly (when terminally ill and no longer facing trial): "Himmler wanted to use the people released from euthanasia who were experts in gassing, such as myself, in the great gassing program getting underway in the east." Before being assigned in December 1941 to supervise gas vans operating with the *Einsatzgruppen* in Russia, Becker had already heard talk in Berlin that other members of the euthanasia program were being sent to Lublin to start "something similar," only this time according to rumor it would be for the Jews.

If the October documents cited above indicate that middle echelon officials of the Führer's Chancellory, Foreign Office, and *Ostministerium* were then discussing special reception camps and gassing in relation to the Jews, the Chelmno and Belzec testimony indicates that, within the SS, preparation for constructing the death camps was in fact already getting underway in that month. Such evidence makes very compelling the conclusion that by October Hitler had approved the mass-murder plan. It must be kept in mind, however, that the death-camp solution was not self-evident; it had to be invented. Precisely how long the whole process of initiation, invention, and approval took, we do not know. In the accounts of Eichmann and Höss, they learned from Heydrich and Himmler respectively by late summer of 1941 of Hitler's order to destroy the Jews but not yet how that was to be accomplished. If the death-camp solution had been approved and was being implemented in October, it is at least *very probable* that the problem was first posed by Himmler and Heydrich to others in August, and that they themselves were first incited to the task by Hitler in late July.

Furthermore, the evidence concerning the founding of the death camps at Chelmno and Belzec does not support the hypothesis of the primacy of local initiative but rather indicates considerable interaction with central authorities in Berlin. Both camps involved the reassignment of personnel formerly involved in the euthanasia program, which was coordinated in the Führer's Chancellory. Both commandants, Lange and Wirth, made trips back to Berlin before their camps began operating. Both camps received visits from Eichmann on inspection tour from Berlin. Both utilized killing technology developed in Germany — in Belzec the stationary gas chamber on the euthanasia institute model, and in Chelmno the gas van, which was developed, tested, produced, and dispatched with drivers by the RSHA.

These conclusions are not compatible with the theories of Adam and Haffner, who date the decision for the Final Solution to the fall or winter of 1941, nor with Broszat's thesis of the primacy of local

initiative in setting the process in motion. Central to all these theories is the conviction that the failure of the Russian campaign was
crucial in launching the Final Solution: either in forcing Hitler to
choose different priorities, as in Haffner's case, or in forcing the Germans to find a solution to the Jewish question other than "resettlement" in Russia, as with Adam and Broszat. If the death camps were
already approved and the initial steps were being taken in October,
the process involved in launching the Final Solution had to have
begun much earlier, at a point when victory in Russia was still
expected by the end of the year. Aronson's dating of "late fall," sometime after the implications of American Lend-Lease to Russia had
altered Hitler's outlook, likewise is too late to account for this course
of events unless the time between the change he postulates in
Hitler's thinking and the commencement of death-camp construction were almost instantaneous. It would appear that the euphoria of
victory in the summer of 1941 and the intoxicating vision of all
Europe at their feet, not the dashed expectations and frustrations of
the last months of the year, induced the Nazis to set the fateful process in motion. . . .

In conclusion, there was no Hitler order from which the Final
Solution sprang full grown like Athena from the head of Zeus. But
sometime in the summer of 1941, probably before Göring's July 31
authorization, Hitler gave Himmler and Heydrich the signal to draw
up a destruction plan, the completion of which inevitably involved
the exploration of various alternatives, false starts, and much delay.
Considerable "lead time" was needed, for the Nazis were venturing
into uncharted territory and attempting the unprecedented; they had
no maps to follow — hence, a seeming ambivalence surrounding
German Jewish policy in the late summer and autumn of 1941,
which was aggravated by two factors. The first was the decision in
mid-September to deport German Jews before the new killing facilities had been devised. The second was the Byzantine style of government in which initiative from above was informal, information was
shared irregularly, and uncertainty was often deliberately cultivated.
By October, a not unreasonable two or three months after Hitler had
given the green light to proceed, the pieces were falling together.
Many outside the SS were now involved, and there had emerged the
rough outline of a plan involving mass deportation to killing centers
that used poison gas. The first concrete steps for implementing this

plan — beginning construction of the earliest death camps at Belzec and Chelmno and the first transfer of euthanasia personnel, both inconceivable without Hitler's approval — were taken by the end of the month. The decision for the Final Solution had been confirmed.

Bergen-Belsen, 1945. Photographed shortly after the camp's liberation, this scene gives some idea of the catastrophic sanitary conditions there. (AP/WideWorld Photos)

PART

II The Holocaust Experience

Variety of Opinion

The prisoners developed types of behavior which are characteristic of infancy or early youth. . . . When a prisoner had reached the final stage of adjustment to the camp situation, he had changed his personality so as to accept various values of the SS as his own.

Bruno Bettelheim

The assumption that there was no moral or social order in the concentration camps is wrong. . . . Through innumerable small acts of humanness, most of them covert but everywhere in evidence, survivors were able to maintain societal structures workable enough to keep themselves alive and morally sane.

Terrence Des Pres

It wasn't ruthlessness that enabled an individual to survive — it was an intangible quality, . . . an overwhelming thirst — perhaps, too, a talent for life, and a faith in life. . . .

Richard Glazar, as told to Gitta Sereny

Maidanek was hell . . . where the art of cruelty was refined to perfection and every facility of modern technology and psychology was combined to destroy men mentally and physically.

Alexander Donat

What it was like to be swept up in the Nazi whirlwind of violence and misery has been told in the memoirs of hundreds of survivors. Although each one presents only a small piece of the puzzle, together they give us a sense of the variety of what were, after all, many millions of Holocaust experiences. How were the victims treated, and how did they react in the camps? Was there anything they could do to enhance the chances of living through this terror? This section briefly contrasts two conflicting views on these issues and then, at greater length, delves into two of the most revealing and memorable survivors' accounts.

Bruno Bettelheim, for many decades until his death in 1990 one of the world's leading child psychologists, was himself an inmate of Nazi concentration camps for about a year in the late 1930s. Although he escaped the Holocaust itself, he called on his own experiences and those of others to formulate an influential view of the experience. The systematic dehumanization of the victims in Nazi camps, Bettelheim argues, crippled inmates psychologically and caused them to regress to childlike behavior. The conclusion implied by this line of reasoning seems inescapable: utterly at the mercy of a pitiless totalitarian leviathan, the victims could do little to influence their fate one way or another. Those who survived until they could be liberated by outside forces were, above all, incredibly lucky.

Terrence Des Pres, an American professor of literature, has drawn on accounts by survivors in an effort to refute Bettelheim's claims. Rejecting the psychological method, Des Pres attributes the inmates' behavior to raw necessity rather than regression. Moreover, he observes that many acts of mutual kindness and aid were decisive in determining whether individuals lived or died. Survival was to some degree in the victims' own hands. It was more a matter of being determined to outlast one's tormentors, and of helping and being helped, than it was of luck.

Gitta Sereny sought to illuminate the Holocaust experience by interviewing Franz Stangl, commandant at Treblinka, who was sentenced to life imprisonment in Germany after his extradition from Brazil in 1967. Stangl told her that his most vivid memory of the death camp was that the victims went to their fate passively, like cattle in a slaughterhouse. Sereny attempted to round out Stangl's story by interviewing several of his surviving victims. One of them, Richard Glazar, was a young Jewish student from Prague when he was sent to Treblinka in October 1942. Glazar's story, reproduced here, begins with his arrival at the death camp and ends with his escape during a revolt by the inmates on August 2, 1943. Glazar made his way to Germany where he survived the war disguised as an ordinary foreign laborer.

Alexander Donat survived the Warsaw ghetto uprising, imprisonment in the Maidanek camp, and forced labor in the Radom ghetto and in Germany. His experiences as a slave worker at Maidanek are presented here. A Warsaw journalist, Donat and his wife watched the doomed resistance in the Warsaw ghetto from an attic hiding place. They were then sent to Maidanek where Donat nearly succumbed to brutal forced labor on the road building detail. What probably saved his life was being sent to work in the camp kitchen and later the motor pool. "I was one of the lucky ones," Donat writes of his assignment to the kitchen.

Was that merely a casual turn of phrase or something to be taken literally? Both of these memoirs should lead us to reflect on the nature of the camp experience, the reactions of the victims, and the qualities that preserved life in the Holocaust. Was survival largely fortuitous or did it depend in great part on the attitudes and actions of the inmates? In thinking about these matters, remember that the survivors' stories are not necessarily typical. Most of the Jews who fell into Nazi hands did not live to tell their stories, and no one can be certain how much their experiences differed from those of the survivors. It is also well to keep in mind that the Holocaust was a vast and complex process that involved millions of people. It can never be neatly encompassed in the accounts of two, or even two hundred, survivors.

Bruno Bettelheim

Helpless Victims

The prisoners developed types of behavior which are characteristic of infancy or early youth. Some of these behaviors developed slowly, others were immediately imposed on the prisoners and grew only in intensity as time went on. Some of these more-or-less infantile behaviors have already been discussed, such as ambivalence toward one's family, despondency, finding satisfaction in daydreaming rather than in action.

Whether some of these behavior patterns were deliberately produced by the gestapo is hard to ascertain. Others were definitely produced by it, but again we do not know whether this was consciously done. It has been mentioned that even during the transportation the prisoners were tortured in the way in which a cruel and domineering father might torture a helpless child; here it should be added that the prisoners were also debased by techniques which went much further into childhood situations. They were forced to soil themselves. In the camp defecation was strictly regulated; it was one of the most important daily events, discussed in great detail. During the day, prisoners who wanted to defecate had to obtain the permission of a guard. It seemed as if education to cleanliness would be once more repeated. It also seemed to give pleasure to the guards to hold the power of granting or withholding the permission to visit the latrines. (Toilets were mostly not available.) The pleasure of the guards found its counterpart in the pleasure the prisoners derived from visiting the latrines, because there they usually could rest for a moment, secure from the whips of the overseers and guards. However, they were not always so secure, because sometimes enterprising young guards enjoyed interfering with the prisoners even at these moments. . . .

In speaking to each other, the prisoners were forced to employ the familiar *du* ("thou") — a form which in Germany is indiscriminately used only among small children; they were not permitted to address one another with the many titles to which middle- and upper-class Germans are accustomed. On the other hand, they had to address the guards in the most deferential manner, giving them all their titles.

The prisoners lived, like children, only in the immediate present; they lost feeling for the sequence of time; they became unable to plan for the future or to give up immediate pleasure satisfactions to gain greater ones in the near future. They were unable to establish durable object-relations. Friendships developed as quickly as they broke up. Prisoners would, like early adolescents, fight one another tooth and nail, declare that they would never again look at one another or speak to one another, and become close friends once more within a few minutes. They were boastful, telling tales about what they had accomplished in their former lives, or how they succeeded in cheating foremen or guards, and how they sabotaged the work. Like children, they felt not at all set back or ashamed when it became known that they had lied about their prowess.

Another factor contributing to the regression into childhood behavior was the work the prisoners were forced to perform. New prisoners particularly were forced to perform nonsensical tasks, such as carrying heavy rocks from one place to another, and after a while back to the place where they had picked them up. On other days they were forced to dig holes in the ground with their bare hands, although tools were available. They resented such nonsensical work, although it ought to have been immaterial to them whether or not their work was useful. They felt debased when forced to perform "childish" and stupid labor, and preferred even harder work when it produced something that might be considered useful. There seems to be no doubt that the tasks they performed, as well as the mistreatment by the gestapo which they had to endure, contributed to their disintegration as adult persons.

The author had a chance to interview several prisoners who before being brought into the camp had spent a few years in prison, some of them in solitary confinement. Although their number was too small to permit valid generalizations, it seems that to spend time in prison does not produce the character changes described in this paper. As far as the regression into childhood behaviors is concerned, the only feature prison and camp seem to have in common is that in both the prisoners are prevented from satisfying their sexual desires in a normal way, which eventually leads them to the fear of losing their virility. In the camp this fear added strength to the other factors detrimental to adult types of behavior and promoted childlike types of behavior.

When a prisoner had reached the final stage of adjustment to the camp situation, he had changed his personality so as to accept various values of the SS as his own. A few examples may illustrate how this acceptance expressed itself.

The SS considered, or pretended to consider, the prisoners to be the scum of the earth. It insisted that none of them was any better than the others. One of the reasons for fostering this attitude was probably to convince the young guards who received their training in the camp that they were superior to even the most outstanding prisoner, and to demonstrate to them that the former foes of the Nazis were now subdued and not worthy of any special attention. If a formerly prominent prisoner had been treated better than the others, the simple guards would have thought that he still had influence; if he had been treated worse, they might have thought that he still was dangerous.

The Nazis wanted to impress on the guards that even a slight degree of opposition to the system led to the complete destruction of the person who dared to oppose, and that the *degree* of opposition made no difference in the punishment. Occasional talks with these guards revealed that they really believed in a Jewish-capitalistic world conspiracy against the German people. Whoever opposed the Nazis was supposed to be participating in it and was therefore to be destroyed, independent of his role in the conspiracy. So it can be understood that the guards' behavior to the prisoners was to treat them as their vilest enemies.

The prisoners found themselves in an impossible situation, due to the steady interference with their privacy on the part of the guards and other prisoners. So a great amount of aggression accumulated. In the new prisoners this aggression vented itself in the way it might have done in the world outside the camp. But slowly prisoners accepted, as the expression of their verbal aggressions, terms which definitely did not originate in their previous vocabularies, but were taken over from the very different vocabulary of the SS. From copying the verbal aggressions of the SS to copying its form of bodily aggressions was one more step, but it took several years to make this step. It was not unusual to find old prisoners, when in charge of others, behaving worse than the SS. In some cases they were trying to win favor with the SS in this way, but more often they considered it the best way to behave toward prisoners in the camp.

Practically all prisoners who had spent a long time in the camp took over the attitude of the SS toward the so-called unfit prisoners. Newcomers presented the old prisoners with difficult problems. Their complaints about the unbearable life in camp added new strain to the life in the barracks, as did their inability to adjust to it. Bad behavior in the labor gang endangered the whole group. So a newcomer who did not stand up well under the strain tended to become a liability for the other prisoners. Moreover, weaklings were those most apt to eventually turn traitor. Weaklings usually died during the first weeks in the camp anyway, so to some it seemed as well to get rid of them sooner. Old prisoners were therefore sometimes instrumental in getting rid of the "unfit" — in this way incorporating Nazi ideology into their own behavior. This was one of many situations in which old prisoners would demonstrate toughness, having molded their treatment of these "unfit" prisoners to the example set by the SS. Self-protection required elimination of the "unfit" prisoners, but the way in which they were sometimes tortured for days by the old prisoners and slowly killed was taken over from the gestapo.

Old prisoners who identified themselves with the SS did so not only in respect to aggressive behavior. They would try to acquire old pieces of SS uniforms. If that was not possible, they tried to sew and mend their uniforms so that they would resemble those of the guards. The length to which prisoners would go in these efforts seemed unbelievable, particularly since the SS punished them for their efforts to copy SS uniforms. When asked why they did it, the old prisoners admitted that they loved to look like the guards. . . .

The satisfaction with which some old prisoners enjoyed the fact that, during the twice-daily counting of the prisoners — which often lasted for hours and always seemed interminable — they had stood really well at attention can be explained only by the fact that they had entirely accepted the values of the SS as their own. These prisoners prided themselves on being as tough as the SS. This identification with their torturers went so far as copying their leisure-time activities. One of the games played by the guards was to find out who could stand to be hit longest without uttering a complaint. This game was copied by some of the old prisoners, as though they had not been hit often and long enough not to need to repeat this experience by inflicting pain on fellow prisoners.

Often the SS would enforce nonsensical rules, originating in the whims of one of the guards. These rules were usually forgotten very quickly, but there were always some old prisoners who would continue to follow the rules and try to enforce them on others long after the gestapo had forgotten about them. Once, for instance, a guard inspecting the prisoners' apparel found that the shoes of some of them were dirty on the inside. He ordered all prisoners to wash their shoes inside and out with water and soap. The heavy shoes, when treated this way, became hard as stone. The order was never repeated, and many prisoners did not even execute it when given. Nevertheless there were some old prisoners who not only continued to wash the inside of their shoes every day but cursed all others who did not do so as negligent and dirty. These prisoners firmly believed that the rules set down by the SS were desirable standards of human behavior, at least within the camp situation. . . .

Among the old prisoners one could observe other developments which indicated their desire to accept the SS along lines which definitely could not originate in propaganda. It seems that once prisoners adopted a childlike attitude toward the SS, they had a desire for at least some of those whom they accepted as all-powerful father-images to be just and kind. They divided their positive and negative feelings — strange as it may be that they should have had positive feelings, they had them — toward the SS in such a way that all positive emotions were concentrated on a few officers who were rather high up in the hierarchy of camp administrators, although hardly ever on the governor of the camp. The old prisoners insisted that these officers hid behind their rough surfaces a feeling of justice and propriety; he, or they, were supposed to be genuinely interested in the prisoners and even trying, in a small way, to help them. Since nothing of these supposed feelings and efforts ever became apparent, it was explained that the officer in question hid them so effectively because otherwise he would not be able to help the prisoners. The eagerness of these prisoners to find support for their claims was pitiful. A whole legend was woven around the fact that of two non-commissioned officers inspecting a barracks, one had cleaned his shoes of mud before entering. He probably did it automatically, but it was interpreted as a rebuff to the other man and a clear demonstration of how he felt about the concentration camp.

After so much has been said about the old prisoners' tendency to conform and to identify with the SS, it ought to be stressed that this was only part of the picture. The author has tried to concentrate on interesting psychological mechanisms in group behavior rather than on reporting types of behavior which are either well known or could reasonably be expected. These same old prisoners who identified with the SS defied it at other moments, demonstrating extraordinary courage in doing so.

Terrence Des Pres

The Will to Survive

With only one exception, so far as I know, psychoanalytic studies of the camp experience maintain that it was characterized by regression to "childlike" or "infantile" levels of behavior. This conclusion is based primarily on the fact that men and women in the concentration camps were "abnormally" preoccupied with food and excretory functions. Infants show similar preoccupations, and the comparison suggests that men and women react to extremity by "regression to, and fixation on, pre-oedipal stages." Here, as in general from the psychoanalytic point of view, context is not considered. The fact that the survivor's situation was itself abnormal is simply ignored. That the preoccupation with food was caused by literal starvation does not count; and the fact that camp inmates were *forced* to live in filth is likewise overlooked.

The case for "infantilism" has been put most forcefully by Bruno

From *The Survivor: An Anatomy of Life in the Death Camps* by Terrence Des Pres. Copyright © 1976 by Oxford University Press, Inc. Reprinted by permission. Footnotes omitted.

Bettelheim. A major thesis of his book *The Informed Heart* is that in extreme situations men are reduced to children; and in a section entitled "Childlike Behavior" he simply equates the prisoners' objective predicament with behavior inherently regressive. Bettelheim observes, for example — and of course this was true — that camp regulations were designed to transform excretory functions into moments of crisis. Prisoners had to ask permission in order to relieve themselves, thereby becoming exposed to the murderous whim of the SS guard to whom they spoke. During the twelve-hour workday, furthermore, prisoners were often not allowed to answer natural needs, or they were forced to do so *while* they worked and on the actual spot *where* they worked. As one survivor says: "If anyone of us, tormented by her stomach, would try to go to a nearby ditch, the guards would release their dogs. Humiliated, goaded, the women did not leave their places — they waded in their own excrement." Worst of all were the days of the death marches, when prisoners who stopped for any reason were instantly shot. To live they simply had to keep going:

> *Urine and excreta poured down the prisoners' legs, and by nightfall the excrement, which had frozen to our limbs, gave off its stench. We were really no longer human beings in the accepted sense. Not even animals, but putrefying corpses moving on two legs.*

Under such conditions, excretion does indeed become, as Bettelheim says, "an important daily event"; but the conclusion does not follow, as he goes on to say, that prisoners were therefore reduced "to the level they were at before toilet training was achieved." Outwardly, yes; men and women were very much concerned with excretory functions, just as infants are, and prisoners were "forced to wet and soil themselves" just as infants do — except that infants are not forced. Bettelheim concludes that for camp inmates the ordeal of excremental crisis "made it impossible to see themselves as fully adult persons any more." He does not distinguish between behavior in extremity and civilized behavior; for of course, if in civilized circumstances an adult worries about the state of his bowels, or sees the trip to the toilet as some sort of ordeal, then neurosis is evident. But in the concentration camps behavior was governed by immediate death-threat; action was not the index of infantile wishes but of response to hideous necessity.

The fact is that prisoners were *systematically* subjected to filth. They were the deliberate target of excremental assault. Defilement was a constant threat, a condition of life from day to day, and at any moment it was liable to take abruptly vicious and sometimes fatal forms. The favorite pastime of one *Kapo* was to stop prisoners just before they reached the latrine. He would force an inmate to stand at attention for questioning; then make him "squat in deep knee-bends until the poor man could no longer control his sphincter and 'exploded'"; then beat him; and only then, "covered with his own excrement, the victim would be allowed to drag himself to the latrine." In another instance prisoners were forced to lie in rows on the ground, and each man, when he was finally allowed to get up, "had to urinate across the heads of the others"; and there was "one night when they refined their treatment by making each man urinate into another's mouth." In Birkenau, soup bowls were periodically taken from the prisoners and thrown into the latrine, from which they had to be retrieved: "When you put it to your lips for the first time, you smell nothing suspicious. Other pairs of hands trembling with impatience wait for it, they seize it the moment you have finished drinking. Only later, much later, does a repelling odor hit your nostrils." And as we have seen, prisoners with dysentery commonly got around camp rules and kept from befouling themselves by using their own eating utensils. . . .

The condition of life-in-death forced a terrible paradox upon survivors. They stayed alive by helping to run the camps, and this fact has led to the belief that prisoners identified not with each other but with their oppressors. Survivors are often accused of imitating SS behavior. Bruno Bettelheim has argued that "old prisoners" developed "a personality structure willing and able to accept SS values and behavior as its own." But that needs clarification, for in order to act like an SS man the prisoner had to occupy a position of real power. A cook could lord it over other prisoners, a locksmith could not. Among *Kapos*, block-leaders and other high camp functionaries, there were indeed prisoners who accepted SS standards as their own — this man for instance:

> His specialty was strangling prisoners with the heel of his boot, and he would stand erect in the pose of a Roman gladiator, enjoying the approval of the other Kapos, who would speak admiringly of a "good, clean job."

Almost certainly, however, that man had been a killer before he came to the camps. For prisoners like him the camps did not cause brutality so much as simply endorse it. Bettelheim's observations are based on camp conditions in the late 1930's, a time when positions of power were held exclusively by criminals — by men and women who, prior to imprisonment, had been murderers, prostitutes, thieves. The concentration camps had long been a dumping ground for criminals, both in Russia and in Germany, and in the Nazi camps this type was exploited by the SS as the most suitable channel for the delegation of power.

But this is not a case of imitation: such prisoners were like their masters from the start. The Nazis knew their own kind and naturally established an order reflecting SS values. That criminals had so much power was one of the most deadly conditions in the camp world; and only slowly, through years of intrigue, threat, bribery and assassination, were underground resistance groups able to replace the criminal *Kapos* with men of their own. This kind of maneuvering was most successful in Buchenwald, least effective in the Soviet camps. One of the cardinal facts about the camps was that everywhere a battle raged between the "greens" and the "reds" — between those imprisoned for real crimes and those imprisoned for opposition to the regime.

The assumption that survivors imitated SS behavior is misleading because it generalizes a limited phenomenon, but also because it overlooks the duality of behavior in extremity. Eugen Kogon, a member of the Buchenwald underground, points out that "the concentration-camp prisoner knew a whole system of mimicry toward the SS," an "everpresent camouflage" which concealed true feelings and intentions. *Strategic* imitation of the SS was enormously important because thereby political prisoners held positions of power which would otherwise have gone to the criminals. In the following instance, a new prisoner, a baker, is attacked by a passing SS guard:

> With purely animal rage, he pulled off the baker's upper garments and tore them to shreds, and then whipped his bare back until the blood oozed. . . . Then the overseer, a Czech-German "political," noticed what was going on. He immediately rushed over and began shouting "You god-damned Jewish dog! You'll work for the rest of the day without clothes! I'm sick of the trouble you lousy Jews give me!" He made a threatening gesture, and then roared, "Come with me!"

> *The SS guard left, confident that the baker was in good hands.*
> *Then the overseer took the baker into a tool-shed where it was warm,*
> *dressed him, washed his wounds, and gave him permission to stay in*
> *the shed until it was time to quit work.*

Or take Franz, the *Kapo* of an SS storeroom in Auschwitz. Every day crates of food were "accidentally" dropped and reported as "shipment damage." The contents were then "organized" — for Franz, for his men and others in need. In the "open," however, there was another Franz:

> *As we walked . . . past other kapos and SS men he began roaring at us.*
> *. . . As he shouted, he swung at us with his club. To the passing SS*
> *men he looked and sounded a splendid kapo, heartless, brutal, effi-*
> *cient; yet never once did he hit us.*

Imitation of SS behavior was a regular feature of life in the camps, and large numbers of prisoners benefited because positions of power were secretly used in ways which assisted the general struggle for life. Even small jobs — working as a locksmith for instance — dovetailed into the larger fabric of resistance. . . .

Prisoners survived through concrete acts of mutual aid, and over time these many small deeds, like fibers in the shuttle of a clumsy loom, grew into a general fabric of debt and care. At roll-call, for instance, or *Appel*, as it was called in the Nazi camps, prisoners had to form up hours before dawn and stand at attention in thin rags through rain and snow. This occurred again in the evening, and took at least two hours, sometimes three and four, and every survivor remembers roll-calls which lasted all night. Prisoners had to stand there the whole time, caps off, caps on, as SS officers strolled past the ranks. Any irregularity was punished savagely, and irregularities were numerous. Prisoners fainted, collapsed from exhaustion and sickness, simply fell dead on the spot. "Those winter *Appels*," says a survivor of Buchenwald, "were actually a form of extermination. . . . In addition to those who regularly fell dead during *Appel*, there were every day a number who contracted pneumonia and subsequently died."

To fall and be noticed by an SS man was to be beaten or shot, and the universal practice among prisoners was to use their own bodies to prop up inmates no longer able to stand. Almost all reports by survivors include moments at roll-call when an individual either gave, or was given, this kind of support: "I was so weakened that during roll call I could scarcely stay on my feet. But the others pressed close on either side and supported me with the weight of their bodies."

Help was forbidden, of course, but there was some safety in numbers, for among so many thousands of prisoners packed together, the SS could view any particular rank only briefly. But despite danger, the need to help persisted, often in elaborate ways. It regularly happened that sick prisoners were carried to roll-call by comrades, who then took turns supporting them. Sometimes this went on for days, and care for the sick did not end with roll-call. Many men and women were nursed back to health by friends who "organized" extra food; who shuffled the sick man back and forth from barracks to barracks; who propped him up at roll-call, and kept him out of sight during "selections" and while he was delirious. In one case a prisoner with typhus was smuggled every day into the "Canada" work detail and hidden in the great piles of clothing where he could rest. This particular rescue involved getting the sick man through a gate guarded by a *Kapo* whose job was to spot sick and feeble prisoners and club them to death. Each day, therefore, two prisoners supported the sick man almost to the gate, and then left him to march through on his own. Once past the guard they propped him up again.

Prisoners in the concentration camps helped each other. That in itself is the significant fact. Sometimes it was help individually given, as in the case of a girl in Birkenau who, "at the risk of being severely beaten if her absence in the potato-peeling room was discovered, every evening . . . brought coffee to the sick. The last time she brought it was on the eve of her own death." Sometimes it took the form of one group helping another, as when a work squad had to carry sacks of cement from the storeroom to a building site:

> I was equal to the job, but working with us were weaker men who grew exhausted after a few trips. The younger of us, myself included, pitched in to help them. We had agreed among our group that we would help one another to whatever extent was possible, rather than surrender to the dog-eat-dog philosophy which poisoned the minds of some prisoners.

And sometimes help came collectively, unplanned and uncalled for, where and when it was needed:

> *For example, five women are pushing a conveyor car loaded to the brim with gravel . . . the car jumps the track . . . then it gets stuck in the sand. The women stop, completely helpless. Fortunately the chief is not around. All efforts to replace the car on the tracks are fruitless; the heavy-laden car will not budge and the chief may appear at any moment. A clandestine congregating begins. Stealthily, bent figures sneak toward the derailed car from all directions: the women who work on the mound of sand, those who level the gravel, a group just returned from delivering a track. A common exertion of arms and backs raises the car, the spades dig into the sand under the wheels and heave — and the loaded car moves, shivers. Fear gives strength to the workers. With more pushing, one wheel is on the track. A Kapo comes rushing from afar, she has noticed people missing at various points of work. But before she can get there, one more tug, one more push — and the gravel-laden conveyor car proceeds smoothly along the tracks.*

The survivor's experience is evidence that the need *to* help is as basic as the need *for* help, a fact which points to the radically social nature of life in extremity and explains an unexpected but very widespread activity among survivors. In the concentration camps a major form of behavior was gift-giving. Inmates were continually giving and sharing little items with each other, and small acts like these were enormously valuable both as morale boosters and often as real aids in the struggle for life. Sometimes the gift was given outright, with no apparent relation between donor and receiver:

> *One evening we were served a soup made with semolina. I drank this with all the more relish since I often had to forgo the daily cabbage soup because of my bowels. Just then I noticed a woman, one of the prostitutes, who always kept very much to themselves, approaching my bunk, holding her bowl out to me with both hands.*
> *"Micheline, I think this is a soup you can eat; here, take mine too."*
> *She emptied her bowl into mine and went without food that day.*

The assumption that there was no moral or social order in the concentration camps is wrong. Except peripherally and for brief periods similar to the "initial collapse" of individuals, the general condition we call chaos or anomie — what philosophers designate as the "state of nature" — did not exist. Certainly it did not prevail. Through innumerable small acts of humanness, most of them covert but everywhere in evidence, survivors were able to maintain societal structures workable enough to keep themselves alive and morally sane. The "state of nature," it turns out, is not natural. A war of all against all must be imposed by force, and no sooner has it started than those who suffer it begin, spontaneously and without plan, to transcend it. . . .

The survivor is the figure who emerges from all those who fought for life in the concentration camps, and the most significant fact about their struggle is that it depended on fixed activities: on forms of social bonding and interchange, on collective resistance, on keeping dignity and moral sense active. That such thoroughly *human* kinds of behavior were typical in places like Buchenwald and Auschwitz amounts to a revelation reaching to the foundation of what man is.

Richard Glazar, as Told to Gitta Sereny

Surviving Extermination Camp Treblinka

"I saw men with blue armbands on the platform, but without insignia. One of them carried a leather whip — not like any whip I'd ever seen, but like something for big animals. These men spoke very strange German. There were loud announcements, but it was all fairly restrained: nobody did anything to us [the prescribed pattern for transports arriving from the West]. I followed the crowd: 'Men to the right, women and children to the left,' we had been told. The women and children disappeared into a barrack further to the left and we were told to undress. One of the SS men — later I knew his name, Küttner — told us in a chatty sort of tone that we were going into a disinfection bath and afterwards would be assigned work. Clothes, he said, could be left in a heap on the floor, and we'd find them again later. We were to keep documents, identity cards, money, watches and jewellery with us.

The queue began to move and I suddenly noticed several men fully dressed standing near another barrack further back, and I was wondering who they were. And just then another SS man (Miete was his name) came by me and said, 'Come on, you, get back into your clothes, quick, special work.' That was the first time I was frightened. Everything was very quiet, you know. And when he said that to me, the others turned around and looked at me — and I thought, my God, why me, why does he pick on me? When I had got back into my clothes, the line had moved on and I noticed that several other young men had also been picked out and were dressing. We were taken through to the 'work-barrack,' most of which was filled from floor to ceiling with clothes, stacked up in layers. Many of the clothes were filthy — we had to tear them apart by force, they stuck together with dirt and sweat. The foreman showed me how to tie the things together into bundles, wrapped up in sheets or big cloths. You understand, there was no time, not a moment between the instant we were taken in there and put to work, to talk to anyone, to take stock of what was happening . . . and of course, never forget that we had no idea at all what this whole installation was for. One saw these stacks of clothing — I suppose the thought must have entered our minds, where do they come from, what are they? We *must* have connected them with the clothes all of us had just taken off outside . . . but I cannot remember doing that. I only remember starting work at once making bundles, I *thought* as the foreman had told me, but then he shouted, 'More, more, put more in if you want to stay around.' Even then I didn't know what he meant; I just put more in. Even though stuff was being carried in from outside, the very clothes the people who had arrived with me had taken off minutes before, I think I still didn't think; it seems impossible now, but that's how it was. I too went outside to pick up clothes and suddenly something hit me on the back — it was like being struck by a tree-trunk: it was a Ukrainian guard hitting me with one of these awful huge whips. . . . 'Run,' he screamed, 'run' — and I understood from that moment on that all work in Treblinka was done at a run."

Later somebody whispered the truth about Treblinka, "But carefully, carefully," Richard said.

Life in Treblinka was always incredibly dangerous, always hung on a thread, but perhaps the most dangerous time was each morning, after the arrival of the transports, while the queues were moving up through the tube towards the death-camp and while the gas chambers were in operation.

"There was an incredible rivalry amongst the SS men," Richard said. "You see, they weren't just an amorphous mass, as people now like to imagine them; they were, after all, individual men, with individual personalities. Some were worse, some better. Almost every one of them had their protégés amongst the prisoners, whom they played off against each other. Of course, one can't look at this in the same way one might consider other 'organizations' where heads of sections have their favourites. Obviously, no ordinary standards of emotion or behaviour can apply; because all of existence, for us especially, and up to a point, at least by reflection, also for them, was reduced to a primeval level: life and death. Consequently all ordinary reactions became special, or at least very different. Perhaps some SS men developed a kind of 'loyalty' to one prisoner or another — though one hesitates to call it that; there really was almost invariably another, and usually nefarious, reason for any act of kindness or charity. One must always measure whatever they did against the deep fundamental indifference they felt towards all of us. It was of course more than indifference, but I call it that for want of a better word. Really, when one wants to evaluate how they behaved and what they were, one must not forget their incredible power, their autonomy within their narrow and yet, as far as we were concerned, unlimited field; but also the isolation created by their unique situation and by what *they* — and hardly anyone else even within the German or Nazi community — had in common. Perhaps if this isolation had been the result of good rather than evil deeds, their own relationships towards each other would have been different. As it was, most of them seemed to hate and despise each other and do anything — almost anything — to 'get at' each other. Thus, if one of them selected a man out of a new transport for work, in other words to stay alive at least for a while, it could perfectly easily happen — and often did — that one of his rivals, and make no mistake about it, in one sense or another they were all rivals, would come along and kill that man just to spite him [send him into the queue to be killed] or else 'mark' him, which was tantamount to death [anybody 'marked' went with the next transport]. All this created a virtually indescribable atmosphere of fear. The most important thing for a prisoner in Treblinka, you see, was not to make himself conspicuous. To this, too, there were degrees — which I will tell you about later. But basically it meant, first of all, not to do anything 'wrong' — the 'wrongest' thing being to work at anything remotely less than one's top capacity. And there were a hundred and one other arbitrary 'wrong' things, depending only on who saw you. Of course, I am not talking about any kind of insubordination; I mean in the context of our lives that would have been impossible — simply unthinkable. What one had to do was to develop to a fine art one's understanding of how to remain alive.

"All this applied much more during the first six months than the second. The whole Treblinka time needs to be divided into four phases. The first one was the months under Dr. Eberl [before Glazar himself — or Stangl — arrived]. The second one, already under Stangl, but in the beginning of his rule, was still a period of utter arbitrariness where one SS might select a man for work and an hour later, he might be dead, sent 'up' by another. Phase three — after the beginning of 1943 — was one of comparative stability: there were less transports; the SS by then knew their comparatively safe jobs far from the shooting war *depended* on their proving themselves indispensable by running efficient camps, so they began to value useful workers. And by that time, too, the prisoners had become individuals of sorts to them. They had, so to speak, 'tenure' in their jobs; there was a terrible kind of communality of basic purpose between the murderers and the victims — the purpose of staying alive.

"Finally phase four was the two, three months before the uprising in August 1943 — a period of increasing insecurity for the Germans when the Russians were approaching and the SS had begun to realize what it would mean if the war was lost and the outside world learned of what had been done in Treblinka, and that they were in fact individual men, individually accountable. And that it followed that they might, eventually, be able to make use of individual prisoners [to speak in their defence].

"However, these are generalizations; the reason why, the morning of our arrival, it was fifteen or thirty minutes before somebody managed to whisper to us what Treblinka was for, was that this was phase two of the camp's existence and fear dictated every move."

Richard Glazar, as I had learned to understand by then, has an extraordinary capacity for recall, and for relative detachment — essential if this particular story is to be bearable — and, in a wider sense, of value.

"How can one say how one reacted?" he said. "What I remember best about the first night is that I decided not to move; to . . . how can I say it . . . stand, sit, lie very very still. Was it already an unconscious realization that the main thing was not to be noticed? Did I instinctively connect being 'noticed' with 'movement'? I don't know. I told myself, 'Swim along with the current . . . Let yourself be carried . . . if you move too much, you'll go under. . . .'

"That night I wasn't hungry. I mean, there *was* food — there was always food after the arrival of 'rich' [Western] transports — but I couldn't eat. I was terribly terribly thirsty, a thirst that continued all evening, all night. . . .

"I remember, that evening in the barrack, the others watching us new ones. 'How are you going to behave?' they wondered. 'Are you going to scream, shout, sob? Are you going to go mad, hysterical, melancholy?' All these things happened; and from the next night on, when I myself was one of the 'old' ones, I watched the 'new' ones in exactly the same way. It was not curiosity — nor was it compassion. Already we were beyond such simple feelings; we did it in response to a need within ourselves; we needed to prove to ourselves, over and over, that everyone was the same as oneself, with the same fears, the same aggressions — perhaps not quite the same capacities. There was a kind of reassurance in both these things, and watching the new arrivals became a kind of rhythm, every night. . . ."

Richard spoke a great deal about "relationships" and how important they were to survival. "My friend Karel arrived in a transport the day after I had come. His whole family were killed at once but he was twenty-one years old and strong like me, so he too was among the lucky ones to be selected for work. From that moment we were never apart until 1945 when we returned to Prague together — they used to call us the twins. . . ."

The small Czech contingent of which Glazar was a part, so important in the life of the camp, is even today spoken of by other survivors, and by former SS men too, with a kind of awe. "They were special," said Samuel Rajzman, who lives in Montreal and is, in terms of wisdom and achievement, a rather "special" man himself. "They had a special kind of strength, a special life force." "The

Czechs?" said Suchomel. "Oh yes, I remember them very well. They *were* a special group: Masarek, Willie Fürst — they worked in the tailor shop under me. And then there was Glazar. Those lads slept on and under feather comforters. They were tidy — really tidy." And Berek Rojzman in Poland, also mentioned the Czechs. "I slept next to them. They were — they were a sort of élite group. Masarek," he said with awe, "and of course Glazar. I knew them all." It is gratifying to him to speak of them.

Richard says they were aware of this feeling in the other prisoners. "At the time," he said, "it was shaming for us. They seemed to feel we were superior to them. One of the Poles, David Bart, said once, 'You must survive; it is more important than that we should.' But there were very few of us. At the 'peak period' of the camp — autumn and winter of 1942 — there were a thousand work-Jews, eighteen of them us Czechs. Two of us survived, that's all." (Altogether about 250,000 Czech Jews were killed during the "Final Solution.")

At the beginning of what Glazar called phase two, the SS (Stangl, no doubt, with his talent for organization) decided they could use certain professionals and people with qualities of leadership to improve efficiency. With few exceptions (one of them a woman, and an informer who was later "executed" by the revolt committee) the members of this "élite" were Warsaw Poles over forty; doctors, engineers, architects and financiers. They were given the best, and slightly segregated accommodation, and arm-bands with the word *Hofjude* — "Court Jew" (derision even in privilege) — the main purpose of which was to protect them from some SS man's murderous whim. (Of the Czechs, only Rudolf Masarek — much younger than the others — was eventually to be appointed a "Court Jew.")

"Later, when we were in phase three," said Richard, "the arm-bands became unnecessary; they took them off then because they found it embarrassing to flaunt them before the rest of the slaves when they came back at night, half dead from exhaustion."

Six of the young Czechs, all arriving within days of each other, became close friends; but even within the six, they paired off in twos. "There was Karel and me," said Richard. "We worked from October until March in the warehouse, more specifically in 'men's clothing' — they called us 'Karel and Richard from Men's Better Overcoats.'

The one who arrived next was Robert Altschuh, a twenty-seven-year-old medical student, and after him thirty-two-year-old Hans Freund; he'd worked in textiles in Prague. Five days after us Rudi Masarek arrived; he was twenty-eight, tall, blond, blue-eyed; his family had owned one of the most exclusive men's shirt shops in Prague. . . ." (When Suchomel first saw Masarek, he said, "What the hell are *you* doing here? You aren't a Jew, are you?")

"Rudi was a sort of 'golden youth,'" said Richard. "You know what I mean? His had been the world of sports-cars, tennis, country-house weekends, summers on the Riviera. He was a half-Jew; there really was no reason for him to be there. Except that in 1938, after the Austrian Anschluss, he had fallen in love with a girl from Vienna who was Jewish. He married her the day before the regulation came into effect that Jews had to wear Stars of David on their clothes. Of course, he didn't have to wear it, but the day after his wedding he had the Star sewn on all his suits and coats. When she (though not he) was ordered to Theresienstadt, he went with her. And when she (not he) was ordered to Treblinka, he came with her there too. She was killed immediately. Rudi was an officer, a lieutenant in the Czech army, and he was later of decisive importance in the planning and execution of the revolt. But after his wife was killed it was three weeks before he would speak to anyone; he had been assigned to work in the tailor shop under Suchomel, who, by comparison to some, was relatively decent," Richard shrugged his shoulders. "That doesn't mean Suchomel didn't beat us; all of them beat us.

"The last arrival of our particular group, ten days or so later, was Zhelo Bloch — a photographer in ordinary life. He too was a Czech officer, also good-looking, with brown hair, a strong square sort of face and a muscular body. He was the military brain behind the planning for the uprising — for a long time. Both he and Rudi — and Robert too in other ways — were immensely important to us and to the camp as a whole. Zhelo and Robert became inseparable; and Rudi Masarek and Hans Freund. All of us had great respect for Galewski, the Polish camp-elder; he was an engineer of note, in his forties I think, tall, slim, with dark hair. He looked and behaved like a Polish aristocrat, a very remarkable man.

"Our daily life? It was in a way very directed, very specific. There were various things which were absolutely essential to survival: it was essential to fill oneself completely with a determination to survive; it was essential to create in oneself a capacity for dissociating oneself to some extent from Treblinka; it was important *not* to adapt completely to it. Complete adaptation, you see, meant acceptance. And the moment one accepted, one was morally and physically lost.

"There were, of course, many who did succumb: I have read more or less everything that has been written about this subject. But somehow no one appears to have understood: it wasn't *ruthlessness* that enabled an individual to survive — it was an intangible quality, not peculiar to educated or sophisticated individuals. Anyone might have it. It is perhaps best described as an over-riding thirst — perhaps, too, a *talent* for life, and a faith in life. . . ."

"If I speak of a thirst, a talent for life as the qualities most needed for survival," said Richard Glazar, "I don't mean to say that these were deliberate acts, or even feelings. They were, in fact, largely unconscious qualities. Another talent one needed was a gift for relationships. Of course, there *were* people who survived who were loners. They will tell you now they survived *because* they relied on no one but themselves. But the truth is probably — and they may either not know it, or not be willing to admit it to themselves or others — that they survived because they were carried by *someone*, someone who cared for them as much, or almost as much as for themselves. They are now the ones who feel the guiltiest. Not for anything they did — but for what they didn't do — for what . . . and this cannot be any reflection on them . . . for what simply wasn't in them to be."

It was quite clear that Richard did not mean to say that people died because they didn't have these qualities. To be chosen to live even for an extra day was nothing but luck, one chance in a thousand: it was only that if they had this incredible luck, then these qualities, he thought, gave them a chance to survive longer. . . .

"In our group," said Richard Glazar, "we shared everything, and the moment one of the group ate something without sharing it, we knew it was the beginning of the end for him. *Food* was uppermost in our minds; for a long time eating was an end in itself; we'd be given tin plates of soup at lunchtime, and bread and coffee. While the Western transports went on, there was so much food around, we used to throw the soup and bread away. There was a huge mountain of mouldy camp bread around [confirming what Suchomel had already told me, and contradicting Stangl's story]. We only drank the coffee. No, they didn't mind our taking food from the transports [presumably as long as they didn't know] — there was so much, you see. Of course, the SS and the Ukrainians had first choice, but there was much much more than that. We stole it, and we bought it too. That is, the Ukrainians would help themselves to most of it and then sell it back to us for gold, American dollars or jewellery. They had no means of getting at the valuables — they guarded the outside work details and the camp itself, but the work camp, inside, was worked by Jews, and guarded by the SS. The group who actually worked on registering the valuables — millions in money and stones — were called the 'gold-Jews.' SS-man Suchomel supervised them too; he did that and the tailor-shop. . . ."

"Later in the autumn," Richard Glazar went on, "we were allowed a thirty-minute lunch break when we could talk, and everybody would ask each other, 'What have you "organized" today?' And that always referred to gold, money and food. After a while we did begin to think that we must *do* something; plan something, resist. But the work and the unremitting tension made us fearfully tired, just tired you know, and one used to say to oneself, or to close friends, 'We *must* think — we *must* plan,' but then we'd add, 'We'll think tomorrow, not today.'

"Did we become hardened, callous to the suffering, the horror around us? Well, one can't generalize; as with everything in life, people reacted differently. One did, I think, develop a kind of dullness, a numbness where the daily nightmarish events became a kind of routine, and only special horrors aroused us, reminded us of normal feelings; sometimes this would be connected with specific and special people, sometimes with special events.

"There was the day when Edek arrived — he was a small fourteen-year-old boy. Perhaps he arrived with his family, perhaps alone, I don't know; when he got off the train and stood on the ramp, all one could see of him was his head and his shoes; in between was the accordion he'd brought, and that was all he brought. An SS saw him and said right away, 'Come, come,' and from that day on he played for them. They made a kind of mascot of him; he played everywhere, at all hours, and almost nightly in their mess. And just about the same time a famous opera singer arrived — a young one, from Warsaw — and somebody drew him to the attention of the SS and he too was pulled out. It wasn't long after that that they started the fires; we saw them for the first time in December, one night, through the barred window of the barrack; the flames rose high, high above the camp, flames in all colours: red, orange, blue, green, purple. And in the silence of the camp, and the terrible brightness of the flames, one heard nothing except little Edek playing his accordion and the young singer singing *Eli Eli*.

"Robert Altschuh said later that night — and that was the first time we had thought of it that way — 'They are trying to find ways to hide the traces; they are burning the corpses. But they aren't going to find it so easy — even one corpse doesn't burn easily, and hundreds of thousands of corpses. . . ?'

"So you see, that night, on the one hand we had allowed ourselves to be emotionally overwhelmed by this 'special event' — the fires. But then, only minutes afterwards, it was in a way cancelled out — and perhaps, although we may not have realized it, deliberately so — by Robert's scientific consideration of the problem of how to burn hundreds of thousands of corpses. He had a lot of ideas on it; he analysed the human body for us, what burned and what didn't burn, who would be easier and who more difficult to burn. And we listened, you know — with interest.

"Secrecy? Good heavens, there was no secrecy about Treblinka; all the Poles between there and Warsaw must have known about it, and lived off the proceeds. All the peasants came to barter, the Warsaw whores did business with the Ukrainians — it was a circus for all of them. . . ."

I asked Richard Glazar whether there were girls among the "work-Jews" and he said "Yes, there were girls. They worked in the kitchen and the laundry, in both the lower and upper camps. Of course, anyone who was sent to work in the upper camp, girls or men, knew they'd never come down again." (There is one single case on record — the carpenter Yankiel Wiernik — of someone moving back and forth between both parts of Treblinka. And although several people from the "upper camp" survived the August uprising, an authentic escape from there before then is unknown and considered impossible.)

"Yes," said Richard, "of course most of the — few — girls who were there paired off with somebody. Love? It's hard to say; relationships, strong friendships, yes — and yes, perhaps love; Kapo Kuba was in love — or lived with, if you like, a girl called Sabina. All the girls who were there were young and attractive; they only picked young and attractive ones, many of them blondes or redheads. Anyway, Sabina was found in bed, I think, with Kuba once, or something like that, and Küttner, one of the very bad SS men, said, 'We can't have all this whoring about,' and sent her up to work in the laundry at the death camp. Well, Kapo Kuba volunteered to go up too, to be with her. They didn't let him. But what would you call that? Not love? [Kuba is dead; "Sabina" is one of the two girls who survived, and lives in Israel.]

"Then there was Tchechia. She was in love with Rakowski, the former camp elder. And he, they said, was in love with her. Stadie shot him when he discovered (through an informer) that he had planned an escape for himself and Tchechia, and found gold on him. Perhaps Tchechia slept with other men afterwards. But can you wonder? Did it really matter? . . .

"Escapes?" said Richard Glazar. "Yes, there were a few, three I think which were successful, all in phase two; afterwards it became impossible."

He was to tell me later that two young men — "they were twenty-four and twenty-five, I think," he said — were smuggled out of the camp in the very first train to be sent out of Treblinka with the victims' clothes and other belongings. "It was the last two days of October or the very first of November. We helped to hide them; it was all very carefully organized to get the news out to Warsaw.

"At the end of November, beginning of December, seven men from the Blue Command tried and were caught. Kurt Franz shot them in the *Lazarett* and then called a special roll-call and said that if anybody else tried, particularly if they succeeded, ten would be shot for each one who escaped. . . .

"[T]he revolt was being planned from November 1942. Very very few people knew about it, and even fewer were actually on the planning committee. It was headed of course by the camp elder, Galewski, and until March, when catastrophe struck us, Zhelo Bloch was the military expert on it.

"The period between late October and the beginning of January was the peak period — that was when most of the transports arrived, sometimes six of them — 20,000 people a day. At first mostly Jews from Warsaw and the West, with their riches — above all enormous quantities of food, money and jewels. It was really incredible how much and what we ate; I remember a sixteen-year-old boy who, a few weeks after his arrival, said one night he'd never lived as well as here in Treblinka. It was — you know — very very different from the way people have written about it.

"You see, we weren't dressed in striped uniforms, filthy, lice-ridden, or, for much of the time, starving, as the concentration camp inmates mostly were. My own group — the Czechs — and the 'court-Jews' dressed extremely well. After all, there was no shortage of clothes. I usually wore jodhpurs, a velvet jacket, brown boots, a shirt, a silk cravat and, when it was cool, a sweater. In hot months I wore light trousers, shirt and a jacket at night. I shone my boots once or twice every day until you could see yourself in them, like in a mirror. I changed shirts every day and of course underclothes. We had no body-lice ourselves, but there were of course vermin all over the barracks — it was inevitable with all that was brought in by the transports. I'd wear a pair of pyjamas for two nights or so and then they'd be full of blood spots where I had killed bugs that crawled up on us in the night, and I'd think to myself, 'Tomorrow I must get new ones; hope they are nice silk ones; they are still on the way now.' That sounds terrible, doesn't it? Well, that is how one became. One was very concerned with the way one *looked*; it was immensely important to look clean on roll-call. One thought of small things all the time, like, 'I must shave; if I shave again, I have won another round.' I always had a little shaving kit on me. I still have it. I shaved up to seven times a day. And yet, this was one of the most torturing uncertainties; one never knew how the mood of the Germans 'ran' — whether, if one was *seen* shaving or cleaning one's boots, that wouldn't get one killed. It was an incredible daily roulette; you see, one SS might consider a man looking after himself in this way as making himself 'conspicuous' — the cardinal sin — and then another might not. The *effect* of being clean always helped — it even created a *kind* of respect in them. But to be seen doing it might be considered showing off, or toadying, and provoke punishment, or death. We finally understood that the maximum safety lay in looking much — but not *too* much — like the SS themselves and the significance of this went even beyond the question of 'safety.'

"At the beginning of winter the huge transports from the East started coming," Richard said. "The [Eastern] Polish Jews; they were people from a different world. They were filthy. They knew nothing. It was impossible to feel any compassion, any solidarity with them. Of course, I am not talking about the Warsaw or Cracow intellectuals; they were no different from us. I am talking about the Byelorussian Jews, or those from the extreme east of Poland. . . ."

"Things changed very much towards the middle of January," said Richard Glazar. "That was the beginning of phase three: fewer and fewer transports; less food and of course no new clothes. This was when the plans for the uprising were being worked on very intensely. And then, in the very beginning of March 1943, real catastrophe struck us.

"Küttner smelled something — there is no other way of putting it. He sensed that something was going on, and with perfect instinct he picked on the one person who was almost irreplaceable for us: Zhelo Bloch, the revolt committee's military expert. What Küttner took as a pretext was that some men's coats had disappeared, and Zhelo was in charge of them. He came to our barracks and raged; two men were shot on the spot, several were beaten. And Zhelo was sent up to Camp II.

"It was the most terrible blow to our morale, an anti-climax which is indescribable now. It wasn't only, you see, that he was so necessary, in a planning sense; it was that he was loved. Contrary perhaps to some of us, he was very much one of the people. Don't misunderstand me, I only mean that, of all of us, he was the one person who could talk to anybody, give anybody a sense of faith in himself and his capacities; he was a born leader, of the best kind.

"The evening he went was the end of hope for us — for a long time. I remember that night so clearly; it was the one time in all those months that we nearly lost control; that we gave way to emotion. It could have been the end for us.

"Robert Altschuh cried like a child. Of course, he had been closest to Zhelo; they needed each other. Zhelo was essential to Robert because he was a *doer*, but Robert was just as essential to Zhelo because he was an intellectual; they complemented and reassured each other. Zhelo had relied utterly on Robert intellectually. It was Robert who was the 'psychological' planner; who would explain the Nazis' psychology to us; he who advised us when to lie low and when to make ourselves noticed. He had an unfailing instinct for what was the right approach, and when. On the other hand, he was physically frail, and Zhelo of course was very strong. Without Zhelo's physical strength, Robert collapsed. Hans Freund, too, despite his closeness to Rudi Masarek, somehow couldn't recover from the psychological blow of Zhelo's going. It took some weeks before Rudi came into his own as a leader — by that time much of Hans's effectiveness had gone." ("Freund and Altschuh," he was to write later, "were still alive at the time of the revolt. But in all probability they died in the course of it.")[1]

"The evening of the day Zhelo was sent up to Camp II, I remember we were lying on our bunks; it was not quite dark. It was very very quiet. And suddenly Hans Freund said, 'We aren't human beings any more. . . .' It was something we had ceased to — or never did — think about. Certainly we had never talked about it; regret for the loss of one's sensitivity and compassion was something one just couldn't afford, just as one couldn't afford remembering those we had loved. But that night was different. . . .

"'I can only think of my wife and boy,' said Hans, who had never, with a word, spoken of his young wife and small boy from the day he arrived. 'I never felt anything that first night after we had come. There they were — on the other side of the wall — dead, but I felt nothing. Only the next morning, my brain and stomach began to burn, like acid; I remember hearing about people who could feel everything inside but couldn't move; that was what I felt. My little boy had curly hair and soft skin — soft on his cheeks like on his bottom — that same smooth soft skin. When we got off the train, he said he was cold, and I said to his mother, "I hope he won't catch a cold." A cold. When they separated us he waved to me. . . .'"

During the many many hours Richard and I talked, he never faltered; this was the only time. It was late at night, his family had gone to bed; his house is so deep in the country, there wasn't a sound except the occasional shuffle or wheezing from a cow in a nearby field. We sat in his living room which was dark except for a lamp on his desk. He hid his face in his hands for long minutes. I poured

---

[1] Although the lists of survivors of Treblinka and Sobibor are believed to be complete, it is impossible to place accurately the circumstances of the deaths of those who perished during or after the revolts.

some coffee his wife had made before she went to bed. We drank it without talking. "Did you see this?" he asked then after a while, pointing to something behind me. I turned around. In a cabinet, on a shelf by itself, a beautiful small Bristol-blue glass jar. "How lovely," I said. He shook his head, stood up, walked over, picked it up and handed it to me. "What do you think it is?" There was half an inch or so of something in the bottom of the jar. I didn't know. "Earth," he said. "Treblinka earth."

"Things went from bad to worse that month of March," he went on. "There were no transports — in February just a few, remnants from here and there, then a few hundred gypsies — *they* were really poor; they brought nothing. In the storehouses everything had been packed up and shipped — we had never before seen all the space because it had always been so full. And suddenly everything — clothes, watches, spectacles, shoes, walking-sticks, cooking-pots, linen, not to speak of food — everything went, and one day there was nothing left. You can't imagine what we felt when there was nothing there. You see, the *things* were our justification for being alive. If there were no *things* to administer, why would they let us stay alive? On top of that we were, for the first time, hungry. We were eating the camp food now, and it was terrible and, of course, totally inadequate [300 grammes of coarse black bread and one plate of thin soup a day]. In the six weeks of almost no transports, all of us had lost an incredible amount of weight and energy. And many had already succumbed to all kinds of illness — especially typhus. It was the strain of anxiety which increased with every day, the lack of food, and the constant fear of the Germans who appeared to us to be getting as panic-stricken as we were.

"It was just about when we had reached the lowest ebb in our morale that, one day towards the end of March, Kurt Franz walked into our barracks, a wide grin on his face. 'As of tomorrow,' he said, 'transports will be rolling in again.' And do you know what we did? We shouted, 'Hurrah, hurrah.' It seems impossible now. Every time I think of it I die a small death; but it's the truth. That is what we did; that is where we had got to. And sure enough, the next morning they arrived. We had spent all of the preceding evening in an excited, expectant mood; it meant life — you see, don't you? — safety and life. The fact that it was their death, whoever they were, which meant our life, was no longer relevant; we had been through this over and over and over. The main question in our minds was, where were they from? Would they be rich or poor? Would there be food or not?

"That morning, all of us stood around everywhere, waiting. The SS did too; for once they didn't care whether we worked or not. Everybody was discussing where they would be from; if only it were from somewhere rich like Holland.

"When the first train pulled in, we were looking out through the cracks in the wall of our barrack, and when they got out, David Bart called to one of the Blue Command, 'Where are they from?' and he answered, 'The Balkans.' I remember them getting off the train, and I remember Hans Freund saying, 'Ah yes, you can see they are rich. But they won't burn well, they are too fat.' This was a very, very special transport of rich Bulgarians who had lived in Salonika — 24,000 of them. They had already spent some time in a camp together; they were organized and disciplined, and they had equipped themselves with a special supply-car for the long journey. When the Blue Command opened those doors, we nearly fainted at the sight of huge pieces of meat, thousands of tins with vegetables, fats and fish, jars of fruit and jams, and cakes — the black earth of the ramp was yellow and white with cakes. Later, after the Bulgarians had been taken away, the Ukrainians fought us for the food; we managed 'accidentally-on-purpose' to drop some of the big wooden chests in which the jams were packed. They burst open, the Ukrainians beat us with their horrible whips, and we bled into the jam. But that was later; oh, the SS were very, very careful with this transport; if the Bulgarians had had the slightest idea what awaited them, they wouldn't have stood still for it. It would have been a bloodbath. But they hadn't a clue; even then, in March, almost April, 1943 — with nearly a million already killed in Treblinka, . . . three million or so by then in all the extermination and other camps in Poland — they were as full of illusions as we Czechs had been six months before. They still didn't know. The mind just boggles — with all the hundreds, the thousands of people who by then knew — how could they not have known? Marvellous-looking people they were; beautiful women, lovely children; stocky and strong-looking men; marvellous specimens. It took three days to kill them all. And ten days later we had processed all their belongings. Imagine, at fifty kilograms a person — that's what each was 'allowed' to bring for this 'resettlement' —

there were 720,000 kilograms of *things*; incredible, how the machine proved itself in those ten days.

"This is something, you know, the world has never understood; how perfect the machine was. It was only lack of transport because of the Germans' war requirements that prevented them from dealing with far vaster numbers than they did; Treblinka alone could have dealt with the 6,000,000 Jews and more besides. Given adequate rail transport, the German extermination camps in Poland could have killed all the Poles, Russians and other East Europeans the Nazis planned eventually to kill. . . .

"The revolt was planned for the late afternoon of August 2," said Richard Glazar, "so as to give people the maximum chance to escape in the dark. . . . At 2 P.M., an order came through from the committee that from that moment no Jew would be allowed to die; if there was any threat from anyone, the balloon would have to go up earlier than planned. At ten minutes to four Kuba said something to Küttner and shortly afterwards Küttner started to beat a young boy. That was what started it — at three minutes to four, probably about two hours early. . . .

"My main memory of the revolt," Richard said, "is one of utter confusion; the first moments were of course madly exciting; grenades and bottles of petrol exploding, fires almost at once, shooting everywhere. Everything was just that much different from the way it had been planned, so that we were thrown into utter confusion. . . .

"Within minutes," Glazar said, "it was more or less each man for himself. There were groups who escaped together as planned, but of each group only a few made it. Of the twenty-five of us in the camouflage unit who had planned to stay together, six, possibly eight, got out. Only four of us are alive today. . . ."

Alexander Donat

Surviving Slave Labor at Maidanek

Maidanek was hell. Not the naive inferno of Dante, but a twentieth-century hell where the art of cruelty was refined to perfection and every facility of modern technology and psychology was combined to destroy men physically and spiritually. To begin with, in accord with Germanic efficiency — *Ordnung muss sein!* — the new shipment of prisoners was taken to the camp office (*Schreibstube*) where "scribes," mostly Czech and Slovak Jews, sat behind tables. One of them carefully filled in a long form for which I had to supply my name, date of birth, occupation (I said printer), and then came the question: "When were you arrested?" I looked at him surprised. Was he trying to mock me? Could it be that he didn't know? "Well, when were you arrested?" he repeated impatiently.

"We weren't arrested. We were rounded up during the uprising."

"All right, all right," he said, in a bored voice. "But when?"

I gave him the date. He handed me the form he'd filled out and told me to go to another table. I glanced at the form and had only enough time to read a few words at the end. They gave me a jolt: "S. D. (for *Sicherheitsdienst*, the Nazi security police) . . . sentenced to life imprisonment. . . ." I handed the form to the clerk at the table indicated and he gave me a numbered piece of canvas. I looked at my number: 7,115. From that moment I ceased to be a man, a human being; instead I became camp inmate 7,115.

After the formalities, we were driven to an empty barrack where a few moments later our new master appeared: the Barrack Elder (*Blockälteste*) of Barrack Number Five. Short, heavy-set, and a former policeman, Mietek Szydlower was a native of Lodz who had

From *The Holocaust Kingdom: A Memoir*. New York: Holocaust Library, 1965.

been sent to Maidanek from the Warsaw cauldron in September, 1942. With brutal frankness he told us what it was like there.

"This is a K. L.," he said. "Remember those two initials, K. L. . . . *Konzentrationslager*. This is a death camp, a *Vernichtungslager*. You've been brought here to be destroyed by hunger, beating, hard labor, and sickness. You'll be eaten by lice, you'll rot in your own shit.

"Let me give you one piece of advice: forget who and what you were. This is a jungle and here the only law is the law of the strongest. No one here is a Mr. Director or a *Herr Doktor*. Everyone here is the same; everyone here is shit. All are going to die."

"There's no hope?" someone asked tremulously.

"Ten percent of you may survive. Only those who can get a special job have a chance. Those who have gold, jewels, money, can buy jobs. For the others, only one hope: to organize."

That was the second time I had heard the magic word and I thought it referred to a highly clandestine but ubiquitous organization of the just which protected the most deserving or the most wronged. But Barrack Elder Szydlower quickly dispelled my romantic fantasies. In camp slang, "to organize" merely meant to look after Number One. It was to steal soup from the kitchen, for example; but to steal bread from a fellow inmate, however, was to *really* steal.

"And another thing," Mietek added, "it's important to keep your eyes and ears open all the time. We have a saying here: You'd better have eyes in your ass."

We were all hungry. We hadn't eaten, couldn't remember our last meal, but we were too late to be fed that day; there hadn't been time to put us on the rolls properly. We'd start eating the next day, we were told. Later we learned that this too was another example of organization — by camp officials. Several hundred stolen suppers meant a handsome profit for them.

The barrack was a long wooden shed originally intended as a stable for horses, easily verified by the *Pferdbaracke* inscription over the doorway and the ramps instead of steps at the entrances. A narrow glass opening ran around the building just under the roof to let some daylight in, but there were no windows in the usual sense. Triple-decker bunks stood against both walls and a narrow aisle was kept between bunks and walls, a broader one between the two rows of bunks. At the far end of the building was a second entrance, usually kept locked. Near the main entrance were the bunks of the barrack élite: the Barrack Elder, the Scribe, and a few orderlies (*Stuben-dienst*). The Barrack Elder was master of life and death of his subjects. The Scribe kept the rolls, the life-and-death statistics of the barrack. He recorded the daily increase (*Zugang*) and decrease (*Abgang*), or transfer (*Verlegung*), whether to another barrack, camp, or hospital. He also noted "natural" decreases, *i.e.*, by death. The orderlies kept the barrack swept and in order, and saw to it that no one stayed hidden there during the day. Occasionally they also acted as the Elder's deputies in handing out food rations. Soon after our arrival a new official was appointed to beat up inmates at the Elder's orders, a job usually given to Soviet prisoners of war. In our barrack the job was held by an athletic native of Leningrad named Andrey. In the next barrack it was another Russian, Ivan. Andrey was normally quiet and rather good-natured; but when he was "on duty," he would grow excited and could be terrible.

All these "authorities" were subject to the central authority of the *Lagerschreiber*, or Camp Scribe, who had a dozen clerks working for him. Together these were the clerical office (*Schreibstube*). The *Lagerschreiber's* principal assistant was the official who assigned inmates to specific work parties, the so-called *Kommandos*. As a member of a *Kommando*, each prisoner was subject to another hierarchy of masters. Each *Kommando* had a Kapo, or head. The term was thought to be derived from the Italian *capo* (head); but others maintained it was an abbreviation of *Kazetpolizei*, or *Konzentrationslager Polizei*. The Kapo also had assistants called *Vorarbeiter* (foremen) who in their turn had assistants called *Schieber* (pushers). Although these were all prisoners, too, they had the power of life and death over the workers assigned to them. At the very top of the concentration-camp hierarchy was the so-called *Lagerälteste* or camp warden, also a prisoner, but invariably a German.

These various prisoner authorities were themselves ruled by a parallel SS organization. Every barrack had its own SS barrack leader, every labor project its own SS men, and at the top of their hierarchical pyramid stood the *Lagerführer*, or Camp Commandant, generally a high-ranking SS officer.

Maidanek was divided into five "Fields," each in reality a separate camp, consisting of a gigantic rectangle surrounded by barbed-wire fences. A few yards from the wire, wooden signs warned: "ATTENTION! DEATH ZONE!" Wire was electrified and anyone who touched it was electrocuted. At the four corners of the rectangle stood watchtowers with armed guards at the ready. The first Field housed the central camp offices and the files; the second was occupied by highly skilled prisoners employed in the camp workshops; the other laborers were crowded into the third and fourth Fields, between which there was a large area called Coal Field or In-Between Field. Field Five was reserved for women prisoners. Fields Three, Four, and Five were filled with inmates destined eventually for the crematoria.

Field Three, where I was assigned, had twenty-two numbered barracks, all of the same design, around a large central open space — except for Barrack Nineteen, the *Gamelbaracke*. Entrance to that was obscured by a high wooden fence so that one couldn't see what went on inside, but we soon learned that it was where the old and weak inmates were housed, the vestibule to the gas chamber. To the right of the entrance to the Field was the Field Office barrack, inhabited by the "aristocracy" of the Field; to the left were the automotive workshops (*Fahrbereitschaft*). The last barrack on the left was the kitchen serving all five Fields; across from it was the L-Barrack, which contained washrooms.

In Barrack Number Five we were given sacks and told to go out and fill them with straw. Those were our mattresses. We were each then assigned a bunk. When the soup, bread, and margarine were brought in for the regular inmates, we newcomers ran to the washroom to get a drink of water to stay our hunger, but the crowd around the faucets was so great that we had little hope of getting close to them.

At 9 P.M. we were driven inside the barracks and 9:30 the gong sounded to mark the end of the day. Anyone caught outside after that time could be shot on sight by the guards on the towers. The lights inside went out except for a few small bulbs, but we were not to have a quiet night's sleep. About 10:30 P.M. the noisy *Wagenkolonne*, the working party which took rations from the kitchen to the other Fields, came in. Though this assignment was hard work, those on the work party were given double portions of food and allowed to catch up on their sleep during the day. Moreover, they earned money by such chores as delivering messages between one Field and another, carrying greetings or gifts from husband to wife, or vice-versa. The majority of these men would not have exchanged for anything in the world their privilege of visiting the women's Field three times a day. The *Wagenkolonne* turned in quickly, but then the parade to and from the latrine began and kept up for the rest of the night.

What was called a latrine consisted of a wooden box with handles at both ends similar to what hod carriers use to transport cement. Only one such box was assigned to each barrack, which might house two or three hundred inmates, and sometimes as many as five hundred. The overwhelming majority of the camp inmates suffered from diarrhea and almost everyone also had weakness of the bladder, so that the latrine was soon filled and overflowing. The stinking puddles on the floor were nauseating and when men had to wade through them barefoot because they had been thoughtless enough not to put on their wooden shoes, it was worse. But barefoot or shod the inmates trotting to and from the latrine soon tracked the entire barracks up with filth. To add to the dreadful stench the crowd around the latrine was usually noisy, and for our first few nights at Maidanek we found it very hard to bear. Afterward nothing could disturb our sleep.

At 2:30 A.M. the *Wagenkolonne* left for work, and an hour later, at 3:30 A.M., the gong announced the beginning of a new day. The orderlies yelled, "Everybody up!" and we barely had our eyes open before Andrey was running back and forth pulling sleepers out of bed by their legs, clouting some over the head, speeding along the dawdlers. Over and over again, in his comical mixture of Polish and Russian, he threatened, "You're going to get twenty-five lashes on your bare ass. . . ."

And so the nightmare began first thing in the morning. German *Ordnung* demanded that our bunks be made up in strict military style and rigidly perfect. Since the majority of inmates had no military or even scout training, the demand was rarely met. Though Barrack Elder Szydlower daily rewarded the two best bedmakers with an extra portion of bread, he simultaneously punished at least a dozen by depriving them of their portions. When that proved ineffective, he ordered those whose beds were improperly made to be flogged. The barrack orderlies took immediate advantage of this — "organization" — and for a modest payment in margarine, soup, or a slice of bread, they exempted the untidy or made up their bunks for them.

After making our beds we rushed to the L-Barrack to wash. We soon learned that the washrooms, like everything else in Maidanek, were instruments of torture. Crowds pressed around the building in such numbers that they had to be held back by Kapos with clubs in their hands. When you did finally manage to get inside and close to a faucet, you were likely to be attacked by one of the many Kapos or orderlies standing there. Anyone taking off his shirt was especially liable to be beaten. "What do you think this is, a Roman bath? Or a beach?" A punch in the face was the usual accompaniment to such comments. If, prudently, you kept your jacket on and simply splashed your face, the Kapo would shout, "You filthy shitface, don't you know how to wash?" And you got your punch in the face anyway. Every day men came back from the washroom bleeding from the blows on the head and face, and before long the intended aim was achieved: the number of visitors to the washroom dropped to a minimum and the orderlies no longer had to work so hard cleaning and polishing it. Prisoners themselves, they consequently did not have to be so frightened when the SS inspectors came around, for the SS men had no special consideration for the buttocks or necks of camp "officials."

At 4:30, "coffee" — a light mint infusion without nourishment and with a repulsive taste — was distributed. We often took a few swallows and used the rest for washing, but not all of us were able to do without this poor substitute for coffee and consequently many inmates ceased to wash. This was the first step to the grave. It was an almost iron law: those who failed to wash every day soon died. Whether this was the cause or the effect of inner breakdown, I don't know; but it was an infallible symptom.

After coffee came the daily roll call, in which inmates lined up in ranks of five, dressed and redressed to military perfection, and interminably counted and recounted. The actual number of prisoners had to dovetail with the theoretical number computed by the Barrack Scribe. Prisoners who had died since the previous roll call also had to be counted present so their bodies were dragged out of the barracks and placed on the ground next to their live comrades. When everything had been checked, with continuing screams and blows, the barracks staff took its place in front of the assembled ranks. Two block *Führers* marched briskly from barrack to barrack, and at their approach everyone froze at attention and held his breath. The Barrack Elder always gave the command in an especially dramatic way:

"*Block fünf. Achtung! Mützen* . . . (the pause always seemed to last an eternity) . . . *ab!*" Then he stepped forward, reporting the number of prisoners present. The SS men would inspect the ranks, take their own count, and then pass on to the next barrack.

When the numbers did not tally, there was hell to pay. The barrack staff scurried around like rats and they were urged on by SS men with kicks and blows. The barracks were thoroughly searched and woe to the wretch who had fallen asleep, fainted, or was simply too weak to stir. They fell on him like a pack of mad dogs. If the barrack staff found him before the SS men got there, he had a chance; but once the SS men arrived, he was as good as dead. By the time he was dragged out and propped up in formation, he was half dead from the beating he had been given. As soon as roll call was over he was publicly hanged for "having attempted to escape."

Most often, however, when a man had to be searched for, he was beyond the reach of the SS. He would usually be stretched out staring up at them with fearless, glassy eyes, teeth bared in a mocking grin that no SS man's fist could wipe away. They would kick and curse him nonetheless, but he was beyond their power.

When roll call was completed, the order, "*Arbeitskommandos formieren!*" rang out. The formations would then scatter, and in the big open area dozens of work parties would form and be marched out of the gate under the leadership of the Kapos. Slowly the square was emptied and the barracks staffs would go back inside to their duties. Only the newly arrived who had not yet been assigned to *Kommandos* were left behind. For these there was no hiding or resting in the barracks. Whether in broiling sun or pouring rain it was forbidden to be in the barracks during the day and new arrivals were forced to spend the entire day out of doors. They would be divided into groups of fifty with a Kapo in charge and the drilling would begin. This pitiful and comic spectacle of ragged men in wooden shoes trying to imitate well-drilled military formations was continued beneath a barrage of blows, curses, and orders. The Kapos, young and well fed, did not tire quickly and depending on their mood — and the frequency with which SS men appeared on the square — drill might be more exhausting and sadistic on one day than on another. When the Kapo was in a bad mood or desirous of showing his zeal to the SS men, formations did everything on the double, push-ups, knee-bends, and all the rest, without letup all morning long. The sun rose and beat down pitilessly, we grew increasingly exhausted by the exercise, we were tormented by hunger.

At last noontime came and an hour break for lunch. We stood in formation before the barrack awaiting the return of the work parties. The barrack staff brought kettles of soup from the kitchen and set them up in a row, and we stood in line and one by one went up to the kettle. One of the orderlies took a bowl from a pile, and the Barrack Elder in person ladled some soup into it. One by one the inmates grabbed the bowl with the steaming soup and greedily began to drink it while walking away. There were no spoons at Maidanek: with time, you might organize one, but in the interim you drank the hot soup directly from the bowl and you did it in a hurry because the bowl might be needed for someone else.

The soup line always moved fast. Several hundred starving men kept the closest and most suspicious tabs on the Barrack Elder as he plunged his ladle into the kettle and filled bowl after bowl. To distribute soup from the kettle was a great art and a great mystery. Theoretically, each inmate was entitled to a liter of soup and the ladle did, in fact, hold one liter. But all the Barrack Elder had to do was step up the pace of his serving, tip the ladle ever so slightly to one side or another and he pinched some of the soup from each theoretical "full" liter. Several hundred such fractions add up to a considerable amount of soup. In most cases the thicker and more nourishing ingredients in the soup fell to the bottom of the kettle and the top was little more than water. Naturally the Barrack Elder always left the thickest part of the soup at the bottom for himself, for his own turn came last. Often he would work it so that the spoon literally "stood up" in the bottom of the kettle. A rude voice would yell angrily, "Stir the soup goddam it!" The Elder would seem to give the soup a good swirl with the ladle, but he would be careful not to stir very deeply so that his own share would be nonetheless nourishing for all of the showy exhibition.

Only the newcomers waxed indignant about this; the old-timers knew better, and didn't try to buck the system. Their strategy was based on the type of soup being served. For potato or turnip soup, where the best settled at the bottom, one tactic was necessary; for cabbage or nettles, where the "best" remained on top, another was called for. Each kettle held fifty liters, and for potato or turnip soup, they placed themselves in line at the end of every fifty men, while the newcomers surged forward to be served first. In these matters, the experienced inmates acted with great shrewdness, and one of them initiated me into the soup strategy shortly after my arrival, my basic course in the *Konzentrationslager* University.

After everyone had had his bowl of soup, the Barrack Elder granted his favorites the privilege of scraping the bottom of the kettle and licking it clean, and there was constant competition for that privilege. This one-hour break for soup, served and consumed outside the barrack, was the only break during the working day.

Field Three housed from 5,000 to 8,000 inmates, and during my first lunch break I looked around eagerly for men I had known in Warsaw. I found many and from them I learned that the workers from our printing plant had been sent to the *Flugplatz* only a few days before me; they had been assigned to Poniatowa, Trawniki, the *Flugplatz*, and Maidanek. They had been deported with the personnel of the *Werterfassung*, and only Rachman and a group of nine men had been left behind to dismantle the presses and prepare them for transport by rail. The *Werterfassung* authorities had decided to move the printing plant to Radom and as soon as the machines were installed and ready, all the printers now in the camps would be sent there to operate it. Some of the printers told me that Rachman had given a high SS officer 100,000 zlotys so that the print shop would be moved to Radom and our printers assigned to it.

After the *Kommandos* had been formed and marched away for the afternoon work, the newcomers were ordered to the barracks to be shaved and to have numbers sewed on their clothes. The barracks barber turned out to be my regular barber from Leszno Street, a man named Stopnica. The man who sewed on my number was the well-known Warsaw tailor, Nisson. Inmates were not yet issued striped uniforms in those days but instead wore cast-off civilian clothing; down the back was a wide red band and the letters *K.L.*, with similar stripes on the trouser legs down the front of the left leg and the back of the right one. Inmates who failed to report to the authorities when these stripes faded risked being hanged "for planning to escape."

Each inmate also had a black number on white canvas sewed over the left breast of his jacket and below it a colored triangle with a letter inside designating nationality: P for Pole, U for Ukrainian, F for Frenchman, and so on. The color of the triangle indicated the nature of the inmate's "crime": political prisoners had red triangles, common criminals green, saboteurs black ones, homosexuals pink, religious objectors purple, and Jews yellow triangles. Neither Germans nor Jews wore letters to indicate nationality. The Jews were a group apart and the yellow triangle was a sufficient badge in itself. Only we, the Jews of Warsaw, were singled out for special "distinction": besides the yellow triangle pointed upward we had on top of it a red triangle pointing downward. Together they made a red and yellow six-pointed Star of David which stood for "the Jewish Bandits of Warsaw."

After being shaved and having our numbers sewed on, we were sent out of the barracks to continue drilling. This time we were to learn to take our caps off together, and the practice gave opportunities for endless sadistic beatings of those who put their caps back on a second too soon or too late.

Beating and being beaten was taken for granted at Maidanek, and was an integral part of the system. Everyone could beat an inmate and the more experienced inmates never questioned why. They knew that they were beaten merely because they happened to run into someone who wanted to beat them. In most cases, the beating did not even involve personal anger or hatred; the authorities hated their victims as a group because when you wrong people for no reason, sooner or later you must come to hate them. It is difficult for man to endure the idea he is a beast and maltreats another human being without cause; therefore, he eventually discovers justification for his behavior and imputes the fault to his victim. Thus, beating was part of the system. Thus, also, the victim was expected to take his licks standing rigidly at attention. Attempts to avoid blows, to cover one's face or head, were treated as additional offenses. Some made the mistake of smiling stupidly as if they understood the "joke" being played on them, as if they appreciated the authorities' "sense of humor," which served only to irritate the beaters further. Worst of all were the beatings undertaken for sheer distraction, for there the morbid imagination of the executioners knew no bounds. Some derived their greatest pleasure from refined torture and were delighted by the professional approval of their colleagues. Some were motivated by sadistic curiosity: they wanted to see how a man suffers and dies. Still others achieved a sexual enjoyment from the last fatal spasms of their victims.

One Kapo, for example, lay in wait near the camp latrine, hidden behind a brick pile. When he saw an inmate running for the latrine he would jump out of his hiding place and call the prisoner to him. The unfortunate victim, repressing the pain in his bowels, would stand at attention while the Kapo showered him with questions. "Where are you going, you son-of-a-bitch? Who is your Kapo? What *Kommando*? Where were you born?" By that time the poor wretch would be writhing with pain. Then the Kapo would give him calisthenics, making him squat in deep-knee-bends until the poor man could no longer control his sphincter and "exploded." Then the Kapo would belabor him with kicks and blows until, bruised and bleeding, covered with his own excrement, the victim would be allowed to drag himself to the latrine.

Another Kapo specialized in torturing alleged escapees. All over the area were scattered large cement pipes a yard in diameter. Occasionally, an inmate ready to faint from exhaustion would seek refuge from the hot sun or pouring rain in one of those pipes, where he would usually fall asleep. Which was precisely what the Kapo was waiting for. He would sneak up to the pipe and arouse his victim with a bloodcurdling yell. The prisoner would leap out of the cement pipe and run for his life, the Kapo screaming in hot pursuit. Soon other Kapos and SS men would join the hunt and prolong it deliberately until their victim was surrounded. His pursuers would merely stand there for a time, watching the inmate's agonies, his heaving chest, his maddened eyes, and the smile on his face, the inexplicable smile of a man who knows his end has come but somehow cannot believe it.

Then one of the pursuers would step forward for the kill. The step signified that the victim was his, and his alone, and none of the others would touch him. If the man playing the part of the matador was one Kapo, a native Viennese, he would knock the prisoner down with a lightning blow and then, with a balletlike motion put his heel against the man's throat. His speciality was strangling prisoners with the heel of his boot, and he would stand erect in the pose of a Roman gladiator enjoying the approval of the other Kapos, who would speak admiringly of a "good, clean job." A real master, a strangler who did not need to dirty his hands. If the matador was another

Kapo, named Janusz, his method of killing was different. He would throw himself on his victim and lie on top of him, almost caressingly wrapping his fingers around his victim's throat. To the uninitiated, it might seem that the two bodies were throbbing in erotic ecstasy, and in fact the Kapo did have an orgasm at such moments, while his companions looked on in snickering admiration. This might happen once, or even twice a day.

But most beat their victims because it was the custom of the place. At Maidanek no one could be neutral: either you were victim or executioner. Anyone in authority who failed to take advantage of his privilege to beat inmates undermined his status in the camp elite. Later, we learned that the elite of our tormentors was far from homogeneous; within the hierarchy there were complex factions and conflicts.

At 6 P.M. the *Kommandos* began to return and the gate became lively. Every few minutes a Kapo — some in red cavalry breeches — drew up before the guard, stood at attention, and reported that his team was returning in such-and-such numbers and the guard would scrupulously write that down in his book. Some teams came back like victorious armies, ranks swaying evenly and rhythmically, files on parade. Others came back as from a pogrom, uneven ranks of emaciated and exhausted men driven by the kicks and curses of their foreman and Kapos. At the end of such processions usually came the corpses, carried on stretchers by their comrades. The work parties assigned to road building, about which there were bloodcurdling stories, produced the most corpses. Not only was road construction beyond the strength and endurance of weakened, undernourished men, but the worst sadists were the Kapos and foremen on those *Kommandos*.

The camp was, in fact, a small city, and continually expanding. Administrative work alone required considerable staff. The kitchens for inmates and SS took a small army of potato peelers, dishwashers, cooks, and food handlers, as well as the special detail which carried the rations to the various Fields. The camp kitchen in our Field served at times as many as 30,000 inmates. Workers were required for new buildings, new roads, fences, water conduits, and all the rest. Workshops of all kinds employed tailors, mechanics, cobblers, seamstresses. Only a small part of workshop production went to fulfill camp needs; most of it was devoted to cleaning up and repairing objects looted or confiscated by the Germans so that they could subsequently be sent to the Reich. Hundreds of inmates worked at sorting, disinfecting, and storing the property taken from new arrivals, and choosing the best of it for shipment to the *Vaterland*.

A special team was permanently employed to empty the gas chambers and dispose of the bodies. The normal problem of the murderer — what to do with the body — was one of Maidanek's most difficult "technical" problems, and the task of disposing of the dead frequently lagged behind the constantly stepped-up "output." Some dead were buried in the old-fashioned way in enormous mass graves in the Krepiec Woods — the work of the so-called *Waldkommando* (the forest detail) — and some were burned on special grills in a provisional crematorium — the task of the *Himmelkommando* (the heaven detail). Bones were ground up and mixed with ashes and the latrine excrement to be used eventually as fertilizer. A special *Scheisskommando* (the "shit detail") cleaned up the latrines and carried away the excrement. Of all the work parties this was considered one of the most desirable: men assigned to it were given better rations and the SS men left it alone because of the stench. . . .

After supper Szydlower sent for me to tell me that my middle-tier bunk was now assigned to some "big shot," and I'd have to take one of the top bunks a few rows back. At first I didn't care, but around midnight I was awakened by something wet on my face. The barrack was full of snores and the latrine stench. Outside it was raining heavily and there was a hole in the roof right over my bunk. I moved to the edge of the bunk, but soon it was completely drenched. I got no sleep and finally the gong ended my torment.

Something different was in store for me. After roll call, when the order resounded to form *Kommandos*, the scribe called out the numbers of those inmates assigned to road building, but many of them began to gripe and one had a hysterical fit. He threw himself on the ground, tore his shirt, screamed he would rather be killed on the spot. Others showed the marks of the previous day — a black eye, welts from a riding crop, a bandaged hand. Several Barracks Elders and a Kapo came to the assistance of Szydlower and the "mutiny" was swiftly quelled. "As punishment," thirty additional men from our barracks were assigned to the road-building work party, including me. We joined a large column which soon was marched through the gate, and we sank up to our ankles in the clayey ground still sodden from the all-night downpour. Our wooden shoes stuck to the clay, making every step an effort. Small wonder that road building was a recognized necessity at Maidanek. We marched past Fields Two and One and found ourselves in an open area next to the Chelm highway. Before us were the guardhouse, the kennels with 200 trained police dogs, and the Political Department, whose mention gave the political prisoners the shakes. Nearby was a house said to be the camp garrison's bordello.

We were split into a number of small groups, mine assigned to loading stones on a cart that was mounted on rails and stationed at the top of a small hill. When it was filled with stones, a prisoner got up behind it to steer it. Other prisoners gave the cart a shove and the driver went down the hill, braking the cart with the help of a heavy pole wedged between the back wheels and the body of the cart. In the same way he had to bring the cart to a halt at the bottom of the hill, where another work party unloaded the stones and then four prisoners, of whom I was one, had to push the empty cart back up the hill. Two young Soviet prisoners of war, supervised by a Kapo and an SS man, were our foremen. During the morning all went well, but in the afternoon the SS man and the Kapo for some reason became enraged and began to belabor us with riding crops and sticks, shouting in broken Polish and German: "Quick, quick! Shove hard, you lazy bastards!"

The foreman emulated them and soon we were running up and down hill under a steady stream of blows. The Russians joined the game wholeheartedly, enjoying the beating and adding their native Russian obscenities to the continual stream of *Dreckjude, Judensau,* and other imprecations screamed by the Germans. One of the Russians ran up to the man next to me and smashed him in the face with his fist. When I looked at him surprised — could he be the same man who had spoken so gently that morning? — the Russian screamed at me, "You Jews won't work. In Russia, too, you always pick the cushy office jobs. Well, now we'll teach you a lesson!"

I had made a mistake in attracting his attention. After a moment the cart was ready to descend again, but this time the driver didn't manage to slow down. His pole broke, the cart jumped the rails, turned over, and spilled the load of stones. The driver had jumped off right into the arms of the SS man and was killed on the spot for "sabotage." When his bloody remains were shoved aside to be carried back to camp after work, the Russian pointed to me and said, "You take his place."

I had never done anything like that in my life. With terror in my heart, I tried my best . . ·. and to my surprise was successful. Every time the cart got safely down the hill, I was soaked with sweat and shaking with tension. That evening when our column returned to camp, four stretchers with the dead made up the rear, two of them from our barracks. I could barely stand on my feet at roll call. We were counted, as usual, and the numbers tallied. The Barrack Elder glanced at the corpses sympathetically because they had died conveniently. The barracks staff hated to have inmates die at night, for then they did not profit from the deaths. This way the Barracks Elder and his cronies got the dead men's shares of the supper ration, since the supper roster had already been closed for the day. To die during the night was an uncomradely act and the disappointed jackals showered abuse on the corpse in the morning.

Our misfortunes were not yet over for the day. A slip-up somewhere had left the over-all roll call for Field Three short. In Maidanek, where the main activity was the extermination of hundreds of thousands of people, the slightest bookkeeping error sent everyone scurrying as if the fate of the Third Reich were at stake. At such times the roll call might be prolonged for hours until the missing inmate was found, or the error otherwise accounted for. This time we did not have to wait long. In about half an hour a prisoner ran in through the gate followed by an SS man belaboring him with a club. "Aii, I'm dead. I'm not alive!" the victim screamed at the top of his lungs. The poor man did not know how close to the truth he was. It turned out he had been in the latrine when his *Kommando* had been ordered back to camp. By mistake he had fallen in with another team which ended up at Field Four. He realized this at the gate to Field Four and reported to the sergeant on duty there. Nevertheless, he was summarily sentenced to be hanged for "attempting to escape.". . .

On the night of my first road-building experience, again I could not sleep. It rained and my bed was soaked; I was tormented by rheumatic pains; I had caught cold in the bladder and kept having to run to the latrine all through the night; in the morning I could barely drag my body to roll call. Again I was assigned to the road-building

Kommando. This time we were to dig ditches for sewers, and each group of five prisoners was allotted a length of ditch to dig. My group included two sturdy, well-fed young Polish laborers, two emaciated Jews from the last Warsaw shipment, and myself.

The Polish boys worked so efficiently that our group did better than the others, our sector was ready before the midday break, and the Kapos and SS men who strode back and forth passed us by and did not beat us. After soup, our group was ordered to dig a lateral trench to the main conduit. Our Kapo nudged me, picked up a stick, thrust it into my hand, and said, "You'll be foreman!" The Polish boys glared at me angrily, but dared not protest. Flashing their shovels, they set to work again efficiently, but the two Warsaw Jews at the other end of the ditch could barely move and every other minute they had to stop for rest. The Poles grumbled loudly: "Look at those goddam goldbricks! No wonder the Germans exterminate them like lice." Gradually, they grew bolder and began to urge me on: "What are you standing there for? What kind of a foreman are you? So now we have to work for these dirty Jews? Why don't you use your stick on them?"

I tried to appease them, but failed. When I urged the Jews to greater effort, they replied that I was as much an anti-Semite as those Polish brutes. I knew that to save my own skin I ought to hit them, but I simply couldn't do it. In a camp swarming with sadists and murderers waiting only for a pretext to indulge themselves, and many who did not even need a pretext, I was sure that I would be maimed or killed. What was I to do? I began to shower abuse on my mutineers: "You so-and-sos, shut up, and get back to work!" The Poles and Jews responded in kind, and our Kapo ran up. "*Was ist los?*" he yelled. Examining the ditchdigging at the Polish end and at the Jewish end, he ordered me to bend over and a merciless blow set my whole body afire. A moment later I was in the ditch with a shovel in my hands and a new foreman, one of the Poles, stood over me, brandishing his stick. "You shitty intellectual, so you want to play the good guy, huh? Well, if you don't want to smack them, you'll have to work for them!" I dug with such a passion that the Pole was amazed; I dug as if my salvation depended on it, and my two Warsaw colleagues, encouraged by blows, were working harder, too.

I dragged myself back to camp that night like a beaten dog. When I went into the barrack, Szydlower jeered at me. He had heard about the incident. "Next time you'll know better," he laughed sardonically. "I, too, thought in the beginning that the world would come to an end if I smacked someone, that I was a traitor to humanity, to my people, to God knows what. Jews are sacred, Jews are martyrs. How could I lift my hand against them? But I got used to it. Jews are just shit like everybody else." The two Warsaw Jews who had brought it all on me listened with cynical approval. "Everybody knows you can't be an asshole in the KL. A *schmuck* of a Jew is worse than an apostate. If we get a stupid foreman, why should we work ourselves to death?"

That night it poured again and I lay on my bunk, groaning, in what was no more than a mud puddle. Every muscle and joint of my body ached, and I still had a cold in my bladder. I was close to a complete breakdown. What hurt me most was the attitude of the two Jews I had tried to be decent to. I could not keep up the struggle any longer. I would have welcomed death; I would even have killed myself if the effort had not been too great. I was at my lowest ebb. "You're *kaputt*," I said to myself. "They've finished you off in three days. *Kaputt!*" My instinct of self-preservation summoned up visions of Lena and Wlodek, and of those who had died in the ashes of the Warsaw Ghetto and whose last testament I had determined to transmit to the world, but in vain: my will was broken.

I slept fitfully, in starts, and gradually the will to live won out over my torpor. I was lucky. Had the breakdown come two weeks later I would no longer have had the inner resources to resist, but Maidanek had not yet sucked out my last ounce of strength; there was just enough left to tip the scales. "I am going to live," I said to myself. "Let them jeer, let them call me an asshole, but I will not beat anybody up." Half unconscious I climbed down from my bunk and sat with my back against the wall where the rain could no longer soak me, and so spent the rest of the night until reveille sounded.

Before roll call I went to the Scribe, a man I'd known before the war, and asked him not to send me on the road-building *Kommando* because it was beyond my strength. He looked at me closely, but said nothing. It was a cold morning and I shivered in my wet clothing; I could barely stand at attention. The Scribe assigned me to do garden work near the barracks, the lightest work in the camp. I had to weed the lawn and remove all refuse from it. I picked up every piece of paper, stone, weed, then watered and smoothed the ground. I spent most of the day on my knees. The day grew warmer, too, my wet clothes steamed in the sun, and the warmth assuaged my rheumatic pains.

"I must do something," I kept saying to myself. But what? I had to get less dangerous and exhausting work. But how? Beginning with the Scribe Weinkiper and Barrack Elder Szydlower, all the people who might help me looked at me with what I can only describe as embarrassed compassion. The Barrack Elder in Number Six barrack, who was a prisoner of war, and who was looking for an office worker, told me candidly, "I have at least twenty inmates who'd gladly give me a ten-dollar gold piece to get this job. Have you got anything to offer? If you have, we can talk. If you haven't, you're wasting my time. I'm too poor to afford gifts. I might do it for my brother, or my best friend, but for a stranger . . . ?"

In despair I took a step so bold that later I never did understand how I dared it. The ruling caste among the camp inmates during that period were Czechoslovak Jews. They controlled the central office jobs, kitchen jobs, and most other key jobs. They had been sent to Maidanek in May, 1942, when the camp was "ruled" by Jewish prisoners of war from the Polish army, soldiers who had fought in the 1939 campaign against the *Wehrmacht*. Originally there had been 12,000 Czechoslovak Jews there but by May, 1943, only 800 were alive. The survivors spoke of the past with horror, of roll calls that lasted all night in winter cold so that in the morning the ground was littered with frozen bodies, of the ruthless slaughter of the sick and weak, of endless beatings for the slightest infraction, of unremitting hunger. And all those Czechoslovak Jews remembered was that their torturers had been Polish Jews. Though they knew their tormentors were only tools in the hands of the Germans, their resentment persisted. Those who had survived were the strongest, toughest, and shrewdest, and gradually they had managed to move in on the better jobs as the Polish prisoners of war were sent into Lublin. They were able to do this because most of them spoke fluent German.

In the main office of Field Three, the *Lagerschreiber* who was next in rank to the *Germaner* was a Czech Jew named Horowitz. Small, bald, with a low forehead and jutting jaw, yellowed skin and a bristling beard, he treated the new shipments for the crematorium with contempt rather than hatred. Occasionally he made short speeches at roll call to inform the inmates of the latest orders and, although no one understood the language, he spoke Czech, usually opening with "Pricks!" (*Hújove!*) After summing up the order in Czech, he translated it into German. He did not torture inmates, but he was short-tempered and did occasionally strike out at or kick a prisoner.

I made up my mind to ask Horowitz for help. As he was coming into the administrative barrack, I stopped him and in one breath told him I was an editor and journalist by trade, and that I felt I had a duty to survive to tell the world about the murder of the Jewish people. I appealed to him to help me to survive. When I finished my outburst, I closed my eyes, expecting to be beaten. When I opened them again, Horowitz was looking at me kindly. "Strange," he said in German. "Before the war, I, too, was a journalist. I edited a monthly issued by the Ministry of Foreign Affairs in Prague. I understand you. I'll help. Go back to your barrack. Don't worry." He asked for my number, the number of my barrack and my name. I looked at him incredulously. He smiled and repeated, "Go back to your barrack. And don't worry."

When I got back to my barrack, the Scribe informed me that the big shot who had taken my bunk had been transferred to another barrack and I could have my old bunk back again. But when the road-building *Kommando* returned that night, carrying two dead, my spirits sank again. There was wailing and lamentation, and finally Szydlower made up his mind to take a drastic step. After roll call he negotiated with two Kapos of the road-builders' *Kommando* and concluded a deal which he announced triumphantly to us. For a regular tribute of one bread ration a week — in our barrack of 300 men that meant 40 loaves of bread — the Kapos promised to beat the workers more moderately, and not to death. Needless to say, Szydlower got his cut of the 40 loaves. But even that enormous (by Maidanek standards) bribe did not stop the murders. After two days of relative calm, the torture and murder resumed, allegedly because of intervention by a third Kapo, and the transaction came to nothing.

Szydlower had figured out that it was more profitable to rule over a gang of well-placed inmates than over wretches. Though he would not have hesitated to sacrifice an inmate's life to make his own easier, he was ready to help us as long as our survival did not threaten his interests. With new shipments from Warsaw arriving daily, more men were needed in all branches of the camp administration. Szydlower got busy at the Employment Office, headed by another native of Lodz, a lawyer, and one night announced that he had succeeded in placing about 50 of us in the kitchen as potato peelers.

The very word *kitchen* was a magnet to which everyone was attracted. Szydlower picked out the neatest-looking inmates, and I was one of the lucky ones. We marched eagerly to the kitchen barrack and were met by the foreman of the potato-peeling room, a man generally called Lieutenant Franto, because he had been a lieutenant in the Czech Army. I spoke to him and in him gained a protector. The only Jew in the town in which he lived, his Jewish ties amounted to the fact that once a year, on Yom Kippur, he took his family in a horse-driven carriage to the nearest town where there was a synagogue.

The camp kitchen was in an L-shaped barrack, divided into three rooms: one where potatoes were peeled, a washing-up room which also served as a storeroom, and the kitchen proper. To the last we were forbidden access. At the head of the kitchen department was an SS man with a number of assistants, a crowd of Kapos and foremen and *Schiebers*. Our work was organized so that on each side of a trough of potatoes a group of ten inmates sat peeling. There were troughs at intervals of every two yards. The peeled potatoes were thrown into a small vessel with handles which, when filled, was taken to the wash-up room where a clerk recorded the number of vessels brought in by each group of peelers.

We began work the next day and a few days later our group included teachers, lawyers, rabbis, and other intellectuals, among them my old friend, the historian and former deputy to the Polish parliament, Dr. Isaac Schipper.

After the days spent in calisthenics and drilling and on the road-construction gang, sitting down in a warm room and doing light work was heaven. We were particularly grateful when the weather was bad outside. Yet even here we had to work without letup. The output of each group was carefully watched, and the group which daily peeled the most potatoes received an extra ration of soup. We had to be careful not only to deliver our daily quota of peeled potatoes, but we had to make sure that the parings were not too thick. Anyone caught peeling potatoes uneconomically lost the job. Moreover, we were searched every day to make sure that no one smuggled either potatoes or peelings out with him. Because the rabbis, Dr. Schipper and I were scarcely expert potato peelers, we resorted to a stratagem: in co-operation with some of the other potato-peeling groups, we "borrowed" one filled vessel every day so that each group had its turn at getting the additional soup ration. Thus, even we finally managed to organize something. But like the rest, we were hungry, and being so close to food, smelling its tantalizing odors all day long from the kitchen, was an added torment which gave us dizzy spells and painful stomach spasms.

Aside from the higher-ups, the dominant figure in the potato-peeling room was a former Polish police officer named Germasinski. Dark, squat, with a square-cut face and turned-up nose, Germasinski was, under the guise of joviality, a menace. He had two favorite games. One was to hide and watch the potato-peeling brigades. When he caught someone slowing up or talking to his neighbors, he would throw a potato at the man's head. If he managed to hit his target, joyous shouting and laughter rang through the room. His second game was more dangerous. There was a big water basin at the back of our room and Germasinski would sneak up on his victim and suddenly push his head into the water and hold it under. If the SS man in the kitchen ran up, lured by the victims' struggles and Germasinski's maniacal laughter, the game would end tragically. The victim would be ducked again and again until he drowned. The other prisoners were forbidden to stop working or to look up and watch while that sadistic exhibition was being perpetrated: we had to sit there pretending that nothing was happening.

In the adjoining room, where the potatoes were rinsed before being taken to the kitchen, all the jobs were held by a well-organized group of young Belgian Jews. They spoke French among themselves, lived in the same barrack, and shared all their possessions.

The kitchen proper was run by Slovak Jews, most of them from Carpatho-Ruthenia, superstitiously religious and simple-minded. They took special care of rabbis, so that in Field Three rabbis had a good chance of surviving. From these men the two rabbis who worked with my potato-peeling group often got extra portions of thick soup, slices of salami, meat, and margarine which they hid under their coats. One of the rabbis ate everything he got; the other, a taciturn man involved with his private concerns, exchanged everything — even his soup ration — for bread and boiled potatoes. The former said that Jewishness allowed one to eat nonkosher food if one's life was endangered; the latter merely smiled and remarked that if such was the will of God, he would get by on dry bread rather than eat nonkosher food. The law allows, but does *not compel* such observance, he said.

The Slovak Jews favored children as well as rabbis. There still were a number of children at Maidanek, boys between ten and fourteen who had escaped being gassed on admittance. Most of them were employed by the *Schreibstube* as messengers — *Laufer*. All day long one saw them dashing back and forth in the various Fields, their young voices crying, "Barrack Scribe Number Six wanted at the office!" "Barrack Elder Number Eleven go to the Employment Office." Some had fathers among the prisoners and took care of them affectionately, as if they themselves were grownups and their fathers children. Even the most hardened Maidanek old-timer had a soft spot for the Jewish children, a species being made extinct before our eyes by the Germans. Some of the prisoners showed their affection in the most curious ways, such as teaching the boys obscenities and terms of abuse. When the children used such words, their mentors purred with pleasure.

But some children were not so fortunate. A few days after my arrival I saw eleven-year-old Uri Horensztein, son of one of the *Judenrat* secretaries who, before the liquidation of the Ghetto, had lived in our apartment house on Muranowska Street. Though Uri was big for his age, he had been pampered by his mother and now cried all day for his parents. Because of his experiences and the drastic change of diet, he lost control of his bladder and wet his bed nightly. The Barrack Elder assigned another boy of his own age to keep him company, but the other boy proved no help; instead, he abused Uri, beat him, mocked him, stole his food, and made fun of his bed-wetting in front of everyone. Finally, the Barrack Elder sent the boy to the *Gamelbaracke* where the *Lagerführer* found him one night and personally hanged him with a belt.

By being assigned to the kitchen detail I was better off than before, but I was still tormented by hunger, and in the face of that basic animal deprivation, food became the only subject of conversation, the master of our thoughts. . . .

At long last, Horowitz came one day to tell me he had gotten me the job he'd been waiting for. He took me to a field near the entrance where a single barrack stood surrounded by a high fence. A square sign before it had the inscription: *Fahrbereitschaft.* . . .

The *Fahrbereitschaft* was Maidanek's motor pool. In the barrack was a repair shop with every trade connected with automotive repair represented by at least one specialist: mechanics, glaziers, locksmiths, electricians, painters, carpenters, saddlers, etc. Two noncommissioned SS officers, who looked like twins, were in charge, and they had a Kapo, a Scribe, and a messenger boy. Most of the staff were Poles, there were a few Slovaks, and only two or three Polish Jews, thirty people in all. The Kapo, a Warsaw-born Pole, received me politely, but without enthusiasm. He looked over my clothes and said that first they'd dress me up. We went to the storehouse where I was given a decent suit that almost fit me, clean linen, and a pair of real leather shoes of the right size. After washing myself and putting on the clean clothes, I felt like a pasha. I had caught cold from standing barefoot on the frozen ground in the icy temperatures, and my nose was running. Timidly, I asked the Kapo for a handkerchief and, to my surprise, was given one.

Horowitz had done his level best. I hadn't known there was such a paradise at Maidanek. My companions were decent and courteous. A loaf of bread was divided into four portions instead of eight. You could eat as much soup as you wanted and nobody cared because most of them received food parcels from home. The barrack was heated by an iron stove. We talked about politics and other general subjects. Finally, we got up at 5 A.M. instead of at 3:30 and roll call took no more than a few minutes. Most phenomenal, there were no members of that Maidanek scourge: lice! In short, it seemed like heaven.

Two resistance fighters in the Warsaw ghetto, 1943. (Institute of Contemporary History and Weiner Library, London)

PART

III

The Problem of Jewish Resistance

Variety of Opinion

[O]ver a period of centuries the Jews had learned that in order to survive they had to refrain from resistance. . . . A 2,000-year-old lesson could not be unlearned; the Jews could not make the switch. They were helpless.

Raul Hilberg

Jewish armed resistance was considerably more widespread than has been assumed. . . . The range of Jewish resistance was broad . . . : armed, unarmed but organized, semi-organized or semi-spontaneous.

Yehuda Bauer

Considering their tasks, cooperation was unavoidable for the [Jewish] Councils. . . . When all factors are considered, Jewish participation or nonparticipation in the deportations had no substantial influence — one way or the other — on the final outcome of the Holocaust.

Isaiah Trunk

107

Revolts such as the one at Treblinka described by Richard Glazar were unusual. With few exceptions, Jews in Eastem European ghettos, labor camps, and extermination centers yielded to their fate with minimal resistance. Modern scholars are divided about how to explain the virtual absence of armed Jewish opposition. Was it because the Jews lacked the will or the opportunity to meet violence with violence?

Raul Hilberg, the dean of American Holocaust scholars, argued in his pioneering 1961 history of the Holocaust that the European Jews lacked the will to resist. Steeped in a culture that put a premium on accommodating Gentiles and looking to political authorities for protection against outbreaks of popular anti-semitism, they could not, or would not, adjust to vastly changed circumstances. Now persecution came from the authorities themselves, but the Jews did not draw the only logical conclusion from this state of affairs: they could fight back, die with honor, and have perhaps a chance at surviving; or they could perish like the "cattle" that Franz Stangl recalled from his days as commandant at Treblinka. Hilberg has been criticized for allegedly lacking sensitivity to the Jews' impossible situation, but he remains convinced of his position, restating it in the recent revision of his book. In his view the Jews could have resisted more than they did, and their failure to do so helped to seal the fate of European Jewry.

Yehuda Bauer denies that Jews missed opportunities for armed revolt. They took up arms when they could, he states, noting cases of militant Jewish resistance. But for most the opportunity never came. They lacked arms and outside support, and they were crushed by the brutal Nazi policy of collective responsibility. Moreover, Bauer suggests a far broader definition of resistance, one that places nonviolent group action to save Jewish lives on the same level as armed resistance. Presenting a highly nuanced appreciation of the conditions of life for Jews during the war, he denies that they could have known that the only alternative to death was militant resistance. Bauer is one of several, mainly Jewish, historians who have sought to rehabilitate the reputation of Jewish leaders and argued for a more understanding view of the dilemma of the Jewish masses under Hitler.

Isaiah Trunk responds to accusations by Hilberg (and others) that the Jewish Councils that ran the ghettos during the Holocaust were guilty of groveling compliance in the destruction process. The Councils, created by the Germans but made up of authentic Jewish leaders, typically organized the production of vital military products for the Wehrmacht, delivered Jews for "resettlement," and restrained their fellow Jews from armed resistance. Trunk views all this against the background of unprecedented Nazi violence and deception on one hand and Jewish psychological vulnerability on the other. Noting that Jewish Council members faced death for themselves and massive retaliation against their communities, Trunk argues that they had little choice but cooperation. At the same time, he notes that not all Jewish Councils conformed to this model; there were significant variations, especially regarding resistance in some of the smaller ghettos. Nor is he uncritical of Council members who surrendered to the corrupting influences of power. But Trunk concludes that most were honorably doing everything they could to save at least some of their coreligionists and had little opportunity to alter the outcome.

Evaluating Jewish resistance during the Holocaust poses overlapping questions of definition and opportunity. As we have seen, some scholars concentrate on armed resistance, whereas others adopt broader definitions that include nonviolent measures. Were nonviolent measures reasonable at the time, or did they play into Nazi hands and merely delay the final day of doom? Should Jews in Eastern European ghettos have refused to serve on Jewish Councils, thereby forcing the Germans to rule them directly? Historians are also divided over the chances of Jews carrying out effective armed resistance to the Germans in Eastern Europe. Should we lament failures to fight back on a broader front, or marvel that there was as much armed resistance as there was? To answer these questions with absolute certainty, we would have to know whether and how the Nazis would have coped with more extensive and militant Jewish opposition. That, of course, is impossible. History is no laboratory science in which one can run the experiment over and change the variables. Answers will suggest themselves only through informed and sensitive appreciation of the situation confronting the victims at the time.

Raul Hilberg

Two Thousand Years of Jewish Appeasement

In a destruction process the perpetrators do not play the only role; the process is shaped by the victims too. It is the *interaction* of perpetrators and victims that is "fate." We must therefore discuss the reactions of the Jewish community and analyze the role of the Jews in their own destruction.

When confronted by a force, a group can react in five ways: by resistance, by an attempt to alleviate or nullify the threat (the undoing reaction), by evasion, by paralysis, or by compliance. Let us consider each in turn.

The reaction pattern of the Jews is characterized by almost complete lack of resistance. In marked contrast to German propaganda, the documentary evidence of Jewish resistance, overt or submerged, is very slight. On a Europeanwide scale the Jews had no resistance organization, no blueprint for armed action, no plan even for psychological warfare. They were completely unprepared. In the words of Anti-Partisan Chief and Higher SS and Police Leader Russia Center von dem Bach, who observed Jews and killed them from 1941 to the end:

> *Thus the misfortunate came about. . . . I am the only living witness but I must say the truth. Contrary to the opinion of the National Socialists that the Jews were a highly organized group, the appalling fact was that they had no organization whatsoever. The mass of the Jewish people were taken completely by surprise. They did not know at all what to do; they had no directives or slogans as to how they should act. That is the greatest lie of anti-Semitism because it gives the lie to the slogan that the Jews are conspiring to dominate the world and that they are so highly organized. In reality they had no organization of their own at all, not even an information service. If they had had some*

From *The Destruction of the European Jews*, Vol. 3, by Raul Hilberg (New York: Holmes & Meier, 1985), Copyright © 1985 by Raul Hilberg. Reprinted by permission of the publisher.

> sort of organization, these people could have been saved by the millions; but instead they were taken completely by surprise. Never before has a people gone as unsuspectingly to its disaster. Nothing was prepared. Absolutely nothing. It was not so, as the anti-Semites say, that they were friendly to the Soviets. That is the most appalling misconception of all. The Jews in the old Poland, who were never communistic in their sympathies, were, throughout the area of the Bug eastward, more afraid of Bolshevism than of the Nazis. This was insanity. They could have been saved. There were people among them who had much to lose, business people; they didn't want to leave. In addition there was love of home and their experience with pogroms in Russia. After the first anti-Jewish actions of the Germans, they thought now the wave was over and so they walked back to their undoing.

The Jews were not oriented toward resistance. Even those who contemplated a resort to arms were given pause by the thought that for a limited success of a handful, the multitude would suffer the consequences. Outbreaks of resistance were consequently infrequent, and almost always they were local occurrences that transpired at the last moment. Measured in German casualties, Jewish armed opposition shrinks into insignificance. The most important engagement was fought in the Warsaw ghetto (sixteen dead and eighty-five wounded on the German side, including collaborators). Following the breakout from the Sobibór camp, there was a count of nine SS men killed, one missing, one wounded, and two collaborators killed. In Galicia sporadic resistance resulted in losses also to SS and Police Leader Katzmann (eight dead, twelve wounded). In addition, there were clashes between Jewish partisans and German forces in other parts of the east, and occasional acts of resistance by small groups and individuals in ghettos and killing centers. It is doubtful that the Germans and their collaborators lost more than a few hundred men, dead and wounded, in the course of the destruction process. The number of men who dropped out because of disease, nervous breakdowns, or court martial proceedings was probably greater. The Jewish resistance effort could not seriously impede or retard the progress of destructive operations. The Germans brushed that resistance aside as a minor obstacle, and in the totality of the destruction process it was of no consequence.

The second reaction was an attempt to avert the full force of German measures. The most common means of pursuing this aim were written and oral appeals. By pleading with the oppressor, the Jews sought to transfer the struggle from a physical to an intellectual and moral plane. If only the fate of the Jews could be resolved with arguments rather than with physical resources and physical combat — so Jewry reasoned — there would be nothing to fear. . . .

There was yet another way in which the Jews tried to avoid disaster. They anticipated German wishes, or divined German orders, or attempted to be useful in serving German needs. A Jewish council in Kislovodsk (Caucasus), acting with full awareness of the German threat, confiscated all Jewish valuables, including gold, silver, carpets, and clothing, and handed the property to the German Commander. The council in Šiauliai (Lithuania) had been asked three times whether any births had occurred in the ghetto and, each time it had replied in the negative. At one point, however, the council was confronted with twenty pregnancies. It decided to use persuasion and, if need be, threats on the women to submit to abortions. One woman was in her eighth month. The council decided that in this case a doctor would induce premature birth and that a nurse would kill the child. The nurse would be told to proceed in such a way that she would not know the nature of her act.

The most important mode of anticipatory action was the widespread effort, particularly in Eastern Europe, to seek salvation through labor. Indeed, the records of several ghettos reveal an upward curve of employment and output. The zeal with which the Jews applied themselves to the German war effort accentuated the differences of interests that paired industry and armament inspectorates against the SS and Police, but the Germans were resolving their conflicts to the detriment of the Jews. Generally, Jewish production did not rise fast enough or high enough to support the entire community. In the balance of payments of many an East European ghetto, the gap between income and subsistence living could not be bridged with limited outside relief or finite sales of personal belongings. Starvation was increasing, and the death rate began to rise. The clock was winding down even as German deportation experts were appearing at the ghetto gates. Ultimately, "productivization" did not save the ghettos. The Germans deported the unemployed, the sick, the old, the children. Then they made distinctions between less essential and more essential labor. In the final reckoning, all of Jewish labor was still Jewish.

The Jewish dedication to work was based on a calculation that liberation might come in time. To hold on was the essential consideration also of appeals and the many forms of Jewish "self-help," from the elaborate social services in the ghetto communities to the primitive "organization" in the killing centers. The Jews could not hold on; they could not survive by appealing.

The basic reactions to force are fundamentally different from each other. Resistance is opposition to the perpetrator. Nullification or alleviation is opposition to the administrative enactment. In the third reaction, evasion, the victim tries to remove himself from the effects of force by fleeing or hiding. The phenomenon of flight is more difficult to analyze. . . .

We know that only a few thousand Jews escaped from the ghettos of Poland and Russia; that only a few hundred Jews hid out in the large cities of Berlin, Vienna, and Warsaw; that only a handful of Jews escaped from camps. Von dem Bach mentions that in Russia there was an unguarded escape route to the Pripet Marshes, but few Jews availed themselves of the opportunity. In the main, the Jews looked upon flight with a sense of futility. The great majority of those who did not escape early did not escape at all.

There were instances when in the mind of the victim the difficulties of resistance, undoing, or evasion were just as great as the problem of automatic compliance. In such instances the futility of all alternatives became utterly clear, and the victim was paralyzed. Paralysis occurred only in moments of crisis. During ghetto-clearing operations, many Jewish families were unable to fight, unable to petition, unable to flee, and also unable to move to the concentration point to get it over with. They waited for the raiding parties in their homes, frozen and helpless. Sometimes the same paralytic reaction struck Jews who walked up to a killing site and for the first time gazed into a mass grave half-filled with the bodies of those who had preceded them.

The fifth reaction was automatic compliance. To assess the administrative significance of that cooperation, one must view the destruction process as a composite of two kinds of German measures: those that perpetrated something upon the Jews and involved only action by Germans, such as the drafting of decrees, the running of deportation trains, shooting, or gassing, and those that required the Jews to do something, for instance, the decrees or orders requiring them to register their property, obtain identification papers, report at a designated place for labor or deportation or shooting, submit lists of persons, pay fines, deliver up property, publish German instructions, dig their own graves, and so on. A large component of the entire process depended on Jewish participation — the simple acts of individuals as well as organized activity in councils. . . .

Not all Jewish cooperation was purely reflexive observance of German instructions, nor was all of it the last act of emaciated, forsaken people. There was also an institutional compliance by Jewish councils employing assistants and clerks, experts and specialists. During the concentration stage the councils conveyed German demands to the Jewish population and placed Jewish resources into German hands, thereby increasing the leverage of the perpetrator in significant ways. The German administration did not have a special budget for destruction, and in the occupied countries it was not abundantly staffed. By and large, it did not finance ghetto walls, did not keep order in ghetto streets, and did not make up deportation lists. German supervisors turned to Jewish councils for information, money, labor, or police, and the councils provided them with these means every day of the week. The importance of this Jewish role was not overlooked by German control organs. On one occasion a German official emphatically urged that "the authority of the Jewish council be upheld and strengthened under all circumstances."

Members of the Jewish councils were genuine if not always representative Jewish leaders who strove to protect the Jewish community from the most severe exactions and impositions and who tried to normalize Jewish life under the most adverse conditions. Paradoxically, these very attributes were being exploited by the Germans against the Jewish victims.

The fact that so many of the council members had roots in the Jewish community or had been identified from prewar days with its concerns gave them a dual status. They were officiating with the authority conferred upon them by the Germans but also with the authenticity they derived from Jewry. Day by day they were reliable agents in the eyes of the German perpetrators while still retaining the trust of Jews. The contradiction became sharper and sharper even as they kept on appealing, to the Germans for relief, to the Jews for acquiescence.

Similarly, when the councils endeavored to obtain concessions they made a subtle payment. Placing themselves into a situation of having to wait for German decisions, they increased not only their own subservience but also that of the entire community, which perforce was waiting as well.

The councils could not subvert the continuing process of constriction and annihilation. The ghetto as a whole was a German creation. Everything that was designed to maintain its viability was simultaneously promoting a German goal. The Germans were consequently aided not only by Jewish enforcement agencies but also by the community's factories, dispensaries, and soup kitchens. Jewish efficiency in allocating space or in distributing rations was an extension of German effectiveness, Jewish rigor in taxation or labor utilization was a reinforcement of German stringency, even Jewish incorruptibility could be a tool of German administration. In short, the Jewish councils were assisting the Germans with their good qualities as well as their bad, and the very best accomplishments of a Jewish bureaucracy were ultimately appropriated by the Germans for the all-consuming destruction process.

If we should now review the Jewish reaction pattern, we would see its two salient features as a posture of appeals alternating with compliance. What accounts for this combination? What factors gave rise to it? The Jews attempted to tame the Germans as one would attempt to tame a wild beast. They avoided "provocations" and complied instantly with decrees and orders. They hoped that somehow the German drive would spend itself. This hope was founded in a 2,000-year-old experience. In exile the Jews had always been a minority, always in danger, but they had learned that they could avert or survive destruction by placating and appeasing their enemies. Even in ancient Persia an appeal by Queen Esther was more effective than the mobilization of an army. Armed resistance in the face of overwhelming force could end only in disaster.

Thus over a period of centuries the Jews had learned that in order to survive they had to refrain from resistance. Time and again they were attacked. They endured the Crusades, the Cossack uprisings, and the czarist persecution. There were many casualties in these times of stress, but always the Jewish community emerged once again like a rock from a receding tidal wave. The Jews had never really been annihilated. After surveying the damage, the survivors had always proclaimed in affirmation of their strategy the triumphant slogan, "The Jewish people lives [*Am Israel Chai*]." This experience was so ingrained in the Jewish consciousness as to achieve the force of law. The Jewish people could not be annihilated.

Only in 1942, 1943, and 1944 did the Jewish leadership realize that, unlike the pogroms of past centuries, the modern machinelike destruction process would engulf European Jewry. But the realization came too late. A 2,000-year-old lesson could not be unlearned; the Jews could not make the switch. They were helpless.

Yehuda Bauer

Forms of Jewish Resistance

We have already seen that the basic situation of Jews during the Hitler period was one of political powerlessness. Negotiations to save them, if conducted at all, would have to have been supported by one or more of the major powers; without that there would be little chance of success. Jews could appeal to the powers, they could try to impress public opinion in the Western democracies, but in the end they were perilously dependent upon the mercy of others. In the free world, Jews could appeal or beg for help; behind the barbed wire of Hitler's hell they could cry out in the hope that muted echoes would reach the outside. Was there anything more that the trapped Jews of Europe could do? If so, did they do it? What was the reaction of the victims to the most terrible terror any regime had yet exercised?

Jewish reaction to Nazi rule is of tremendous importance to Jews and non-Jews alike. The Jew wants to know the tradition to which he is heir. How did that tradition, that whole range of historically developed values, stand up to the supreme test of Hitler's death sentence on the Jewish people? Did Jewish civilization, demoralized under the blows of the brutal enemy, surrounded in the East by largely indifferent or hostile populations, simply collapse?

These questions are equally significant for non-Jews. Nothing like the Holocaust had happened before, but there are no guarantees against its recurrence. Jews are not the only possible victims of genocide. It is urgent to know how people react in such extreme circumstances; to find out how people, who were Jews, reacted when it happened to them.

What do we mean by resistance? What, more specifically, do we mean by that term in the context of World War II? What, when we apply it to Jews? Henri Michel, perhaps the most important contemporary historian of anti-Nazi resistance, defines the term negatively: resistance was the maintenance of self-respect. He writes that "acceptance of defeat whilst still capable of fighting, was to lose one's self-respect; self-respect dictated that one should not yield to the blandishments of collaboration." But it is practically useless to analyse Jewish resistance with such categories — the Nazis certainly did not use the blandishments of collaboration on the Jews.

Professor Raul Hilberg, on the other hand, seems to regard armed resistance as the only, or nearly only, legitimate form of real resistance. In his monumental book, *The Destruction of the European Jews* (Chicago, 1961), he stated categorically and, to my mind, mistakenly, that the lack of Jewish armed resistance to the Holocaust was a consequence of the fact that Jews during their long diaspora had not had occasion to learn the art of self-defence.

Let me start off with a definition of my own and we shall then subject it to the test of known facts. I would define Jewish resistance during the Holocaust as any *group* action consciously taken in opposition to known or surmised laws, actions, or intentions directed against the Jews by the Germans and their supporters. I cannot accept Michel's definition because there were in fact very few Jews who consciously collaborated with the Germans, or who were willing to help Germany achieve victory in the hope that they would help themselves or the Jewish people. There were, of course, paid Jewish Gestapo agents and others who helped the Germans having been promised their lives — quite a number of these. But I know of only one clear and one marginal case of collaboration as defined here: I am referring to the group known as the 13 (*Dos Dreizentl*) of Avraham Gancwajch, in Warsaw, and to Moshe Mietek Merin's Judenrat in Zagłębie.

I cannot accept Hilberg's definition or description for two reasons. In the first place, I do not think he is being historically accurate. Jews did defend themselves throughout the ages by force of arms when this was feasible or when they had no other choice — in Polish towns against Chmielnicki's hordes in 1648; in Palestine against the Crusaders; in medieval York. One could cite many such instances. In pre-1939 Poland, moreover, the socialist Bund party had special defence groups that fought street battles with anti-semitic hooligans. Early in this century, Jewish students in Prague, Vienna, and Berlin established fraternities that fought duels against antisemites, and so on.

The second and more important point is surely that armed resistance during the Holocaust was possible only under conditions that most Jews did not enjoy. You either have arms or you do not; for the most part, the Jews did not. Still, the nature of Jewish armed resistance was much more complicated than one might expect.

In the Generalgouvernement (the central area of Poland ruled by the Nazis) there were, according to exhaustive historical accounts, about 5,000 Jewish fighters. Of these about 1,000 fought in the Warsaw ghetto rebellion, 1,000 in the Warsaw Polish uprising in 1944, and the rest as partisans in forests and in a number of ghetto and camp uprisings. There were some 1.5 million Jews in the area in 1939, so one gets a ratio of resisters of 0.33 per cent — not a very high figure — and concludes that Jewish armed resistance was marginal at best. In eastern Poland, where there were about one million Jews before the war, 15,000 armed Jews came out of the forests at liberation — a ratio of 1.5 per cent — which will still not cause one to change the verdict. But during the time Jews were organizing to fight, that is in 1942 and 1943, they accounted for one half of all the partisans in the Polish forests. The other half, about 2,500, were Poles. There were more than 20 million Poles in the Generalgouvernement, so one arrives at a resistance ratio of 0.0125 per cent. The same game can be played regarding other nations in Nazi Europe. One begins to appreciate Mark Twain's adage that there are lies, damned lies, and statistics.

Let us then disregard such futile exercises and examine the real facts concerning Jewish armed resistance in Poland and, subsequently, elsewhere. It is generally accepted that large-scale operations were mainly dependent on two ingredients: the availability of weapons, and the support of a civilian population capable of aiding underground fighters. Neither of these preconditions existed for the Jews. Jews did not have access to the arms buried by the collapsing

Polish army in 1939. There were very few Jewish officers in that army, fewer of them holding high ranks (e.g., one general), and the secrets of the buried arms were kept by right-wing officers who went into hiding.

The Polish government underground, the Armia Krajowa (AK), did not buy any arms from deserting German soldiers until very late in the war. No partisan detachments of any importance were established by it before 1943, and, anyway, not only were Jews not accepted in AK ranks, but a number of AK detachments were actively engaged in hunting down and murdering them. Thus when the Jews realized that they were being threatened with mass murder in 1942, there were no AK detachments for them to join. When these did come into existence, most Jews had already been murdered, and the detachments, in any case, would still not accept the survivors.

The Communist Gwardia Ludowa, later the Armia Ludowa (AL), was founded in the spring of 1942. It was then very weak, had very few arms, and about half its partisan forces were in fact the Jewish detachments in the forests of the Lublin area and elsewhere. By the time the AL grew stronger (in 1943) large numbers of Jews were no longer alive, but survivors did join the AL. Its weapons were bought or captured from peasants or, in most cases, parachuted by Soviet aircraft.

Jews locked in ghettos generally had no way to procure arms. The AK would not provide them; the Communists still did not have them. Controls at the gates were so strict that it was virtually impossible to bring any arms that could be obtained into the ghetto. The best known exception to the rule was in Vilna where Jews worked in German armouries. There, despite very stringent security measures, arms were smuggled into the ghetto from the city. The same general conditions applied in Czestochowa, which explains why the underground there had secured arms despite the obstacles.

Let us now turn to the three basic scenes of armed resistance in the east — the ghettos, the forests, and the camps. In the ghettos, the Jewish population was starved and decimated by disease and forced labour. They were, moreover, surrounded by a gentile population whose reaction to Jewish suffering varied between indifference, mostly hostile, and open enmity toward the victims. As applied to the ghettos Hilberg's thesis seems correct, that so long as the Jews thought they would survive the Nazi rule and the war they could see an incentive to re-enact the modes of passive conduct that in the past had tended to ensure the survival of the community, and they were accordingly reluctant to engage in armed resistance.

Resistance would have met with the disapproval, not only of the Polish population, but even of the Polish underground, the AK. Stefan Rowecki, commander in chief of the AK, issued an order (No. 71) as late as 10 November 1942 which bluntly stated that "the time of our uprising has not come." He mentioned the fact that the "occupant is exterminating the Jews," and warned his people not to be drawn into a "premature" (!) action against the Germans.

An examination of ghetto armed underground organizations shows quite clearly that, indeed, the Jews entered into the phase of practical preparations for armed action only *after* the first so-called *Aktion*, i.e., mass murder operation by the Nazis. Ghetto rebellions never took place when a hope of survival could be entertained — only when the realization finally struck that all Jews were going to be killed anyway. All other armed rebellions during World War II were predicated on the assumption that there was some chance of success. In the ghettos, no such success could be contemplated; the only result of ghetto rebellion would be the annihilation of all Jewish residents and the subsequent plundering of the empty Jewish houses by the surrounding population — that is, when the Germans did not plunder the houses themselves. This plunder, by the way, ensured the cooperation of the local population in the murder of the Jews and also prevented the escape of survivors: the local population had a strong incentive to ensure that no witnesses survived.

By the time of the first major waves of Nazi murder in 1942, only a small remnant (some 15 to 20 per cent) of the Jewish population still lived in the ghettos. This remnant then had to form an organization which might either be opposed by the Judenrat or, if the Judenrat supported a rebellion, would have to coordinate its plans with the latter in some way, and would have to secure arms in the face of supreme diffficulties. In the western and central part of Poland, moreover, there were no forests where partisans could hide, so that escape was impossible. During the summer of 1942 the Warsaw underground did send Jewish groups into forests some distance from the capital, but the hostility of the Poles, the murderous actions of the AK, and German patrols quickly put an end to these attempts.

The situation was different in the eastern parts of Poland, western Byelorussia, and the eastern parts of Lithuania. Here the forests were thick, but in 1942 and early 1943 very few Soviet partisan groups were operating. In Minsk, where there was a ghetto of 84,000 Jews, the Judenrat led by Eliahu Mishkin was part of an underground movement which tried to smuggle Jews out to the forests. Some arms were obtained, luckily, for the few Soviet partisans in the area would not accept Jews without them. But only a small number of persons could be suitably equipped from among the many who were sent out. In the city itself no effective non-Jewish underground was organized for a long time and no help was obtained from the Byelorussians; on the contrary, the ghetto had to hide anti-Nazis who could not hold out in the city. We do not yet know how many Jews were smuggled out to the forests from Minsk; we are working on a list, and it will take a long time yet before the job is finished. But I would guess the number to be between 6,000 and 10,000. About 5,000 survived the war in the forests — which shielded only those bent on escape and capable of bearing arms.

I should now like to address another problem: collective responsibility. The Nazis murdered a great many persons in retribution for the rebellious acts or suspected sedition of the few. In Dolhynov, near Vilna, for instance, two young men who were about to leave the ghetto for the forest were caught, but managed to escape and hide. The Germans told the Judenrat that if these men did not return and surrender, the ghetto would be annihilated immediately. The two men refused to return, knowing that they were endangering the lives of hundreds of others. On the morrow the inhabitants of the ghetto were shot. What would we have done in the place of the youngsters?

Yet the main internal problem for the Jews was not that of the collective responsibility imposed upon them by Nazi reprisals so much as the more fundamental problem of family responsibility. To belong to a resistance group one had to abandon one's family to death — not just leave it at some risk, as with the non-Jewish resister. The young Jewish man had to make the clear-cut decision to leave his parents, brothers, sisters, relatives, and sweethearts, and watch them being transported to death while he stood helpless, albeit wearing the mantle of the resistance fighter. Abba Kovner, the great Israeli poet and former head of the FPO (*Farainikte Partisaner*

Organizacje), the resistance movement in the Vilna ghetto, has told how he gave the order to his people to assemble at an appointed hour: they were to leave the ghetto through the sewers in order to continue the battle in the forests. When the time came, and he stood at the entrance to the sewer, his old mother appeared and asked him for guidance. He had to answer her that he did not know. And, said Kovner, from that time on he did not know whether he deserved the prestige of a partisan fighting the Nazis or the stigma of a faithless son.

Let us then recount, in the face of these facts, what the armed resistance of Jews in the East amounted to. In the Generalgouvernement there were three armed rebellions, at Warsaw, Czestochowa, and Tarnów; four attempted rebellions, at Kielce, Opatów, Pilica, and Tomaszów Lubelski; and seventeen places from which armed groups left for the forests, Chmielnik, Cracow, Iwanska, Józefów, Kalwaria, Markuszew, Miedzyrzec Podlaski, Opoczno, Radom, Radzyn, Rzeszów, Sokolów Podlaski, Sosnowiec, Tomaszów Lubelski, Tarnów, Wlodawa, and Zelechów.

There were moreover rebellions in six concentration and death camps — Kruszyna, Krychów, Minsk Mazowiecki ('Kopernik'), Sobibor, and Treblinka, together with the famous Jewish rebellion in the gas chambers at Auschwitz in late 1944. These were the only rebellions that ever did take place in any Nazi camps, except for that of Soviet prisoners of war at Ebensee at the end of the war. There were armed international undergrounds, in Buchenwald and Auschwitz for instance, but they never acted. (In Buchenwald they took over the camp after the SS withdrew.)

We know also of 30 Jewish partisan detachments in the Generalgouvernement, and a further list of 21 detachments where Jews formed over 30 per cent of the partisans. These latter groups were all part of the AL, because, as I have explained, the AK wouldn't accept them. Individual Jews fulfilled important functions in the AK, but they had to hide their Jewishness and appear under assumed names. A further 1,000 Jews participated in the Polish Warsaw uprising of August 1944. The total number of these fighters was about 5,000, of whom over 4,000 were killed.

The situation in Lithuania, eastern Poland, and Byelorussia is much more complicated, and I cannot render a complete picture. At least sixty ghettos had armed rebellions (such as those in Tuczyn,

Lachwa, and Mir), attempted rebellions (as in Vilna), or armed underground movements which sent people to the forests (as in Kovno, Zetl, and so on). In some ghettos resistance took more than one form, as in Nieswiez, where an armed rebellion was followed by an escape to the forests. An estimate of Jewish partisans in this area is most difficult to make, though, again, we are currently working on a list. We know that there were some 15,000 Jewish partisans in the area towards the end of the war, and many more must have died before that. Some 2,000 Jewish partisans in the Tatra mountains of Slovakia must be added to any account dealing with eastern Europe.

Two further points. First, the problem of defining a "Jewish partisan" is no simple matter. Do we include in that category only Jews who fought in Jewish groups? Or may we include Jews who fought as individuals in non-Jewish groups, such as Soviet partisan units? Moreover, what about Jews who denied their Jewishness and fought as Poles, or Russians? There were, after all, a number of communists (such as Yurgis-Zimanas, the commander of the Lithuanian partisans) who emphatically defined themselves as Soviet or Polish citizens, specifically denying their Jewish backgrounds. This is also true of a few Jews in the AK, and of some of the central figures in the AL command. But these cases were generally few and far between, for Jews were required to identify as such, irrespective of their particular political ideology. Indeed, the attitude toward Jews who refused to identify as anything but Poles or Soviets was often negative in character, so that one is left to wonder whether there is any justification for excluding even communist leaders and assimilationists from an analysis of Jewish resistance. Were not their individual idiosyncrasies overwhelmed by the intruding fate of the Jewish community to which they percieved themselves to belong only by birth?

Second, we cannot ignore antisemitism even in the Soviet partisan detachments, especially those in which Ukrainian partisans had great influence. A large number of such cases have been documented, as have the fatal consequences for a number of Jewish fighters. This hatred was directed not only against Jewish units — which the Soviet partisan command disbanded — but also against individual Jews in general units. Where there were large numbers of Jews in some unit[s], a struggle against antisemitsm was likely; but in smaller detachments with relatively few Jews, defiance was much more difficult.

Let us also deal, albeit summarily, with western Europe. Here the story is less dramatic, first, because the total number of Jews in France, Belgium, and Holland was less than one-sixth of the Jewish population of prewar Poland and, second, because armed resistance movements of a serious kind did not become active until well into 1943. By that time there were not many Jews left to fight. In the west, of course, the same hostility towards the Jews did not exist as in the east, but there were notable exceptions. In France, for instance, the French police effected most of the anti-Jewish measures.

There were Jewish armed groups in the OJC (*Organisation juive de combat*) and the MOI (a communist group) in France, two groups in Belgium, and two communist groups of Jews in Germany. By and large, however, Jews participated as individuals in non-Jewish organizations because no ghettos were set up in western Europe. Should we consider them as Jewish resisters, or as Belgian and French resisters?

I think the answer depends on the way these Jews acted. Was their behaviour more likely the result of specifically Jewish concerns or not? The answer is important because it would help us to measure the depths of Jewish identification among western Jews. It would also help to reveal the extent of integration among Jews and non-Jews. We are still in the middle of these researches, but I would venture the general conclusion that these Jews were usually fighting for "Jewish" reasons.

How many Jews fought? In France there were thousands rather than hundreds and there were probably close to a thousand in Belgium. Moreover, the Jews were usually the first to act — for example, the first urban guerillas fighting against the Nazis in Paris during the spring of 1942 were members of a Jewish unit of the pro-communist MOI. The Guttfreund group in Belgium took up arms as early as September 1941, killing a Jewish Gestapo agent, robbing a factory producing for the Germans, and later burning a card index of Jews at the Judenrat offices in Brussels. Finally, thousands of Jews fought in northern Italy in 1943–4, and thousands more fought with Tito's army in Jugoslavia.

Let me summarize: Jewish armed resistance was considerably more widespread than has been subsequently assumed. In eastern Europe, a high proportion of those who survived the first wave of murders participated in armed activities. Jewish rebellions in Warsaw and elsewhere were the first urban struggles against the Germans anywhere in Europe, and the Jewish rebellions in the camps were the only ones of their kind. Michel's conclusion that Jewish armed resistance was proportionately higher than that of other people, with few exceptions, is probably true. This is remarkable in light of the greater difficulties Jews encountered and of their lack of modern military tradition. Surely the radical nature of the Nazi threat to Jewish communities is pertinent here. But persecution does not explain resistance, especially when the former is attended by elaborate forms of control and coercion. At any rate, it seems easier to explore the ways Jews in Palestine and then Israel met their military challenges in the light of the above analysis than to believe, with Hilberg, that there was little struggle in Europe and then a sudden inexplicable upsurge of martial skills that enabled the Jews of Israel to fight for their existence.

I have dealt with armed resistance first because unarmed active resistance is best explained against the background of armed struggle. Let us now therefore consider the problem of resistance without weapons.

Unarmed struggle took place largely before the murder actions began. In such situations, when Jews were unaware of any Nazi intentions to murder them, Jewish behaviour was at least in some measure comparable to the behaviour of non-Jewish populations under Nazi rule. Such comparisons are important as measuring-rods for the behaviour of populations subject to the rule of terror. On the other hand, differences between Jewish and non-Jewish situations will stand out clearly as time moves on, and we cannot avoid approaching both comparable and noncomparable situations with the knowledge that the Jews were later subjected to Holocaust, whereas other nationalities were not.

What, then, did these other subject nationalities in Europe do? Did they obey German law, even those laws forbidding education in Poland and Russia? Yes, they did. Did they resist the shipment of slave labour to Germany? No, they did not.

By and large the Jews, on the other hand, proved recalcitrant. History had taught them the art of evasion, and they showed themselves to be highly skilled practitioners. In the first place, contrary to conventional wisdom, most German and Austrian Jews, some 410,000 out of 700,000, did manage to leave the Third Reich. (Some of these, tragically, were caught again as the German armies advanced.)

In Poland, after the war had begun, German rules were so brutal that, had the Jews passively acquiesced — even though every infringement of Nazi law was punishable by death — they would have died out in no time at all. Let me give a few examples. Official German food allocations distributed by the Warsaw Judenrat came to 336 calories daily in 1941. It is unlikely that the Warsaw Jews could have survived longer than a few months on such rations. But smuggling, illicit production on a considerable scale, and great inventiveness produced an average of 1,125 calories daily. Unfortunately, a large population of unemployed Jewish refugees who had been expelled by the Germans from their homes in the provinces into Warsaw slowly died because their food supplies fell below that average. Many others managed to survive on these rations nevertheless. I would consider this stubbornness, this determination to survive in defiance of Nazi authority, to be an act of resistance under the definition I offered at the beginning of this essay. In Kovno, similar smuggling was organized by groups that were controlled by the Judenrat and the Jewish police — the police here were the very heart of the armed resistance organization. It was thus an organized act, under public supervision of sorts, and the aim was very definitely to subvert German laws.

Consider the question of education. Until the late autumn of 1941, education of any kind was forbidden in Jewish Warsaw. But it took place clandestinely, in so-called *complets* where small groups of pupils would meet either in the soup kitchen or in the home of the teacher. We find evidence for this, in fact, in a large number of places in Poland. There were also clandestine high schools in Warsaw which received some funds from illegal JDC (American Jewish Joint Distribution Committee) sources. The activities of such schools are documented. Their older students passed official matriculation exams under conditions which were, to put it mildly, unusual.

Also, according to Ringelblum, there were in Warsaw alone some 600 illegal *minyanim*, groups of Jews praying together throughout the period when all public religious observance was forbidden. Political parties were of course proscribed, as were newspapers or printing of any description. But we now know of more than fifty titles of underground newspapers in Warsaw alone, and most of the political parties continued their clandestine existence.

There is, one is inclined to think, something typically Jewish or — more profoundly — *traditionally* Jewish, in the importance that cultural institutions achieved in such a time. There was, for instance, YIVO, the Yiddish Scientific Institute in Vilna, where Kovner and the poet Abraham Sutzkever were active in preserving materials, establishing a library system, and encouraging literary output in a conscious effort to maintain morale. It was no accident that the YIVO group was a recruiting ground for FPO, the resistance movement in Vilna. The most famous of these cultural institutions was the Oneg Shabbat group in Warsaw. Founded and headed by Dr Emmanuel Ringelblum, the historian and public figure, it methodically assembled reports and diaries and initiated research in order to preserve documentary evidence of the life of the Jews in the Warsaw ghetto. Among its studies were the famous medical investigations into the effects of hunger on the human body under the direction of Dr Milejkowski, which were published after the war in 1946 in Poland.

Oneg Shabbat did not know of the speech in Poznan in 1943 in which Himmler boasted that nothing would ever become known of the Final Solution. But the basic idea of Oneg Shabbat was that knowledge and documentation were forms of defiance of Nazi intent. In this the group succeeded. Despite the fact that only two-thirds of the Oneg Shabbat archives were found after the war, they are our main source of knowledge regarding Jewish life in Poland during the Holocaust.

Of all active unarmed resistance, most intriguing, I believe, were the activities of the "Joint" (the Joint Distribution Committee), the American-based social welfare agency. The Joint was actually just an office which, in Poland, distributed American funds to local Jewish agencies such as TOZ, a health agency, Centos, a society for the care of orphans, Cekabe, a network of free-loan banks, and Toporol, a society for agricultural vocational training. On the face of it, nothing more tame could be devised. But when war came the Joint offices in Warsaw happened to be headed by a group of men with leftist political convictions, among whom Dr Ringelblum is perhaps the best known today. They very early on realized that it would be their job to fight against Nazi-imposed starvation, humiliation, and gratuitous cruelty.

Until the end of 1941, certain sums still arrived from America through a complicated transfer system; although no dollars were actually sent to Nazi-controlled territory, German marks left behind by Jewish emigrants were sent to Warsaw from Berlin and Vienna. This stopped in December 1941, and the Joint became an illegal institution. But even before this, additional funds were being obtained by illegal means. In 1941, the Joint fed 260,000 Jews in the Generalgouvernement, including some 42,000 children. Centos and TOZ, which had themselves been declared illegal, still maintained their operations under the cover of an official welfare organization. Kitchens and children's homes became the centres of illegal political activities, including party meetings, clandestine presses, and illegal schooling. All this was consciously activated by the Joint.

Parallel to this was Joint support for so-called house committees, of which over 1,000 existed in the ghetto of Warsaw. Residences in eastern Europe were usually built around a courtyard, so that in each instance the "house" included four apartment buildings, about 200 or 300 families. These groups of people organized spontaneously, outside any Judenrat groupings, to institute mutual aid, schooling for children, cultural activities, and so on. (Unfortunately these groups included Warsaw Jews only; the refugees, crammed in their shelters, were dependent on the woefully insufficient feeding of Joint soup kitchens which were meant to provide only supplementary nourishment.) The house committees sprang up from below, but the Joint quickly realized their potential and Ringelblum set up a roof organization called Zetos. This body tried to create a central fund through which more affluent house committees would help the poorer ones, and encouraged activity essentially opposed to the Judenrat. The steering committee of Zetos became the political base for the resistance movement. The Joint was also behind the preparations for the Warsaw ghetto rebellion, and financed the uprising to a large degree. Giterman, the Joint's chief director, also helped to finance resistance movements in Bialystok and elsewhere by sending them money explicitly for this purpose.

The Joint's was a mass activity which embraced hundreds of thousands of Jews. Still, it obviously could not stand up to the forces of mass murder. Giterman was killed on 19 January 1943 in Warsaw, and Ringelblum was murdered in March 1944 when the Germans finally found his hiding place. They shared the fate of the millions whom they had tried to feed, encourage, and lead. But we cannot be concerned here with their ultimate fate; we are concerned rather with their behaviour prior to their murder. We want to know how widespread was unarmed active opposition to Nazi rule among the Jews; and we discover that owing to the work of men like Ringelblum and Giterman the range of such resistance was considerable. . . .

I have dealt with eastern Europe; but it would be wrong to disregard the 500,000 Jews of western Europe, or indeed the Jews of Germany, Austria, and Czechoslovakia. The Joint, Zetos, and various cultural institutions could be classified as self-governing institutions interposed between the Judenrat and the Jewish masses. Similar groups and organizations existed in western and central Europe as well.

Take for example the OSE. This was a general Jewish health organization which had a rather modest branch in prewar France. During the Holocaust, OSE became the main child-care organization in the Jewish sector. In France, of course, the gentile population had a much more positive attitude toward Jews than that which prevailed in Poland. German rule was comparatively less oppressive; Nazi police and SS were less numerous, while German Army interests, which did not always parallel those of the SS, were more important. In this climate OSE and some other groups managed to hide about 7,000 Jewish children, some in Catholic and Protestant institutions but mostly among peasants, and we do not know of one single case where children were betrayed by those undertaking to hide them. OSE, the Jewish Scout movement, and some other groups managed to smuggle some 2,000 people into Switzerland and a smaller number into Spain. In Belgium, the Comité de défense des juifs, headed by a Jewish member of the Belgian underground, hid thousands of Jews as well.

Let us now turn, very briefly, to what is probably the most important, but also the most diffuse, form of resistance: that of popular, mass reaction. Here we are on uncertain ground, because this form barely comes within our own definition. Can one speak of an unorganized, spontaneous action of Jews as expressing true resistance to Nazi enactments?

Well, up to a point it seems one can. Let us cite a few examples. In Holland, which had a Judenrat of the Lodz type, the Jewish proletariat of Amsterdam reacted forcefully in February 1941 to provocations by Dutch Nazis. A Dutch Nazi died in the scufffle, and Jewish and non-Jewish inhabitants of the Jewish quarter chased the Nazis out. This was the immediate cause for the famous strike of Dutch workers in support of the Jews. It failed, largely because of the intervention of the Jewish leaders who were told by the Nazis that, if the strike did not stop, large numbers of Jews would be taken to concentration camps and killed. The Dutch desisted, and the same Jewish leaders became the nucleus of the Dutch Judenrat. But what should concern us here is the popular Jewish reaction, especially since the story of the anti-Nazi acts in Amsterdam had further instalments.

Nazi documents record that after the first deportations from Holland in July 1942, the Jews ceased to appear at the appointed time and place when called. From the summer of 1942 on the Nazi and the Dutch police had to ferret the Jews out. This was popular unarmed resistance. We know, of course, that this tactic did not succeed; but the measure of resistance is not its success but its incidence. Was the moral backbone of the Dutch-Jewish population broken? It appears, rather, that their desire to live as free human beings was maintained.

Turning to the east, let us inspect another example. The so-called Slovak National Uprising broke out in the hills of Slovakia in August 1944. The Jews from some Slovak towns and camps fled there in large numbers. Those who could, fought; those who could not tried to hide. As the German troops advanced into the Slovak mountains suppressing the uprising, the Jews refused to obey Nazi orders and certainly avoided concentrating in places where they could be picked up by the Germans. This was typical unarmed resistance.

Some of the popular mood of this kind of resistance is captured in diaries which have survived: the young boy who believes that his father is being taken away and will not come back but writes that he believes his own place is with his father; the young man who jumps out the window of the deportation train only when he is already separated from his mother, whom he had not dreamed of leaving to face her fate alone; Chaim A. Kaplan, in Warsaw, who is sorry he will not see the Nazis' downfall which he is sure will come. Such acts and sentiments are beyond our definition of resistance, to be sure; but they form the background to those acts of unarmed circumspect defiance which I have tried to relate.

Let us not exaggerate. There were communities that collapsed. One cannot even find the dignity of quiet defiance in some Jewish responses. In Copenhagen, for example, the whole Jewish community was saved without its lifting a finger to help itself; in Vienna, but for a few hundred people in hiding, nothing but abject submission was the rule. Unfortunately it is impossible to explore here the reasons behind this apparent lethargy.

The range of Jewish resistance was broad, as I have shown: armed, unarmed but organized, semi-organized or semi-spontaneous. Let me conclude with a form of resistance which I have saved to the last because it is the most poignant. My example is from Auschwitz, and I am relating it on the authority of the late Yossel Rosensaft, head of the Bergen-Belsen Survivors' Association. Yossel was also a "graduate" of Auschwitz, and he testified that in December 1944 he and a group of inmates calculated when Hanukka would occur. They went out of their block and found a piece of wood lying in the snow. With their spoons, they carved out eight holes and put pieces of carton in them. Then they lit these and sang the Hanukka song, "Ma Oz Tsur Yeshuati."

None of the people who did this were religious. But on the threshold of death, and in the hell of Auschwitz, they demonstrated. They asserted several principles: that contrary to Nazi lore, they were human; that Jewish tradition, history, and values had a meaning for them in the face of Auschwitz; and that they wanted to assert their humanity in a Jewish way. We find a large number of such instances in concentration and death camps. Of course, there were uncounted instances of dehumanization in a stark fight for survival: bread was stolen from starving inmates by their comrades, violent struggles broke out over soup, over blankets, over work details — struggles which only too often ended with death. In the conditions of the camps, incidents of this kind are not surprising or unusual, but examples such as the one mentioned are. The few Jews who did survive could not have done so without the companionship and cooperation of friends. And friendship under such conditions is itself a remarkable achievement.

I think the story of Kosów is also appropriate. It exemplifies most vividly the refusal of so many Jewish victims to yield their humanity in the face of impending murder. Kosów is a small town in eastern Galicia, and it had a Judenrat which was not very different from others. On Passover 1942, the Gestapo announced it would come into the ghetto. The Judenrat believed that this was the signal for the liquidation of the ghetto, and told all the Jews to hide or flee. Of the twenty-four Judenrat members, four decided to meet the Germans and offer themselves as sacrificial victims — to deflect the wrath of the enemy. With the ghetto empty and silent, the four men sat and waited for their executioners. While they were waiting one of them faltered. The others told him to go and hide. The three men of Kosów prepared to meet the Nazis on Passover of 1942. Was their act less than firing a gun?

Isaiah Trunk

Why the Jewish Councils Cooperated

Utter lawlessness and virtual anarchy prevailed in he territories under German occupation during World War II. With respect to the civil population in general and the Jews in particular, the German authorities applied no legal norms such as are commonly understood and practiced in the relations between governments and governed or in human relations in the civilized world. The Jews were just plain outlawed as soon as the Germans caught up with them in any given town, township, or hamlet that came under their rule. Unheard-of acts of terror against the Jews by the German army and police bear witness to a bloody wave of degradation, spoliation, and murder. . . .

We shall now endeavor to analyze . . . "rescue-through-work" as a fundamental element in the strategy of the Councils vis-à-vis the Germans before "resettlements" and even after "resettlements" were partially completed. The practical implementation of this strategy stemmed from the assumption that the work of Jews within and outside the ghetto for the benefit of German war industry could serve as a basis for survival, or at least for a reprieve from extermination. One finds these theoretical considerations in the preserved speeches of prominent leaders in a few larger ghettos.

The most outspoken propagator of the idea that the lives of ghetto inmates could be preserved only by work was the Elder of the Łódź ghetto, Rumkowski. On innumerable occasions, in all his public utterances both before and during the "resettlements," he untiringly repeated that the physical existence of the ghetto depended solely on labor useful to the Germans and that under no circumstances, even the most tragic ones, should the ghetto give up this justification for its continuation. In an address delivered to deportees from Central Europe on November 1, 1941, barely one month before preparations for deportations from Łódź had begun, he said, *inter alia:*

> *When I moved into the ghetto on April 6, 1940, I told the mayor that I was moving in the belief that this was a gold mine. When he, aston- ished, asked for an explanation, I told him: "I have forty thousand hands for work in the ghetto and this is my gold mine." As I began successfully to organize work, the authorities gradually began to deal with me and to count on me more and more. . . . Today there are 52 factories in the ghetto testifying to my success in creating places of employment. These factories have been visited by the highest represen- tatives of the authorities on many occasions, and they have been amazed. They repeatedly have told me that up to now they had known of only one type of Jew — the merchant or middleman — and had never realized that Jews were capable of productive work. I shall never forget the reaction of one of the dignitaries from Berlin. Noticing a patrol of the ghetto police in the factory, he was sure that their duty was to chase people to work. I informed this gentleman that the duty of the policemen was rather to chase away the many people constantly searching for some kind of work. . . . Work provides the best publicity for the ghetto and enhances confidence in it. . . .*

Despite the fact that the ghettos had veen sealed off, the assumption that employment might make rescue possible spread from ghetto to ghetto through escapees, special emissaries, and other channels. . . .

When people in the town of Łúków (Lublin district) complained that the Jewish Council had done nothing to prevent imminent dis- aster, they received the answer that "it is nescessary to work. . . . it is possible that the Germans will not bother workers at employment premises, and that they will live." A frantic search for the places to work ensued. People tried by giving bribes and gifts to find better, more secure German employment places. It is alleged that Hendler, the chairman of the Jewish Council at Brzesko (Cracow district), advised the Jewish population on the second day of the "resettlement" to clench their teeth and continue working, since labor was the only res- cue possibility available. . . ."

The policy of employment as a rescue strategy was probably encouraged by the attitude of certain circles of the occupation authorities, notably the military, who had sometimes expressed their opposition to the rapid and total physical extermination of the Jews. Though on the whole the *Wehrmacht* and the *Einsatzgruppen* in the occupied territories of Soviet Russia cooperated in the Final Solution, this cooperation was not always smooth. The intra-office correspondence of some occupation authorities in areas invaded by the Germans after June 1941 (when mass murder of the Jews began to take place concurrently with the victorious advance of the German army) indicates that the contradiction between the economic interests of the *Wehrmacht* and the political exigencies of carrying out the Final Solution appeared very early. When the Germans occupied the Ukraine and Ostland they found that Jewish artisans and skilled workers were predominant. In a number of small towns the only artisans and skilled workers were Jews. . . .

Skepticism regarding the advisability of the mass physical extermination of the Jews, including skilled labor (which, incidentally, cost the Germans next to nothing) was also expressed by the Nazi bureaucratic and military machines in the occupied territories of Poland, both in the Government General and the Wartheland. It was particularly evident in the middle of 1942, when the German war economy began to feel a pinching scarcity of reserves. The net result of the sudden mass elimination of Jewish laborers was a drastic decrease in production, which caused uneasiness among the economic and administrative authorities responsible for production output. . . .

German firms working for the army were reluctant to let their Jewish workers go and tried to intercede with the SS and police in order to exempt them from "resettlements." In their secret reports, various German labor offices sounded the alarm, warned against drastic reduction of the labor crews, and requested new workers to replace "resettled" ones. Interventions followed on the part of the economic agencies of the German army directly affected by negative results of the "resettlements" for war production potential. . . .

We know now that the Jewish Councils made a great mistake in believing that Nazi policy with respect to the Jews had been motivated by rational or utilitarian considerations of any kind. Now we know for sure that the difference of opinion between the *Wehrmacht* and the SS had been *only about slowing down* the tempo of the Final Solution and *not about stopping* the total physical destruction of the Jews. The army was interested solely in the exploitation of Jewish slave labor for the benefit of the German war machine until the time when replacement of Jews with non-Jewish workers from the native population would become feasible. . . .

Admittedly, however, in those times of unprecedented calamity the Jewish Councils, groping toward means to cope with the "resettlements," had no choice but to try the mass employment strategy. It should be added that wide circles of the working segments of the population shared this strategy, though perhaps under the influence of the Councils. In retrospect we find that those who remained in the ghettos perished almost to a man, having been deported to extermination camps or killed on the spot. On the other hand, a certain percentage survived from among those who, before or during the liquidation of the ghettos, were shipped to various labor or concentration camps. There is no doubt that the decisive factor in extending the lives of some of the ghettos was the measure of their contribution to the German war economy. Thus the final liquidation of the Łódź Ghetto took place as late as the end of August 1944 (except for Theresienstadt, Łódź was the last ghetto in occupied Europe to be liquidated). Among the relatively long-lived ghettos, important for the German war economy, were those of Białystok and Vilna, which were liquidated in August and September 1943 respectively. The ghettos of Kaunas and Šiauliai, which were converted into concentration camps, were liquidated in July 1944. These few ghettos were almost the last remaining ones in occupied Eastern Europe at the time. Each of them was what the Germans called an *Arbeitsgetto* ("labor ghetto").

Had the war ended earlier, a sizable number of the labor elements might have survived. Let us take the case of the Łódź Ghetto. In August 1944, when the Soviet armies had already reached the environs of Warsaw, approximately 70,000 Jews still lived in Łódź (at a distance of some 75 miles). Had the Soviet army not stopped its advance till January 1945, a large number of these 70,000 people would certainly have escaped the gas chambers of Auschwitz. . . .

What were the tactics used by the Jewish Councils vis-à-vis the ghetto population during the "resettlement actions"? What answers could they give to placate frightened people inquiring in a state of terror about the alarming news from neighboring ghettos of disaster descending upon them?

At first the Councils had no hint whatsoever what the intentions of the Germans were. At most they may have guessed intuitively that this was not a simple matter and that the "resettled" people were in danger. It simply was humanly impossible to perceive that "resettlement" meant physical destruction of the entire Jewish population, particularly since the police and the officials of the civil administration used elaborate tricks before and during the course of the "actions" to keep the Jews in the dark about their monstrous intentions. A few examples will suffice to illustrate German fraud and deceit.

On July 20, 1942, barely two days before the Gestapo men came to the office of the Jewish Council in Warsaw to dictate the order for mass "resettlement" to Adam Czerniakow,[1] he noted in his diary:

> [I visited] the Gestapo at 7:30 in the morning. I inquired of Mende [in charge of Jewish affairs] how much truth there was in the rumors [about pending resettlement]. He answered that he knew nothing about it. To my question whether this was at all possible, he again answered that he knew nothing about it. I left unconvinced. I then asked his chief, Kommissar Boehm, who answered that this was not within his competence, that Höhnemann [a leading Gestapo man] might be in a position to give some information. I stressed that, according to rumors, the "resettlement" was to start today at 19:30 [7.30 P.M.]. [He] answered that he would certainly have had some information if this were so. Having no recourse, I approached Scherer, the deputy chief of Department III [of the Gestapo]. He showed surprise and said that he too knew nothing. I then asked whether I might inform the [Jewish] population that there was no foundation for the alarm. [He] answered that I could do so. Everything that has been rumored is unsubstantiated gossip and groundless talk. I have [therefore] instructed [Jacob] Lejkin [commandant of the ghetto police] to inform the population accordingly through the area committees.

Czerniakow supplemented the entry by stating that when First, the chief of the economic department of the Jewish Council, inquired of two other Security Police officials, they got very angry because of the rumors and said that an investigation would be

[1] Chairman of the Jewish Council in Warsaw. — Ed.

ordered about the whole thing. A mere two days later the "resettlement" began and Czerniakow committed suicide. . . .

All this intentional fraudulence and cheating in cold blood during the Final Solution process was used by the Germans in order to soothe the panic-stricken Jews, reduce their alertness, and entirely disorient them so that to the very last minute they had no inkling of what "resettlement" really meant. The instinct of self-preservation, which prompts people to resist the thought of imminent destruction and to cling to even a spark of hope, here played into the hands of the executioners. A vast number of ghettos fell prey to this combination of circumstances. To a large degree the age-old Jewish optimism that a miracle might yet occur even at the very last moment itself contributed to the fatalistic attitudes of Council members and of the ghetto population as well, particularly since no other solution to their tragic situation was in sight. . . .

The Jewish Councils faced a particularly grave dilemma when the fateful time of the "resettlements" came. It was perhaps the most excruciating moral predicament encountered by a representative body in history.

The German authorities forced the Councils to make all the preliminary preparations for "resettlements" on their behalf: deliver data on the demography and employment of the ghetto population; prepare, in accordance with their strict guidelines, lists of suggested candidates for deportation; order the Jews to report at the places designated for "selection"; search for deportation candidates who tried to conceal themselves and deliver them in person, or order the ghetto police to find them according to lists prepared by the Councils or given to them by the authorities.

During these most awful times, the Councils realized that it was impossible to save the entire ghetto community. Though they may have reasoned that, thanks to their "rescue-through-work" strategy, the working segment of the ghetto population, the young men and women, would have a better chance of survival, they understood at the same time that people on welfare or otherwise not working had no chance at all — people like the elderly and the feeble, who faced death or illness anyway, and large families with small children as well as the children themselves. Beset by the impending ordeal, a sizable number of Councils fearfully came to the fateful conclusion that since not all Jews could be saved, it was better to deliver to the Nazi Moloch those ghetto dwellers with little or no chance of survival in order to save others. This desperate reasoning, that in the calamity that had befallen them it was necessary as a kind of rescue strategy to sacrifice some to save others, emerged within many ghettos. . . .

A vivid description of the crushing moral dilemma that overpowered the Jewish Councils during the "resettlements" comes from the Kaunas Ghetto. On October 26, 1941, there arrived in the ghetto its newly appointed boss, the Gestapo man Rauke, who ordered the entire Jewish population, without exception, to assemble at the Democratic Square two days later. All were to bring their working papers. A check would be made, and those unable to work would be transported elsewhere. Whoever was found at home after 6 A.M. on the day of the assembly would be shot. Only the ill were exempt; however, they had to produce a certificate from a doctor. The vice chairman of the Council thus describes the anguish that tortured its members.

> The Council faced problems of conscience and responsibility at the same time. . . . [There were two alternatives:] . . . either to comply, announce the Gestapo order to the ghetto inhabitants, and issue proper instructions to the Ghetto police; or openly to sabotage the order by disregarding it. The Council felt that if it followed the first alternative, part, or perhaps the majority, of the ghetto might yet be rescued at least for a time. Should however, the other alternative be chosen, heavy measures of persecution would follow against the entire ghetto, and possibly its immediate liquidation [might result].

Aware of the situation and of this burden of responsibility for the lives of thousands whom it might yet be possible to save, the Council at the same time felt the traditional Jewish optimism that, perhaps, a miracle might yet mercifully come at the last minute. These considerations influenced the Council once more not to choose the path of open sabotage against the Germans. A resolution to this effect was adopted in Kaunas after an agonizing moral struggle during a long meeting and following a night of consultation with the old Kaunas rabbi, the late Abraham Duber Shapiro. The rabbi fainted when he heard what the Council members told him. When he came to, he asked for a few hours to search the holy books for advice on how one is to act in times of such a calamity, according to Jewish ethics. In the morning, he gave the following opinion to the

Jewish Council: "If a Jewish community (may God help it) has been condemned to physical destruction, and there are means of rescuing part of it, the leaders of the community should have courage and assume the responsibility to act and rescue what is possible." Of the 26,400 Jews remaining in Kaunas after three previous "actions" (on August 18, September 26, and October 4, 1941), some 9,000 persons were taken away during this "selection" on the next day. . . . and killed. . . .

Considering their tasks, cooperation with the authorities was unavoidable for the Councils. The very rationale for their existence would have vanished without it.

The Councils had to maintain daily contacts with the Germans in such matters as food, delivery of forced laborers, collection of imposed material *Leistungen* [contributions], filling production orders for ghetto industry, permission for import of raw materials, carrying out of some welfare activities — medical or sanitary services, education of children, etc.

It was stated in official German pronouncements that the Councils represented the interests of the Jews. . . . Thus the Councils were made to believe that they would really be able to protect Jewish interests.

For purposes of comparison, it should be remembered that cooperation between the indigent non-Jewish population and the authorities took place throughout the occupied territories. Hundreds of thousands of officials and workers from among the local population (in the Government General alone their number reached 260,000 persons . . .) served in the German administrative, economic, judicial, and even police apparatuses. Without their assistance it would have been impossible for the Germans to administer and dominate the occupied lands. No accusations of collaboration were advanced against these people after the war, except in some individual cases of overt criminal acts committed against the population in the occupied territories.

There were however, basic differences between non-Jewish collaboration and Jewish cooperation.

1.   Collaboration of non-Jews was on a *voluntary* basis, either because of sharing the National Socialist ideology, or because of opportunity for personal gain (career, authority, etc.) or in order to

let off pent-up hatred toward the Jews, or because of a lust to rob and kill. This category includes Jewish Gestapo agents and the demoralized members of the Councils and the ghetto police who served the German authorities in order to gain privileges and material goods for themselves and their families. In contrast, the cooperation of the Councils with the Germans was forced upon the Jews and was maintained in an atmosphere of ever-present merciless terror.

2. Diametrically different were German aims with regard to non-Jewis collaborations, as compared to Jewish ones. Toward the former their aims were political and tactical: to infect with propaganda and morally disarm the local population in order to neutralize the anti-Nazi movement. But with respect to the Jews, the imposed cooperation was aimed at accomplishing the special tasks of an instrument for carrying out all anti-Jewish persecution measures, including self-destruction, with the Council members and the Jewish Police themselves as the final victims.

3. The non-Jewish collaborationists greatly profited from the fruits of their cooperation, sharing the material privileges of the German authority apparatus. They were considered allies in the future "New Europe," while the Councils, as a rule, acted under conditions of constant physical and spiritual degradation, always on the brink of the abyss, with the threat of being thrown into it hanging over them all the time. They were treated as enemies by the Nazis, and were all Jews.

However, cooperation with the Germans was a threat to spineless Council members. They were in danger of going to the extreme in cooperationg the the Nazis, not so much in the illusory belief of interceding for the common good of the Jews as for their own benefit. In an atmosphere of moral nihilism, corruption of Nazi officialdom, and inhuman terror, it was not easy for such Council members to be on guard against crossing the fine demarcation line between cooperation and collaboration. Compelled to adjust themselves to the mentality of their German bosses, some of the Council members were disposed to adopt their methods. They were often forced to do so. There were also Councilmen with a compulsive urge to rule, and participation in the Councils provided them with the opportunity of relieving their lust for authority and honor; for this they felt obligated to the Germans.

Here we come to yet another aspect characteristic of the cooperation of the Jewish Councils with the Germans: the seeming "authority." The Jewish Councils got from the Nazis functions which had not been carried out for ages by Jewish community representatives. Since the Middle Ages, no other Jewish body had exercised so much economic, administrative, judicial, and police authority. This alleged "authority" could corrupt many Council members or chairmen. For the price of continuing in office (and this could happen only at the mercy of the Nazis) they entered into open or covert collaboration. . . .

Two periods can be discerned in the history of the Jewish Councils, with the "resettlement actions" as a borderline. During the initial period, when the authorities requested cooperation in the seizure of Jewish property and delivery of Jewish laborers to places of work or to labor camps, the moral responsibility that weighed on the Councils was still bearable. They could justify their cooperation by reasoning that in carrying out German demands they helped prolong the life of the ghetto, making it useful to the authorities as a source of material gain, and of slave labor for the Nazi war economy, almost free of charge. The situation became morally unbearable when, during the mass "resettlement actions," the Germans forced the Councils and the Jewish police to carry out the preparatory work and to participate in the initial stages of the actual deportation. The latter task was forced mainly upon the Jewish police. The Councils then faced a tragic dilemma never before experienced by a community representative organ. Cooperation then reached the morally dangerous borderline of collaboration. The Councils were called upon to make fateful decisions on the life and death of certain segments of their coreligionists. There were Council chairmen in the large ghettos who even then found justification for cooperating with the authorities. However, there were numerous instances where Council members, including chairmen, resisted this delusive temptation, committing suicide or going to execution in the gas chambers together with their families. Others took the perilous path of resistance. . . .

It is clear from available sources that the majority of the Councils were against the idea of organized resistance. There were Councils that actively opposed underground groups and denounced them to the Germans. They were afraid that open resistance might spoil their strategy of making the ghetto inmates useful to the Germans. Collective reprisals against the ghettos after Jews had been caught with arms or waging other forms of resistance confirmed these Councils in their negative attitudes. To give only one instance of many: On July 22, 1943, members of a group of the Jewish United Partisan Organization in the Vilna Ghetto left for the Narotch Forest. Fourteen people joined them on the way. During an encounter with the Germans, some of the fighters fell. Two were taken prisoners and perished in Ponary. In retribution, the Gestapo chief, Neugebauer, ordered that the families of the escapees be delivered to him. He also ordered that the brigadiers of the labor unit where the escapees had been employed be delivered together with their families. Thirty-two persons were taken from their homes in the night and brought to the prison and, later, to Ponary. Neugebauer issued an order of collective responsibility: the entire family of each escapee was to be seized. In case an escapee had no family, all the persons living with him in the same room were to be seized. If these persons were not found, all the tenants of his building were to be shot. All Jews leaving the ghetto for work were to be separated into groups of 10; if one was missing on return from work, all of his group were to be shot. After this tragic event in which 32 persons were murdered, there appeared in the *Geto-yedies* the following item under the headline "Wrath and Grief" (*Tsar un tsorn*):

> *The responsibility for these deaths falls onto those who betrayed our ghetto community and all its serious tasks in the full knowledge that they were endangering the existence of our entire ghetto and the lives of their loved ones in the first place. They are responsible for the spilt blood.*

. . .

There were Councils that adopted a positive attitude to resistance and rescue endeavors by all those able to escape from the ghetto, dangerous consequences notwithstanding. There were individual Council members and entire Councils involved in underground activities against the Germans even before the "resettlement actions." . . .

Positive attitudes to resistance took various shapes: some Councils granted young people financial assistance, some encouraged them to organize groups for resistance when the time came to join the partisans. The highest degree of cooperation was achieved when chairmen or other leading Council members themselves actively participated in preparing and executing acts of resistance, particularly in the course of liquidations of ghettos. Here are a few examples.

Jacob Lazebnik, a member of the Lenin Jewish Council (near Pińsk), called upon the youth to organize themselves. In Radomsko the Council chairman Gutgesztalt in January 1943 warned members of the Zionist Youth Organizations Hechalutz and Hashomer Hatzair not to trust German assurances that there was a possibility of their going to Palestine as part of a special exchange program. He labeled this another Gestapo trick and advised them to flee the ghetto. He himself escaped into the forest.

One of the most prominent members of the Warsaw Jewish Council, Abraham Gepner, adopted a positive attitude toward the resistance movement and contributed money to buy arms.

When the Sasów Jewish Council (Distrikt Galizien) got an order to deliver people for "resettlement," it warned the inmates to escape and itself escaped to the forest. When the Gestapo arrived, they found the Jewish homes empty.

Jewish Councils or their individual members suspected of cooperating with the underground were mercilessly persecuted. According to a witness, Shmuel Zalcman, second chairman of the Chmielnik Jewish Council, maintained contact with the underground circles, advising them on how to organize the underground in the ghetto. Zalcman was arrested because of an informer. Fastened to a horse-drawn cart, he was dragged all over town and died a horrible death. . . .

The sources mention instances of Council members actively taking part in acts of armed resistance against the Germans and physically resisting the "actions." One of these was Bert Lopatyn, chairman of the Council at Lachwa Ghetto (Pińsk area). Based on facts contained in four eyewitness accounts collected independently, this is what took place. On September 3, 1942, the ghetto was unexpectedly shut off by the Byelorussian militia. Next day, the SD men began chasing inmates through the ghetto gate to prepared graves nearby. The SD men entered the Council building, demanding that Dubski, a Council member, give them the list of Jews in the ghetto (probably in order to carry out a "selection"). When Dubski refused, he was shot on the spot. Before the "action" began, Lopatyn unsuccessfully tried to pay off the *Kommandant* of the SD unit. In company with a member of the underground group, he then went from house to house telling ghetto inmates that when he sees that the end had come he would set fire to the Council building as a signal for all inmates to do the same [to their homes]. It seems that on his advice many people armed themselves with knives and axes. A large number of armed ghetto inmates waited at the assembly place for the signal. When the Council building began to burn, people put their own homes to flame. In the turmoil that broke out one of the inmates, Yitzhak Rechstein, split the head of a gendarme with his hatchet. As if on signal the crowd surged forward, trying to reach the ghetto gate. Lopatyn snatched an automatic gun from a German but did not know how to use it and began shooting at random. The German wounded him in the arm. A former soldier of the Polish army, Hajfec, snatched a gun from another German and began shooting in the direction of the German cordon, which opened fire on the Jews. The crowd, armed with knives and bottles of lye, attacked the ghetto sentries. Some escaped, taking along some arms from the watchmen. Many others escaped from the burning ghetto, but the majority perished. One eyewitness, Leon Slutski, related that of 2,000 ghetto inmates some 600 escaped, of whom only 100 or 120 remained alive and met in the forest. Lopatyn was among these, and later on he fought in the Stalin squad of the Kirow Brigade (operational area: Lida-Nowogródek). Hit by a mine, he perished on April 1, 1944. . . .

The material cited is sufficient to illustrate how complicated the problem of objective evaluation is, both with respect to the behavior of individual members of Councils and of Councils as a whole. The researcher faces grave psychological problems grappling with the analysis, particularly so because it is not easy to perceive now the specific climate of those "times with no precedent" and the spirit of people who lived and acted under unimaginable conditions of stress, on the brink of an abyss that constantly threatened to swallow them up. Considering the behavior and deeds of the Councilmen one has always to bear in mind that they were under the pressure of cynical, merciless terror by the Nazis at all times, that the prospect of being killed sooner or later was a concrete eventuality, and that every step they took was liable to postpone or hasten it. . . . Only in the context of this extraordinary situation with its relentless psychological stress is it possible to grasp at all or explain the activities and behavior of the Councils and their members. . . .

[Trunk's associate and collaborator, Jacob Robinson, wrote the introduction to the book in which he commented on the significance of Trunk's findings. Here are Robinson's final thoughts. — Ed.]

Was the Jewish Council a positive or a negative factor in the final outcome of the Holocaust? The problem refers to the broad outcome of the Holocaust, not to the isolated individual cases of casualties charged — rightly or wrongly — to the Councils or the individual cases of rescue attributed — rightly or wrongly — to them. Did their participation or nonparticipation influence the dreadful statistics? The following facts should help in formulating an enlightened answer:

1.   In large areas of Eastern Europe at least two million victims were murdered without any participation at all on the part of Jews. This refers particularly to victims of the *Einsatzgruppen* in both the initial phase of the war and during the later stages.

2.   In the larger ghettos in Poland and in the Baltic states where there was Jewish participation it was of importance in the initial, not in the final, stages of deportations; the later deportations, as has been indicated above, were carried out by German forces, while the Jewish police played only a secondary role.

3.   With few exceptions the process of extermination was finished by early 1943, a year and a half prior to Himmler's autumn 1944 "stop extermination" order. Whatever survivors of the fatal year (spring 1942–spring 1943) remained or could have remained alive were destroyed (one may even say at a leisurely pace) during the following months.

4.   Above all, the German will to destroy the Jewish people (*Vernichtungswille*) was directed with particular fury against Eastern European Jewry. The Nazi official statements are full of warnings of the dangers to Germany of East European Jewry, which is represented as the greatest source of Jewish power, a mighty stream from which Jews spread out to all corners of the world, as the reservoir for the existence and constant renewal of world Jewry. The Nazis claimed that without the addition of fresh East European Jewish

blood, Jewry in the West would long ago have disappeared. It is difficult to believe that with this determination the Nazis would not have used every day and every device to implement the Final Solution to the letter.

It would appear, then, that when all factors are considered, Jewish participation or nonparticipation in the deportations had no substantial influence — one way or the other — on the final outcome of the Holocaust in Eastern Europe.

SS men having their picture taken with a Polish Jew as he says the last prayer for his dead brothers. He, too, probably was shot soon afterwards. (Archive Photos)

The Motivations of the Killers

Variety of Opinion

The key to understanding how Nazi doctors came to do the work of Auschwitz is the psychological principle I call "doubling": the division of the self into two functioning wholes, so that a part-self acts as an entire self. An Auschwitz doctor could, through doubling, not only kill . . . but organize . . . all aspects of his behavior.

Robert Jay Lifton

To break ranks and step out, to adopt overtly nonconformist behavior, was simply beyond most of the men. It was easier for them to shoot. . . . If the men of Reserve Police Battalion 101 could become killers under such circumstances, what group of men cannot?

Christopher R. Browning

Not economic hardship, not the coercive means of a totalitarian state, not social psychological pressure, not invariable psychological propensities, but ideas about Jews that were pervasive in Germany, and had been for decades, induced ordinary Germans to kill . . . systematically and without pity.

Daniel Jonah Goldhagen

149

What drove the men who were directly involved in killing Jews, Gypsies, and others during the Holocaust? Earlier views of them as the personification of unalloyed evil have not proved very satisfying. After all, thousands of Germans participated in the killings, and they could not all have been morally depraved brutes (although some certainly were). We now know that they were not all SS men. Even those who were could be loving family men and decent human beings capable of acts of kindness to some victims. How, then, could they participate in mass murder?

Robert Jay Lifton examines the motivations of Nazi doctors who selected who would live and who would die in the camps, supervised the gassings, and performed experiments on prisoners that ended in fatal injections when the victims no longer were useful. What transformed men dedicated to healing into killers? Lifton, a leading American psychiatrist, sought to answer this question by interviewing dozens of surviving Nazi doctors and nonmedical professionals, as well as former concentration camp inmates. He concluded that the doctors had gone through the process of "doubling," the separation of a person's self into two functioning wholes, a phenomenon he distinguished from multiple personalities and split ("Dr. Jekyll/Mr. Hyde") personalities. Lifton underscored the central role of Nazi ideology in doubling. Killing Jews, who were viewed as embodying all that was evil in the world, would heal the Aryan race. By adopting an "Auschwitz self" while simultaneously maintaining their professional identity, the doctors could murder with a clear conscience. After 1945 they could return to their "prewar self" and resume normal lives and careers — unburdened, it seems, by guilt or remorse. As Lifton makes clear, this analysis has implications that go well beyond the medical profession and the Nazi era.

Christopher Browning reaches both similar and different conclusions about the members of Reserve Police Battalion 101, older men (and "ordinary men," not SS) drafted to keep order behind German lines in Eastern Europe and unexpectedly ordered to murder Jews. Although they were given the choice of other assignments in the unit and did not have to fear being punished or sent away for noncompliance, most joined in the killing and grew used to it. Browning examined their testimony to a postwar German court and found that Nazi ideology played little part in determining their behavior. Few of the men had been enthusiastic Nazis, and their ideological indoctrination had been rudimentary. In exploring the complex web of motivation, Browning concludes that deference to authority and conformity to the group are what made killers out of "ordinary men."

Daniel Jonah Goldhagen believes that the perpetrators did not need to "double," blindly obey orders, or bow to peer pressure. They passionately *wanted* to kill Jews. Products of a society that long had been permeated with venomous antisemitism, in Goldhagen's view, these "ordinary Germans" (not "ordinary men") actually took the initiative in mistreating Jews and enjoyed themselves while doing it. Goldhagen's study of both SS officers and members of police battalions challenges the reliability of their postwar testimony. He attributes their occasional reluctance to kill to distaste over having to become personally involved in a messy business, not to principled opposition to murdering Jews. The perpetrators, he concludes, were zealous racists and as such faithfully represented a German nation that had wanted to get rid of the Jews even before Hitler came to power.

Did Holocaust perpetrators have to be *made into* killers, or did they jump at the chance to murder? Although antisemitism was certainly at the heart of the Holocaust, is it sufficient in itself to explain German conduct? Or were the circumstances more important in conditioning the killers? If the latter was true, did perpetrators adopt a psychological defense mechanism, such as "doubling," to avoid consciousness of how their deeds clashed with humane values? Or did they simply subordinate those values to authority and group loyalty and then become acclimatized to killing?

Robert Jay Lifton

The Nazi Doctors

In Nazi mass murder, we can say that a barrier was removed, a boundary crossed: that boundary between violent imagery and periodic killing of victims (as of Jews in pogroms) on the one hand, and systematic genocide in Auschwitz and elsewhere on the other. My argument in this study is that the medicalization of killing — the imagery of killing in the name of healing — was crucial to that terrible step. At the heart of the Nazi enterprise, then, is the destruction of the boundary between healing and killing.

Early descriptions of Auschwitz and other death camps focused on the sadism and viciousness of Nazi guards, officers, and physicians. But subsequent students of the process realized that sadism and viciousness alone could not account for the killing of millions of people. The emphasis then shifted to the bureaucracy of killing: the faceless, detached bureaucratic function originally described by Max Weber, now applied to mass murder. This focus on numbed violence is enormously important, and is consistent with what we shall observe to be the routinization of all Auschwitz functions.

Yet these emphases are not sufficient in themselves. They must be seen in relation to the visionary motivations associated with ideology, along with the specific individual-psychological mechanisms enabling people to kill. What I call "medicalized killing" addresses these motivational principles and psychological mechanisms, and permits us to understand the Auschwitz victimizers — notably Nazi doctors — both as part of a bureaucracy of killing and as individual participants whose attitudes and behavior can be examined.

Medicalized killing can be understood in two wider perspectives. The first is the "surgical" method of killing large numbers of people by means of a controlled technology making use of highly poisonous gas; the methods employed became a means of maintaining distance between killers and victims. This distancing had considerable importance for the Nazis in alleviating the psychological problems experienced (as attested over and over by Nazi documents) by the *Einsatzgruppen* troops who carried out face-to-face shooting of Jews in Eastern Europe . . . — problems that did not prevent those troops from murdering 1,400,000 Jews.

I was able to obtain direct evidence on this matter during an interview with a former *Wehrmacht* neuropsychiatrist who had treated large numbers of *Einsatzgruppen* personnel for psychological disorders. He told me that these disorders resembled combat reactions of ordinary troops: severe anxiety, nightmares, tremors, and numerous bodily complaints. But in these "killer troops," as he called them, the symptoms tended to last longer and to be more severe. He estimated that 20 percent of those doing the actual killing experienced these symptoms of psychological decompensation. About half of that 20 percent associated their symptoms mainly with the "unpleasantness" of what they had to do, while the other half seemed to have moral questions about shooting people in that way. The men had the greatest psychological difficulty concerning shooting women and children, especially children. Many experienced a sense of guilt in their dreams, which could include various forms of punishment or retribution. Such psychological difficulty led the Nazis to seek a more "surgical" method of killing.

But there is another perspective on medicalized killing that I believe to be insufficiently recognized: *killing as a therapeutic imperative.* That kind of motivation was revealed in the words of a Nazi doctor quoted by the distinguished survivor physician Dr. Ella Lingens-Reiner. Pointing to the chimneys in the distance, she asked a Nazi doctor, Fritz Klein, "How can you reconcile that with your [Hippocratic] oath as a doctor?" His answer was, "Of course I am a doctor and I want to preserve life. And out of respect for human life, I would remove a gangrenous appendix from a diseased body. The Jew is the gangrenous appendix in the body of mankind."

The medical imagery was still broader. Just as Turkey during the nineteenth century (because of the extreme decline of the Ottoman empire) was known as the "sick man of Europe," so did pre-Hitler ideologues and Hitler himself interpret Germany's post–First World War chaos and demoralization as an "illness," especially of the Aryan race. Hitler wrote in *Mein Kampf*, in the mid-1920's, that *"anyone who wants to cure this era, which is inwardly sick and rotten, must first of all summon up the courage to make clear the causes of this disease."* The diagnosis was racial. The only genuine "culture-creating" race, the Aryans, had permitted themselves to be weakened to the point of endangered survival by the "destroyers of culture," characterized as "the Jew." The Jews were agents of "racial pollution" and "racial tuberculosis," as well as parasites and bacteria causing sickness, deterioration, and death in the host peoples they infested. They were the "eternal bloodsucker," "vampire," "germ carrier," "peoples' parasite," and "maggot in a rotting corpse." The cure had to be radical: that is (as one scholar put it), by "cutting out the 'canker of decay,' propagating the worthwhile elements and letting the less valuable wither away, . . . [and] 'the extirpation of all those categories of people considered to be worthless or dangerous.'"

Medical metaphor blended with concrete biomedical ideology in the Nazi sequence from coercive sterilization to direct medical killing to the death camps. The unifying principle of the biomedical ideology was that of a deadly racial disease, the sickness of the Aryan race; the cure, the killing of all Jews.

Thus, for Hans Frank, jurist and General Governor of Poland during the Nazi occupation, "the Jews were a lower species of life, a kind of vermin, which upon contact infected the German people with deadly diseases." When the Jews in the area he ruled had been killed, he declared that "now a sick Europe would become healthy again." It was a religion of the will — the will as "an all-encompassing metaphysical principle;" and what the Nazis "willed" was nothing less than total control over life and death. While this view is often referred to as "social Darwinism," the term applies only loosely, mostly to the Nazi stress on natural "struggle" and on "survival of the fittest." The regime actually rejected much of Darwinism; since evolutionary theory is more or less democratic in its assumption of a common beginning for all races, it is therefore at odds with the Nazi principle of inherent Aryan racial virtue.

Even more specific to the biomedical vision was crude genetic imagery, combined with still cruder eugenic visions. . . . Here Heinrich Himmler, as high priest, spoke of the leadership's task as being "like the plant-breeding specialist who, when he wants to breed a pure new strain from a well-tried species that has been exhausted by too much cross-breeding, first goes over the field to cull the unwanted plants."

The Nazi project, then, was not so much Darwinian or social Darwinist as a vision of absolute control over the evolutionary process, over the biological human future. Making widespread use of the Darwinian term "selection," the Nazis sought to take over the functions of nature (natural selection) and God (the Lord giveth and the Lord taketh away) in orchestrating their own version of human evolution.

In these visions the Nazis embraced not only versions of medieval mystical anti-Semitism but also a newer (nineteenth- and twentieth-century) claim to "scientific racism." Dangerous Jewish characteristics could be linked with alleged data of scientific disciplines, so that a "mainstream of racism" formed from "the fusion of anthropology, eugenics, and social thought." The resulting "racial and social biology" could make vicious forms of anti-Semitism seem intellectually respectable to learned men and women.

One can speak of the Nazi state as a "biocracy." The model here is a theocracy, a system of rule by priests of a sacred order under the claim of divine prerogative. In the case of the Nazi biocracy, the divine prerogative was that of cure through purification and revitalization of the Aryan race: "From a dead mechanism which only lays claim to existence for its own sake, there must be formed a living organism with the exclusive aim of serving a higher idea." Just as in a theocracy, the state itself is no more than a vehicle for the divine purpose, so in the Nazi biocracy was the state no more than a means to achieve "*a mission of the German people on earth*": that of "*assembling and preserving the most valuable stocks of basic racial elements in this* [Aryan] *people . . . [and] . . . raising them to a dominant position.*" The Nazi biocracy differed from a classical theocracy in that the biological priests did not actually rule. The clear rulers were Adolf Hitler and his circle, not biological theorists and certainly not the doctors. (The difference, however, is far from absolute: even in a theocracy, highly politicized rulers may make varying claims to priestly authority.) In any case, Nazi ruling authority was maintained in the name of the higher biological principle.

Among the biological authorities called forth to articulate and implement "scientific racism" — including physical anthropologists, geneticists, and racial theorists of every variety — doctors inevitably found a unique place. It is they who work at the border of life and death, who are most associated with the awesome, death-defying, and sometimes death-dealing aura of the primitive shaman and medicine man. As bearers of this shamanistic legacy and contemporary practitioners of mysterious healing arts, it is they who are likely to be called upon to become biological activists.

I have mentioned my primary interest in Nazi doctors' participation in medicalized or biologized killing. We shall view their human experiments as related to the killing process and to the overall Nazi biomedical vision. At Nuremberg, doctors were tried only limitedly for their involvement in killing, partly because its full significance was not yet understood.

In Auschwitz, Nazi doctors presided over the murder of most of the one million victims of that camp. Doctors performed selections — both on the ramp among arriving transports of prisoners and later in the camps and on the medical blocks. Doctors supervised the killing in the gas chambers and decided when the victims were dead. Doctors conducted a murderous epidemiology, sending to the gas chamber groups of people with contagious diseases and sometimes including everyone else who might be on the medical block. Doctors ordered and supervised, and at times carried out, direct killing of debilitated patients on the medical blocks by means of phenol injections into the bloodstream or the heart. In connection with all of these killings, doctors kept up a pretense of medical legitimacy: for deaths of Auschwitz prisoners and of outsiders brought there to be killed, they signed false death certificates listing spurious illnesses. Doctors consulted actively on how best to keep selections running smoothly; on how many people to permit to remain alive to fill the slave labor requirements of the I. G. Farben enterprise at Auschwitz; and on how to burn the enormous numbers of bodies that strained the facilities of the crematoria.

In sum, we may say that doctors were given much of the responsibility for the murderous ecology of Auschwitz — the choosing of victims, the carrying through of the physical and psychological mechanics of killing, and the balancing of killing and work functions in the camp. While doctors by no means ran Auschwitz, they did lend it a perverse medical aura. As one survivor who closely observed the process put the matter, "Auschwitz was like a medical operation," and "the killing program was led by doctors from beginning to end."

We may say that the doctor standing at the ramp represented a kind of omega point, a mythical gatekeeper between the worlds of the dead and the living, a final common pathway of the Nazi vision of therapy via mass murder. . . .

The key to understanding how Nazi doctors came to do the work of Auschwitz is the psychological principle I call "doubling": the division of the self into two functioning wholes, so that a part-self acts as an entire self. An Auschwitz doctor could, through doubling, not only kill and contribute to killing but organize silently, on behalf of that evil project, an entire self-structure (or self-process) encompassing virtually all aspects of his behavior.

Doubling, then, was the psychological vehicle for the Nazi doctor's Faustian bargain with the diabolical environment in exchange for his contribution to the killing; he was offered various psychological and material benefits on behalf of privileged adaptation. Beyond Auschwitz was the larger Faustian temptation offered to German doctors in general: that of becoming the theorists and implementers of a cosmic scheme of racial cure by means of victimization and mass murder.

One is always ethically responsible for Faustian bargains — a responsibility in no way abrogated by the fact that much doubling takes place outside of awareness. In exploring doubling, I engage in psychological probing on behalf of illuminating evil. For the individual Nazi doctor in Auschwitz, doubling was likely to mean a choice for evil.

Generally speaking, doubling involves five characteristics. There is, first, a dialectic between two selves in terms of autonomy and connection. The individual Nazi doctor needed his Auschwitz self to function psychologically in an environment so antithetical to his previous ethical standards. At the same time, he needed his prior self in order to continue to see himself as humane physician, husband, father. The Auschwitz self had to be both autonomous and connected to the prior self that gave rise to it. Second, the doubling follows a holistic principle. The Auschwitz self "succeeded" because it was inclusive and could connect with the entire Auschwitz environment: it rendered coherent, and gave form to, various themes and mechanisms, which I shall discuss shortly. Third, doubling has a life-death dimension: the Auschwitz self was perceived by the perpetrator as a form of psychological survival in a death-dominated environment; in other words, we have the paradox of a "killing self" being created on behalf of what one perceives as one's own healing or survival. Fourth, a major function of doubling, as in Auschwitz, is likely to be the avoidance of guilt: the second self tends to be the one performing the "dirty work." And, finally, doubling involves both an unconscious dimension — taking place, as stated, largely outside of awareness — and a significant change in moral consciousness. These five characteristics frame and pervade all else that goes on psychologically in doubling. . . .

The way in which doubling allowed Nazi doctors to avoid guilt was not by the elimination of conscience but by what can be called the *transfer of conscience*. The requirements of conscience were transferred to the Auschwitz self, which placed it within its own criteria for good (duty, loyalty to group, "improving" Auschwitz conditions, etc.), thereby freeing the original self from responsibility for actions there. . . . The Auschwitz self of the Nazi doctor similarly assumed the death issue for him but at the same time used its evil project as a way of staving off awareness of his own "perishable and mortal part." It does the "dirty work" for the entire self by rendering that work "proper" and in that way protects the entire self from awareness of its own guilt and its own death.

In doubling, one part of the self "disavows" another part. What is repudiated is not reality itself — the individual Nazi doctor was aware of what he was doing via the Auschwitz self — but the meaning of that reality. The Nazi doctor knew that he selected, but did not interpret selections as murder. One level of disavowal, then, was the Auschwitz self's altering of the meaning of murder; and on another, the repudiation by the original self of *anything* done by the Auschwitz self. From the moment of its formation, the Auschwitz self so violated the Nazi doctor's previous self-concept as to require more or less permanent disavowal. Indeed, disavowal was the life blood of the Auschwitz self.

Doubling is an active psychological process, a means of *adaptation to extremity*. That is why I use the verb form, as opposed to the more usual noun form, "the double." The adaptation requires a dissolving of "psychic glue" as an alternative to a radical breakdown of the self. In Auschwitz, the pattern was established under the duress of the individual doctor's transition period. At that time the Nazi doctor experienced his own death anxiety as well as such death equivalents as fear of disintegration, separation, and stasis. He needed a functional Auschwitz self to still his anxiety. And that Auschwitz self had to assume hegemony on an everyday basis, reducing expressions of the prior self to odd moments and to contacts with family and friends outside the camp. Nor did most Nazi doctors resist that usurpation as long as they remained in the camp. Rather they welcomed it as the only means of psychological function. If an environment is sufficiently extreme, and one chooses to remain in it, one may be able to do so *only* by means of doubling.

Yet doubling does not include the radical dissociation and sustained separateness characteristic of multiple or "dual personality." In the latter condition, the two selves are more profoundly distinct and autonomous, and tend either not to know about each other or else to see each other as alien. . . .

While individual Nazi doctors in Auschwitz doubled in different ways, all of them doubled. Ernst B.,[1] for instance, limited his doubling; in avoiding selections, he was resisting a full-blown Auschwitz self. Yet his conscious desire to adapt to Auschwitz was an accession to at least a certain amount of doubling: it was he, after all, who said that "one could react like a normal human being in Auschwitz only for the first few hours;" after that, "you were caught and had to go along," which meant that you had to double. His own doubling was evident in his sympathy for Mengele[2] and, at least to some extent, for the most extreme expressions of the Nazi ethos (the image of the Nazis as a "world blessing" and of Jews as the world's "fundamental evil"). And despite the limit to his doubling, he retains aspects of his Auschwitz self to this day in his way of judging Auschwitz behavior.

In contrast, Mengele's embrace of the Auschwitz self gave the impression of a quick adaptive affinity, causing one to wonder

[1]"Dr. Ernst B." (real name Wilhelm Münch), an Auschwitz physician described as "a human being in an SS uniform," was the only death-camp doctor acquitted in a postwar trial. Former prisoners, including prisoner doctors, testified in his behalf. — Ed.

[2]Dr. Josef Mengele, a fanatical Nazi, performed macabre experiments on twins at Auschwitz. He escaped capture and died in hiding in Brazil in 1979. — Ed.

whether he required any doubling at all. But doubling was indeed required in a man who befriended children to an unusual degree and then drove some of them personally to the gas chamber; or by a man so "collegial" in his relationship to prisoner doctors and so ruthlessly flamboyant in his conduct of selections. Whatever his affinity for Auschwitz, a man who could be pictured under ordinary conditions as "a slightly sadistic German professor" had to form a new self to become an energetic killer. The point about Mengele's doubling was that his prior self could be readily absorbed into the Auschwitz self; and his continuing allegiance to the Nazi ideology and project probably enabled his Auschwitz self, more than in the case of other Nazi doctors, to remain active over the years after the Second World War.

Wirth's[3] doubling was neither limited (like Dr. B's) nor harmonious (like Mengele's): it was both strong and conflicted. We see Auschwitz's chief doctor as a "divided self" because both selves retained their power. Yet his doubling was the most successful of all from the standpoint of the Auschwitz institution and the Nazi project. Even his suicide was a mark of that success: while the Nazi defeat enabled him to equate his Auschwitz self more clearly with evil, he nonetheless retained responsibility to that Auschwitz self sufficiently to remain inwardly divided and unable to imagine any possibility of resolution and renewal — either legally, morally, or psychologically.

Within the Auschwitz structure, significant doubling included future goals and even a sense of hope. Styles of doubling varied because each Nazi doctor created his Auschwitz self out of his prior self, with its particular history, and with his own psychological mechanisms. But in all Nazi doctors, prior self and Auschwitz self were connected by the overall Nazi ethos and the general authority of the regime. Doubling was a shared theme among them.

Indeed, Auschwitz as an *institution* — as an atrocity-producing situation — ran on doubling. An atrocity-producing situation is one so structured externally (in this case, institutionally) that the average

---

[3]Dr. Eduard Wirth was chief physician at Auschwitz. A dedicated physician capable of showing compassion to individual prisoners, he also set up the camp's machinery of mass murder. He hanged himself in 1945. — Ed.

person entering it (in this case, as part of the German authority) will commit or become associated with atrocities. Always important to an atrocity-producing situation is its capacity to motivate individuals psychologically toward engaging in atrocity.

In an institution as powerful as Auschwitz, the external environment could set the tone for much of an individual doctor's "internal environment." The demand for doubling was part of the environmental message immediately perceived by Nazi doctors, the implicit command to bring forth a self that could adapt to killing without one's feeling oneself a murderer. Doubling became not just an individual enterprise but a shared psychological process, the group norm, part of the Auschwitz "weather." And that group process was intensified by the general awareness that, whatever went on in other camps, Auschwitz was the great technical center of the Final Solution. One had to double in order that one's life work there not be interfered with either by the corpses one helped to produce or by those "living dead" (the *Muselmänner*) all around one.

Inevitably, the Auschwitz pressure toward doubling extended to prisoner doctors, the most flagrant examples of whom were those who came to work closely with the Nazis. . . . Even those prisoner doctors who held strongly to their healing ethos, and underwent minimal doubling, inadvertently contributed to Nazi doctors' doubling simply by working with them, as they had to, and thereby in some degree confirmed a Nazi doctor's Auschwitz self.

Doubling undoubtedly occurred extensively in nonmedical Auschwitz personnel as well. Rudolf Höss[4] told how noncommissioned officers regularly involved in selections "pour[ed] out their hearts" to him about the difficulty of their work (their prior self speaking) — but went on doing that work (their Auschwitz self directing behavior). Höss described the Auschwitz choices: "either to become cruel, to become heartless and no longer to respect human life [that is, to develop a highly functional Auschwitz self] or to be weak and to get to the point of a nervous breakdown [that is, to hold onto one's prior self, which in Auschwitz was nonfunctional]." But in the Nazi doctor, the doubling was particularly stark in that a prior healing self gave rise to a killing self that should have been, but func-

---

[4]Höss was commandant of Auschwitz from 1940 to 1943. He was tried and hanged by the Poles in 1947. — Ed.

tionally was not, in direct opposition to it. And as in any atrocity-producing situation, Nazi doctors found themselves in a psychological climate where they were virtually certain to choose evil: they were propelled, that is, toward murder.

Beyond Auschwitz, there was much in the Nazi movement that promoted doubling. The overall Nazi project, replete with cruelty, required constant doubling in the service of carrying out that cruelty. The doubling could take the form of a gradual process of "slippery slope" compromises: the slow emergence of a functional "Nazi self" via a series of destructive actions, at first more incriminating, if not more murderous, than the previous ones.

Doubling could also be more dramatic, infused with transcendence, the sense (described by a French fascist who joined the SS) of being someone entering a religious order "who must now divest himself of his past," and of being "reborn into a new European race." That new Nazi self could take on a sense of mystical fusion with the German *Volk*, with "destiny," and with immortalizing powers. Always there was the combination noted earlier of idealism and terror, imagery of destruction and renewal, so that "gods . . . appear as both destroyers and culture-heroes, just as the Führer could appear as front comrade and master builder." Himmler, especially in his speeches to his SS leaders within their "oath-bound community," called for the kind of doubling necessary to engage in what he considered to be heroic cruelty, especially in the killing of Jews.

The degree of doubling was not necessarily equivalent to Nazi Party membership; thus, Hochhuth could claim that "the great divide was between Nazis [meaning those with well-developed Nazi selves] and decent people, not between Party members and other Germans." But probably never has a political movement demanded doubling with the intensity and scale of the Nazis.

Doctors as a group may be more susceptible to doubling than others. For example, a former Nazi doctor claimed that the anatomist's insensitivity toward skeletons and corpses accounted for his friend Hirt's grotesque "anthropological" collection of Jewish skulls. . . . While hardly a satisfactory explanation, this doctor was referring to a genuine pattern not just of numbing but of medical doubling. That doubling usually begins with the student's encounter with the corpse he or she must dissect, often enough on the first day of medical school. One feels it necessary to develop a "medical self," which enables one not only to be relatively inured to death but to function reasonably efficiently in relation to the many-sided demands of the work. The ideal doctor, to be sure, remains warm and humane by keeping that doubling to a minimum. But few doctors meet that ideal standard. Since studies have suggested that a psychological motivation for entering the medical profession can be the overcoming of an unusually great fear of death, it is possible that this fear in doctors propels them in the direction of doubling when encountering deadly environments. Doctors drawn to the Nazi movement in general, and to SS or concentration-camp medicine in particular, were likely to be those with the greatest previous medical doubling. But even doctors without outstanding Nazi sympathies could well have had a certain experience with doubling and a proclivity for its further manifestations.

Certainly the tendency toward doubling was particularly strong among *Nazi* doctors. Given the heroic vision held out to them — as cultivators of the genes and as physicians to the *Volk*, and as militarized healers combining the life-death power of shaman and general — any cruelty they might perpetrate was all too readily drowned in hubris. And their medical hubris was furthered by their role in the sterilization and "euthanasia" projects within a vision of curing the ills of the Nordic race and the German people.

Doctors who ended up undergoing the extreme doubling necessitated by the "euthanasia" killing centers and the death camps were probably unusually susceptible to doubling. There was, of course, an element of chance in where one was sent, but doctors assigned either to the killing centers or to the death camps tended to be strongly committed to Nazi ideology. They may well have also had greater schizoid tendencies, or been particularly prone to numbing and omnipotence-sadism, all of which also enhance doubling. Since, even under extreme conditions, people have a way of finding and staying in situations they connect with psychologically, we can suspect a certain degree of self-selection there too. In these ways, previous psychological characteristics of a doctor's self had considerable significance — but a significance in respect to tendency or susceptibility, and no more. Considerable doubling occurred in people of the most varied psychological characteristics.

We thus find ourselves returning to the recognition that most of what Nazi doctors did would be within the potential capability — at least under certain conditions — of most doctors and of most people. But once embarked on doubling in Auschwitz, a Nazi doctor did indeed separate himself from other physicians and from other human beings. Doubling was the mechanism by which a doctor, in his actions, moved from the ordinary to the demonic. . . .

The Auschwitz self depended upon radically diminished feeling, upon one's not experiencing psychologically what one was doing. I have called the state "psychic numbing," a general category of diminished capacity or inclination to feel. Psychic numbing involves an interruption in psychic action — in the continuous creation and re-creation of images and forms that constitutes the symbolizing or "formative process" characteristic of human mental life. Psychic numbing varies greatly in degree, from everyday blocking of excessive stimuli to extreme manifestations in response to death-saturated environments. But it is probably impossible to kill another human being without numbing oneself toward that victim.

The Auschwitz self also called upon the related mechanism of "derealization," of divesting oneself from the actuality of what one is part of, not experiencing it as "real." (That absence of actuality in regard to the killing was not inconsistent with an awareness of the killing policy — that is, of the Final Solution.) Still another pattern is that of "disavowal," or the rejection of what one actually perceives and of its meaning. Disavowal and derealization overlap and are both aspects of the overall numbing process. The key function of numbing in the Auschwitz self is the avoidance of feelings of guilt when one is involved in killing. The Auschwitz self can then engage in medicalized killing, an ultimate form of numbed violence.

To be sure, a Nazi doctor arrived at Auschwitz with his psychic numbing well under way. Much feeling had been blunted by his early involvement with Nazi medicine, including its elimination of Jews and use of terror, as well as by his participation in forced sterilization, his knowledge of or relationship to direct medical killing ("euthanasia"), and the information he knew at some level of consciousness about concentration camps and medical experiments held there if not about death camps such as Auschwitz. Numbing was fostered not only by this knowledge and culpability but by the admired principle of "the new spirit of German coldness." Moreover, early Nazi achievements furthered that hardness; and it is often the case that success breeds numbing. . . .

There has to be a transition from feeling to not feeling — a transition that, in Auschwitz, could be rapid and radical. It began with a built-in barrier toward psychologically experiencing the camp's main activity; killing Jews. The great majority of Jews were murdered upon arrival, without having been admitted to the camp and achieving the all-important status of having a number tattooed on one's arm, which in Auschwitz meant life, however precarious. Numbing toward victims was built in because, in Auschwitz terms, those victims never existed. The large selections brought about that massive non-existence; and the selections themselves became psychologically dissociated from other activities, relegated to a mental area that "didn't count" — that is, both derealized and disavowed. In that sense, there was a kernel of truth to Dr. B.'s claim that selections were psychologically less significant to Nazi doctors than the problems of hunger they encountered from moment to moment.

But only a kernel, since Nazi doctors knew that selections meant killing, and had to do the psychological work of calling forth a numbed Auschwitz self in order to perform them. While Nazi doctors varied in their original will, or willingness, to perform selections, they tended to have to overcome some "block" (as Dr. B. put it) or "scruple" (as Nazi literature has it). With the actual performance of one's first and perhaps second selection, one had, in effect, made a pledge to stay numbed, which meant to live within the restricted feelings of the Auschwitz self.

For this transition, the heavy drinking I have referred to has great significance on several levels. It provided, at the very beginning, an altered state of consciousness within which one "tried on" the threatening Auschwitz realities (the melodramatic, even romanticized declarations of doubts and half opposition described by Dr. B.). In this altered state, conflicts and objections need not have been viewed as serious resistance, need not have been dangerous. One could then explore doubts without making them real: one could derealize both the doubts and the rest of one's new Auschwitz life. At the same time, alcohol was central to a pattern of male bonding through which new doctors were socialized into the Auschwitz community. Men pull togther for the "common good," even for what was perceived among Nazi doctors as group survival. Drinking enhanced the meeting of the minds between old-timers, who could offer models of an Auschwitz self to the newcomer seeking entry into the realm of Auschwitz killing. The continuing alcohol-enhanced sharing of group feelings and group numbing gave further shape to the emerging Auschwitz self.

Over time, as drinking was continued especially in connection with selections, it enabled the Auschwitz self to distance that killing activity and reject responsibility for it. Increasingly, the Jews as victims failed to touch the overall psychological processes of the Auschwitz self. Whether a Nazi doctor saw Jews without feeling their presence, or did not see them at all, he no longer experienced them as beings who affected him — that is, as human beings. Much of that transition process occurred within days or even hours, but tended to become an established pattern by two or three weeks.

The numbing of the Auschwitz self was greatly aided by the diffusion of responsibility. With the medical corpsmen closer to the actual killing, the Auschwitz self of the individual doctor could readily feel "It is not I who kill." He was likely to perceive what he did as a combination of military order ("I am assigned to ramp duty"), designated role ("I am expected to select strong prisoners for work and weaker ones for 'special treatment'"), and desirable attitude ("I am supposed to be disciplined and hard and to overcome 'scruples'"). Moreover, since "the Führer decides upon the life and death of any enemy of the state," responsibility lay with him (or his immediate representatives) alone. As in the case of the participant in direct medical killing ("euthanasia"), the Auschwitz self could feel itself no more than a member of a "team," within which reponsibility was so shared, and so offered to higher authorities, as no longer to exist for anyone on that team. And insofar as one felt a residual sense of responsibility, one could reinvoke numbing by means of a spirit of numerical compromise: "We give them ten or fifteen and save five or six."

Numbing could become solidified by this focus on "team play" and "absolute fairness" toward other members of the team. Yet if the "team" did something incriminating, one could stay numbed by asserting one's independence from it. I have in mind one former Nazi doctor's denial of responsibility for the medical experiments done by a team to which he provided materials from his laboratory, even though he showed up on occasion at a concentration camp and looked over experimental charts and subjects. That same doctor also denied reponsibility for the "team" (committee) decision to allocate large amounts of Zyklon-B for use in death camps, though he was prominent in the decision-making process, because, whatever other members of the team knew, he had not been informed that the gas would be used for killing. In this last example in particular, we sense that numbing can be willed and clung to in the face of the kind of continual involvement of the self in experiences that would ordinarily produce lots of feeling. . . .

The language of the Auschwitz self, and of the Nazis in general, was crucial to the numbing. A leading scholar of the Holocaust told of examining "tens of thousands" of Nazi documents without once encountering the word "killing," until, after many years he finally did discover the word — in reference to an edict concerning dogs.

For what was being done to the Jews, there were different words, words that perpetuated the numbing of the Auschwitz self by rendering murder nonmurderous. For the doctors specifically, these words suggested responsible military-medical behavior: "ramp duty" (*Rampendienst*) or sometimes even "medical ramp duty" (*ärztliche Rampendienst*) or "[prisoners] presenting themselves to a doctor" (*Arztvorstellern*). For what was being done to the Jews in general, there was, of course, the "Final Solution of the Jewish question" (*Endlösung der Judenfrage*), "possible solutions" (*Lösungsmöglichkeiten*), "evacuation" (*Aussiedlung* or *Evakuierung*), "transfer" (*Überstellung*), and "resettlement" (*Umsiedlung*, the German word suggesting removal from a danger area). Even when they spoke of a "gassing *Kommando*" (*Vergasungskommando*), it had the ostensible function of disinfection. The word "selection" (*Selektion*) could imply sorting out the healthy from the sick, or even some form of Darwinian scientific function having to do with "natural selection" (*natürliche Auswahl*), certainly nothing to do with killing.

The Nazi doctor did not literally believe these euphemisms. Even a well-developed Auschwitz self was aware that Jews were not being resettled but killed, and that the "Final Solution" meant killing all of them. But at the same time the language used gave Nazi doctors a discourse in which killing was no longer killing; and need not be experienced, or even perceived, as killing. As they lived increasingly within that language — and they used it with each other

— Nazi doctors became imaginatively bound to a psychic realm of derealization, disavowal, and nonfeeling. . . .

Although doubling can be understood as a pervasive process present in some degree in most if not all lives, we have mainly been talking about a destructive version of it: *victimizer's doubling.* The Germans of the Nazi era came to epitomize this process not because they were inherently more evil than other people, but because they succeeded in making use of this form of doubling for tapping the general human moral and psychological potential for mobilizing evil on a vast scale and channeling it into systematic killing.

While victimizer's doubling can occur in virtually any group, perhaps professionals of various kinds — physicians, psychologists, physicists, biologists, clergy, generals, statesmen, writers, artists — have a special capacity for doubling. In them a prior, humane self can be joined by a "professional self" willing to ally itself with a destructive project, with harming or even killing others. . . .

In light of the recent record of professionals engaged in mass killing, can this be the century of doubling? Or, given the ever greater potential for professionalization of genocide, will that distinction belong to the twenty-first century? Or, may one ask a little more softly, can we interrupt the process — first by naming it?

Christopher R. Browning

"Ordinary Men"

In the very early hours of July 13, 1942, the men of Reserve Police Battalion 101 were roused from their bunks in the large brick school building that served as their barracks in the Polish town of Biłgoraj. They were middle-aged family men of working- and lower-middle-class background from the city of Hamburg. Considered too old to be of use to the German army, they had been drafted instead into the Order Police. Most were raw recruits with no previous experience in German occupied territory. They had arrived in Poland less than three weeks earlier.

It was still quite dark as the men climbed into the waiting trucks. Each policeman had been given extra ammunition, and additional boxes had been loaded onto the trucks as well. They were headed for their first major action, though the men had not yet been told what to expect.

The convoy of battalion trucks moved out of Biłgoraj in the dark, heading eastward on a jarring washboard gravel road. The pace was slow, and it took an hour and a half to two hours to arrive at the destination — the village of Józefów — a mere thirty kilometers away. Just as the sky was beginning to lighten, the convoy halted outside Józefów. It was a typical Polish village of modest white houses with thatched straw roofs. Among its inhabitants were 1,800 Jews.

The village was totally quiet. The men of Reserve Police Battalion 101 climbed down from their trucks and assembled in a half-circle around their commander, Major Wilhelm Trapp, a fifty-three-year-old career policeman affectionately known by his men as "Papa Trapp." The time had come for Trapp to address the men and inform them of the assignment the battalion had received.

Pale and nervous, with choking voice and tears in his eyes, Trapp visibly fought to control himself as he spoke. The battalion, he said plaintively, had to perform a frightfully unpleasant task. This assignment was not to his liking, indeed it was highly regrettable, but the orders came from the highest authorities. If it would make their task any easier, the men should remember that in Germany the bombs were falling on women and children.

He then turned to the matter at hand. The Jews had instigated the American Boycott that had damaged Germany, one policeman remembered Trapp saying. There were Jews in the village of Józefów who were involved with the partisans, he explained according to two others. The battalion had now been ordered to round up these Jews. The male Jews of working age were to be separated and taken to a work camp. The remaining Jews — the women, children, and elderly — were to be shot on the spot by the battalion. Having explained what awaited his men, Trapp then made an extraordinary offer: if any of the older men among them did not feel up to the task that lay before him, he could step out. . . . [Some members of the battalion rounded up three hundred able-bodied Jewish men for shipment to a slave labor camp. Other members systematically murdered the remaining Jews.]

When Trapp first made his offer early in the morning, the real nature of the action had just been announced and time to think and react had been very short. Only a dozen men had instinctively seized the moment to step out, turn in their rifles, and thus excuse themselves from the subsequent killing. For many the reality of what they were about to do, and particularly that they themselves might be chosen for the firing squad, had probably not sunk in. But when the men of First Company were summoned to the marketplace, instructed in giving a "neck shot," and sent to the woods to kill Jews, some of them tried to make up for the opportunity they had missed earlier. One policeman approached First Sergeant Kammer, whom he knew well. He confessed that the task was "repugnant" to him and asked for a different assignment. Kammer obliged, assigning him to guard duty on the edge of the forest, where he remained throughout the day. Several other policemen who knew Kammer well were given guard duty along the truck route. After shooting for some time, another group of policemen approached Kammer and said they could not continue. He released them from the firing squad and reassigned them to accompany the trucks. . . .

With the constant coming and going from the trucks, the wild terrain, and the frequent rotation, the men did not remain in fixed groups. The confusion created the opportunity for work slowdown and evasion. Some men who hurried at their task shot far more Jews than others who delayed as much as they could. After two rounds one policeman simply "slipped off" and stayed among the trucks on the edge of the forest. Another managed to avoid taking his turn with the shooters altogether.

> *It was in no way the case that those who did not want to or could not carry out the shooting of human beings with their own hands could not keep themselves out of this task. No strict control was being carried out here. I therefore remained by the arriving trucks and kept myself busy at the arrival point. In any case I gave my activity such an appearance. It could not be avoided that one or another of my comrades noticed that I was not going to the executions to fire away at the*

victims. They showered me with remarks such as "shithead" and "weakling" to express their disgust. But I suffered no consequences for my actions. I must mention here that I was not the only one who kept himself out of participating in the executions. . . .

For his first victim August Zorn was given a very old man. Zorn recalled that his elderly victim

> *could not or would not keep up with his countrymen, because he repeatedly fell and then simply lay there. I regularly had to lift him up and drag him forward. Thus, I had only reached the execution site when my comrades had already shot their Jews. At the sight of his countrymen who had been shot, my Jew threw himself on the ground and remained lying there. I then cocked my carbine and shot him through the back of the head. Because I was already very upset from the cruel treatment of the Jews during the clearing of the town and was completely in turmoil, I shot too high. The entire back of the skull of my Jew was torn off and the brain exposed. Parts of the skull flew into Sergeant Steinmetz's face. This was grounds for me, after returning to the truck, to go to the first sergeant and ask for my release. I had become so sick that I simply couldn't anymore. I was then relieved by the first sergeant. . . .*

When the men arrived at the barracks in Biłgoraj, they were depressed, angered, embittered, and shaken. They ate little but drank heavily. Generous quantities of alcohol were provided, and many of the policemen got quite drunk. Major Trapp made the rounds, trying to console and reassure them, and again placing the responsibility on higher authorities. But neither the drink nor Trapp's consolation could wash away the sense of shame and horror that pervaded the barracks. Trapp asked the men not to talk about it, but they needed no encouragement in that direction. Those who had not been there likewise had no desire to speak, either then or later. By silent consensus within Reserve Police Battalion 101, the Józefów massacre was simply not discussed. "The entire matter was a taboo." But repression during waking hours could not stop the nightmares. During the first night back from Józefów, one policeman awoke firing his gun into the ceiling of the barracks. . . .

The resentment and bitterness in the battalion over what they had been asked to do in Józefów was shared by virtually everyone, even those who had shot the entire day. The exclamation of one policeman to First Sergeant Kammer of First Company that "I'd go crazy if I had to do that again" expressed the sentiments of many. But only a few went beyond complaining to extricate themselves from such a possibility. Several of the older men with very large families took advantage of a regulation that required them to sign a release agreeing to duty in a combat area. One who had not yet signed refused to do so; another rescinded his signature. Both were eventually transferred back to Germany. The most dramatic response was again that of Lieutenant Buchmann, who asked Trapp to have him transferred back to Hamburg and declared that short of a direct personal order from Trapp, he would not take part in Jewish actions. In the end he wrote to Hamburg, explicitly requesting a recall because he was not "suited" to certain tasks "alien to the police" that were being carried out by his unit in Poland. Buchmann had to wait until November, but his efforts to be transferred were ultimately successful. . . .

In subsequent actions two vital changes were introduced and henceforth — with some notable exceptions — adhered to. First, most of the future operations of Reserve Police Battalion 101 involved ghetto clearing and deportation, not outright massacre on the spot. The policemen were thus relieved of the immediate horror of the killing process, which (for deportees from the nothern Lublin district) was carried out in the extermination camp at Treblinka. Second, while deportation was a horrifying procedure characterized by the terrible coercive violence needed to drive people onto the death trains as well as the systematic killing of those who could not be marched to the trains, these actions were generally undertaken jointly by units of Reserve Police Battalion 101 and the Trawnikis, SS-trained auxiliaries from Soviet territories, recruited from the POW camps and usually assigned the very worst parts of the ghetto clearing and deportation. . . .

When the time came to kill again, the policemen did not "go crazy." Instead they became increasingly efficient and calloused executioners. . . .

With a conservative estimate of 6,500 Jews shot during earlier actions like those at Józefów and Lomazy and 1,000 shot during the "Jew hunts," and a minimum estimate of 30,500 Jews shot at Majdanek and Poniatowa, the battalion had participated in the direct shooting deaths of at least 38,000 Jews. With the death camp depor- tation of at least 3,000 Jews from Międzyrzec in early May 1943, the number of Jews they had placed on trains to Treblinka had risen to 45,000. For a battalion of less than 500 men, the ultimate body count was at least 83,000 Jews. . . .

Why did most men in Reserve Police Battalion 101 become killers, while only a minority of perhaps 10 percent — and certainly no more than 20 percent — did not? A number of explanations have been invoked in the past to explain such behavior: wartime brutaliza- tion, racism, segmentation and routinization of the task, special selection of the perpetrators, careerism, obedience to orders, defer- ence to authority, ideological indoctrination, and conformity. These factors are applicable in varying degrees, but none without qualifica- tion. . . .

War, and especially race war, leads to brutalization, which leads to atrocity. . . . Except for a few of the oldest men who were veterans of World War I, and a few NCOs who had been transferred to Poland from Russia, the men of the battalion had not seen battle or encountered a deadly enemy. Most of them had not fired a shot in anger or ever been fired on, much less lost comrades fighting at their side. Thus, wartime brutalization through prior combat was not an immediate experience directly influencing the policemen's behavior at Józefów. Once the killing began, however, the men became increasingly brutalized. As in combat, the horrors of the initial encounter eventually became routine, and the killing became pro- gressively easier. In this sense, brutalization was not the cause but the effect of these men's behavior. . . .

To what degree, if any, did the men of Reserve Police Battalion 101 represent a process of special selection for the particular task of implementing the Final Solution? . . . By age, geographical origin, and social background, the men of Reserve Police Battalion 101 were least likely to be considered apt material out of which to mold future mass killers. On the basis of these criteria, the rank and file — mid- dle-aged, mostly working-class, from Hamburg — did not represent special selection or even random selection but for all practical pur- poses negative selection for the task at hand. . . . Reserve Police Bat- talion 101 was not sent to Lublin to murder Jews because it was composed of men specially selected or deemed particularly suited for the task. On the contrary, the battalion was the "dregs" of the manpower pool available at that stage of the war. It was employed to kill Jews because it was the only kind of unit available for such behind-the-lines duties. Most likely, Globocnik simply assumed as a matter of course that whatever battalion came his way would be up to this murderous task, regardless of its composition. If so, he may have been disappointed in the immediate aftermath of Józefów, but in the long run events proved him correct. . . .

Those who emphasize the relative or absolute importance of situational factors over individual psychological characteristics invariably point to Philip Zimbardo's Stanford prison experiment. Screening out everyone who scored beyond the normal range on a battery of psychological tests, including one that measured "rigid adherence to conventional values and a submissive, uncritical attitude toward authority" (i.e., the F-scale for the "authoritarian personality"), Zimbardo randomly divided his homogeneous "normal" test group into guards and prisoners and placed them in a simulated prison. Though outright physical violence was barred, within six days the inherent structure of prison life — in which guards operating on three-man shifts had to devise ways of controlling the more numerous prisoner population — had produced rapidly escalating brutality, humiliation, and dehumanization. "Most dramatic and distressing to us was the observation of the ease with which sadistic behavior could be elicited in individuals who were not 'sadistic types'." The prison situation alone, Zimbardo concluded, was "a *sufficient* condition to produce aberrant, anti-social behavior."

Perhaps most relevant to this study of Reserve Police Battlion 101 is the spectrum of behavior that Zimbardo discovered in his sample of eleven guards. About one-third emerged as "cruel and tough." They constantly invented new forms of harassment and enjoyed their newfound power to behave cruelly and arbitrarily. A middle group of guards was "tough but fair." They "played by the rules" and did not go out of their way to mistreat prisoners. Only two (i.e., less than 20 percent) emerged as "good guards" who did not punish prisoners and even did small favors for them.

Zimbardo's spectrum of guard behavior bears an uncanny resemblance to the groupings that emerged within Reserve Police Battalion

101: a nucleus of increasingly enthusiastic killers who volunteered for the firing squads and "Jew Hunts"; a larger group of policemen who performed as shooters and ghetto clearers when assigned but who did not seek opportunities to kill (and in some cases refrained from killing, contrary to standing orders, when no one was monitoring their actions); and a small group (less than 20 percent) of refusers and evaders. . . .

If obedience to orders out of fear of dire punishment is not a valid explanation, what about "obedience to authority" in the more general sense used by Stanley Milgram — deference simply as a product of socialization and evolution, a "deeply ingrained behavior tendency" to comply with the directives of those positioned hierarchically above, even to the point of performing repugnant actions in violation of "universally accepted" moral norms. In a series of now famous experiments, Milgram tested the individual's ability to resist authority that was not backed by any external coercive threat. Naive volunteer subjects were instructed by a "scientific authority" in an alleged learning experiment to inflict an escalating series of fake electric shocks upon an actor/victim, who responded with carefully programmed "voice feedback" — an escalating series of complaints, cries of pain, calls for help, and finally fateful silence. In the standard voice feedback experiment, two-thirds of Milgram's subjects were "obedient" to the point of inflicting extreme pain.

Several variations on the experiment produced significantly different results. If the actor/victim was shielded so that the subject could hear and see no response, obedience was much greater. If the subject had both visual and voice feedback, compliance to the extreme fell to 40 percent. If the subject had to touch the actor/victim physically by forcing his hand onto an electric plate to deliver the shocks, obedience dropped to 30 percent. If a nonauthority figure gave orders, obedience was nil. If the naive subject performed a subsidiary or accessory task but did not personally inflict the electric shocks, obedience was nearly total. In contrast, if the subject was part of an actor/peer group that staged a carefully planned refusal to continue following the directions of the authority figure, the vast majority of subjects (90 percent) joined their peer group and desisted as well. If the subject was given complete discretion as to the level of electric shock to administer, all but a few sadists consistently delivered a minimal shock. When not under the direct surveillance of the scientist, many of the subjects "cheated" by giving lower shocks than prescribed, even though they were unable to confront authority and abandon the experiment.

Milgram adduced a number of factors to account for such an unexpectedly high degree of potentially murderous obedience to a noncoercive authority. An evolutionary bias favors the survival of people who can adapt to hierarchical situations and organized social activity. Socialization through family, school, and military service, as well as a whole array of rewards and punishments within society generally, reinforces and internalizes a tendency toward obedience. A seemingly voluntary entry into an authority system "perceived" as legitimate creates a strong sense of obligation. Those within the hierarchy adopt the authority's perspective or "definition of the situation" (in this case, as an important scientific experiment rather than the infliction of physical torture). The notions of "loyalty, duty, discipline," requiring competent performance in the eyes of authority, become moral imperatives overriding any identification with the victim. Normal individuals enter an "agentic state" in which they are the instrument of another's will. In such a state, they no longer feel personally reponsible for the content of their actions but only for how well they perform.

Once entangled, people encounter a series of "binding factors" or "cementing mechanisms" that make disobedience or refusal even more difficult. The momentum of the process discourages any new or contrary initiative. The "situational obligation" or etiquette makes refusal appear improper, rude, or even an immoral breach of obligation. And a socialized anxiety over potential punishment for disobedience acts as a further deterrent.

Milgram made direct reference to the similarities between human behavior in his experiments and under the Nazi regime. He concluded, "Men are led to kill with little difficulty." Milgram was aware of significant differences in the two situations, however. Quite explicitly he acknowledged that the subjects of his experiments were assured that no permanent physical damage would result from their actions. The subjects were under no threat or duress themselves. And finally, the actor/victims were not the object of "intense devaluation" through systematic indoctrination of the subjects. In contrast, the killers of the Third Reich lived in a police state where the consequences of disobedience could be drastic and they were subjected to intense indoctrination, but they also knew they were not only inflicting pain but destroying human life.

Was the massacre at Józefów a kind of radical Milgram experiment that took place in a Polish forest with real killers and victims rather than in a social psychology laboratory with naive subjects and actor/victims? Are the actions of Reserve Police Battalion 101 explained by Milgram's observations and conclusions? There are some difficulties in explaining Józefów as a case of deference to authority, for none of Milgram's experimental variations exactly paralleled the historical situation at Józefów, and the relevant differences constitute too many variables to draw firm conclusions in any scientific sense. Nonetheless, many of Milgram's insights find graphic confirmation in the behavior and testimony of the men of Reserve Police Battalion 101.

At Józefów the authority system to which the men were responding was quite complex, unlike the laboratory situation. Major Trapp represented not a strong but a very weak authority figure. He weepingly conceded the frightful nature of the task at hand and invited the older reserve policemen to excuse themselves. If Trapp was a weak immediate authority figure, he did invoke a more distant system of authority that was anything but weak. The orders for the massacre had been received from the highest quarter, he said. Trapp himself and the battalion as a unit were bound by the orders of this distant authority, even if Trapp's concern for his men exempted individual policemen.

To what were the vast majority of Trapp's men responding when they did not step out? Was it to authority as represented either by Trapp or his superiors? Were they responding to Trapp not primarily as an authority figure, but as an individual — a popular and beloved officer whom they would not leave in the lurch? And what about other factors? Milgram himself notes that people far more frequently invoke authority than conformity to explain their behavior, for only the former seems to absolve them of personal responsibility. "Subjects deny conformity and *embrace* obedience as the explanation of their actions." Yet many policemen admitted responding to the pressures of conformity — how would they be seen in the eyes of their comrades? — not authority. On Milgram's own view, such admission was the tip of the iceberg, and this factor must have been even more important than the men conceded in their testimony. If so, conformity assumes a more central role than authority at Józefów.

Milgram tested the effects of peer pressure in bolstering the individual's capacity to resist authority. When actor/collaborators bolted, the naive subjects found it much easier to follow. Milgram also attempted to test for the reverse, that is, the role of conformity in intensifying the capacity to inflict pain. Three subjects, two collaborators and one naive, were instructed by the scientist/authority figure to inflict pain at the lowest level anyone among them proposed. When a naive subject acting alone had been given full discretion to set the level of electric shock, the subject had almost invariably inflicted minimal pain. But when the two collaborators, always going first, proposed a step-by-step escalation of electric shock, the naive subject was significantly influenced. Though the individual variation was wide, the average result was the selection of a level of electric shock halfway between no increase and a consistent step-by-step increase. This is still short of a test of peer pressure as compensation for the deficiencies of weak authority. There was no weeping but beloved scientist inviting subjects to leave the electric shock panel while other men — with whom the subjects had comradely relations and before whom they would feel compelled to appear manly and tough — stayed and continued to inflict painful shocks. Indeed, it would be almost impossible to construct an experiment to test such a scenario, which would require true comradely relations between a naive subject and the actor/collaborators. Nonetheless, the mutual reinforcement of authority and conformity seems to have been clearly demonstrated by Milgram.

If the multifaceted nature of authority at Józefów and the key role of conformity among the policemen are not quite parallel to Milgram's experiments, they nonetheless render considerable support to his conclusions, and some of his observations are clearly confirmed. Direct proximity to the horror of the killing significantly increased the number of men who would no longer comply. On the other hand, with the division of labor and removal of the killing process to the death camps, the men felt scarcely any responsibility at all for their actions. As in Milgram's experiment without direct surveillance, many policemen did not comply with orders when not directly supervised; they mitigated their behavior when they could do so without

personal risk but were unable to refuse participation in the battalion's killing operations openly.

One factor that admittedly was not the focal point of Milgram's
experiments, indoctrination, and another that was only partially
touched upon, conformity, require further investigation. Milgram
did stipulate "definition of the situation" or ideology, that which
gives meaning and coherence to the social occasion, as a crucial
antecedent of deference to authority. Controlling the manner in
which people interpret their world is one way to control behavior,
Milgram argues. If they accept authority's ideology, action follows
logically and willingly. Hence "ideological justification is vital in
obtaining willing obedience, for it permits the person to see his
behavior as serving a desirable end."

In Milgram's experiments, "overarching ideological justification" was present in the form of a tacit and unquestioned faith in
the goodness of science and its contribution to progress. But there
was no systematic attempt to "devalue" the actor/victim or inculcate
the subject with a particular ideology. Milgram hypothesized that
the more destructive behavior of people in Nazi Germany, under
much less direct surveillance, was a consequence of an internaliza-
tion of authority achieved "through relatively long processes of
indoctrination, of a sort not possible within the course of a laboratory hour."

To what degree, then, did the conscious inculcation of Nazi
doctrines shape the behavior of the men of Reserve Police Battalion
101? Were they subjected to such a barrage of clever and insidious
propaganda that they lost the capacity for independent thought and
responsible action? Were devaluation of the Jews and exhortations
to kill them central to this indoctrination? . . .

[T]he men of Reserve Police Battalion 101, like the rest of German society, were immersed in a deluge of racist and anti-Semitic
propoganda. Furthermore, the Order Police provided for indoctrination both in basic training and as an ongoing practice within each
unit. Such incessant propagandizing must have had considerable
effect in reinforcing general notions of Germanic racial superiority
and "a certain aversion" toward the Jews. However, much of the
indoctrination material was clearly not targeted at older reservists
and in some cases was highly inappropriate or irrelevant to them.

And material specifically designed to harden the policemen for the personal task of killing Jews is conspicuously absent from the surviving documentation. One would have to be quite convinced of the manipulative powers of indoctrination to believe that any of this material could have deprived the men of Reserve Police Battalion 101 of the capacity for independent thought. Influenced and conditioned in a general way, imbued in particular with a sense of their own superiority and racial kinship as well as Jewish inferiority and otherness, many of them undoubtedly were; explicitly prepared for the task of killing Jews they most certainly were not.

Along with ideological indoctrination, a vital factor touched upon but not fully explored in Milgram's experiments was conformity to the group. The battalion had orders to kill Jews, but each individual did not. Yet 80 to 90 percent of the men proceeded to kill, though almost all of them — at least initially — were horrified and disgusted by what they were doing. To break ranks and step out, to adopt overtly nonconformist behavior, was simply beyond most of the men. It was easier for them to shoot.

Why? First of all, by breaking ranks, nonshooters were leaving the "dirty work" to their comrades. Since the battalion had to shoot even if individuals did not, refusing to shoot constituted refusing one's share of an unpleasant collective obligation. It was in effect an asocial act vis-à-vis one's comrades. Those who did not shoot risked isolation, rejection, and ostracism — a very uncomfortable prospect within the framework of a tight-knit unit stationed abroad among a hostile population, so that the individual had virtually nowhere else to turn for support and social contact.

This threat of isolation was intensified by the fact that stepping out could also have been seen as a form of moral reproach of one's comrades: the nonshooter was potentially indicating that he was "too good" to do such things. Most, though not all, nonshooters intuitively tried to diffuse the criticism of their comrades that was inherent in their actions. They pleaded not that they were "too good" but rather that they were "too weak" to kill.

Such a stance presented no challenge to the esteem of one's comrades; on the contrary, it legitimized and upheld "toughness" as a superior quality. For the anxious individual, it had the added advantage of posing no moral challenge to the murderous policies of the regime, though it did pose another problem, since the difference between being "weak" and being a "coward" was not great. Hence the distinction made by one policeman who did not dare to step out at Józefów for fear of being considered a coward, but who subsequently dropped out of his firing squad. It was one thing to be too cowardly even to try to kill; it was another, after resolutely trying to do one's share, to be too weak to continue.

Insidiously, therefore, most of those who did not shoot only reaffirmed the "macho" values of the majority — according to which it was a positive quality to be "tough" enough to kill unarmed, noncombatant men, women, and children — and tried not to rupture the bonds of comradeship that constituted their social world. Coping with the contradictions imposed by the demands of conscience on the one hand and the norms of the battalion on the other led to many tortured attempts at compromise: not shooting infants on the spot but taking them to the assembly point; not shooting on patrol if no "go-getter" was along who might report such squeamishness; bringing Jews to the shooting site and firing but intentionally missing. Only the very exceptional remained indifferent to taunts of "weakling" from their comrades and could live with the fact that they were considered to be "no man."

Here we come full circle to the mutually intensifying effects of war and racism noted by John Dower, in conjunction with the insidious effects of constant propaganda and indoctrination. Pervasive racism and the resulting exclusion of the Jewish victims from any common ground with the perpetrators made it all the easier for the majority of the policemen to conform to the norms of their immediate community (the battalion) and their society at large (Nazi Germany). Here the years of anti-Semitic propaganda (and prior to the Nazi dictatorship, decades of shrill German nationalism) dovetailed with the polarizing effects of war. The dichotomy of racially superior Germans and racially inferior Jews, central to Nazi ideology, could easily merge with the image of a beleaguered Germany surrounded by warring enemies. If it is doubtful that most of the policemen understood or embraced the theoretical aspects of Nazi ideology as contained in SS indoctrination pamphlets, it is also doubtful that they were immune to "the influence of the times" (to use Lieutenant Drucker's phrase once again), to the incessant proclamation of German superiority and incitement of comtempt and hatred for the Jewish enemy. Nothing helped the Nazis to wage a race war so much as the war itself. In wartime, when it was all too usual to exclude the enemy from the community of human obligation, it was also all too easy to subsume the Jews into the "image of the enemy," or *Feindbild.*

In his last book, *The Drowned and the Saved,* Primo Levi included an essay entitled "The Gray Zone," perhaps his most profound and deeply disturbing reflection on the Holocaust. He maintained that in spite of our natural desire for clear-cut distinctions, the history of the camps "could not be reduced to the two blocs of victims and persecutors." He argued passionately, "It is naive, absurd, and historically false to believe that an infernal system such as National Socialism sanctifies its victims; on the contrary, it degrades them, it makes them resemble itself." The time had come to examine the inhabitants of the "gray zone" between the simplified Manichean images of perpetrator and victim. Levi concentrated on the "gray zone of *protekcya* [corruption] and collaboration" that flourished in the camps among a spectrum of victims: from the "picturesque fauna" of low-ranking functionaries husbanding their miniscule advantages over other prisoners; through the truly privileged network of Kapos, who were free "to commit the worst atrocities" at whim; to the terrible fate of the Sonderkommandos, who prolonged their lives by manning the gas chambers and crematoria. (Conceiving and organizing the Sonderkommandos was in Levi's opinion National Socialism's "most demonic crime.")

While Levi focused on the spectrum of victim behavior within the gray zone, he dared to suggest that this zone encompassed perpetrators as well. Even the SS man Muhsfeld of the Birkenau crematoria — whose "daily ration of slaughter was studded with arbitrary and capricious acts, marked by his inventions of cruelty" — was not a "monolith." Faced with the miraculous survival of a sixteen-year-old girl discovered while the gas chambers were being cleared, the disconcerted Muhsfeld briefly hesitated. In the end he ordered the girl's death but quickly left before his orders were carried out. One "instant of pity" was not enough to "absolve" Muhsfeld, who was deservedly hanged in 1947. Yet it did "place him too, although at its extreme boundary, within the gray band, that zone of ambiguity which radiates out from regimes based on terror and obsequiousness."

Levi's notion of the gray zone encompassing both perpetrators and victims must be approached with a cautious qualification. The perpetrators and victims in the gray zone were not mirror images of one another. Perpetrators did not become fellow victims (as many of them later claimed to be) in the way some victims became accomplices of the perpetrators. The relationship between perpetrator and victim was not symmetrical. The range of choice each faced was totally different.

Nonetheless, the spectrum of Levi's gray zone seems quite applicable to Reserve Police Battalion 101. The battalion certainly had its quota of men who neared the "extreme boundary" of the gray zone. Lieutenant Gnade, who initially rushed his men back from Minsk to avoid being involved in killing but who later learned to enjoy it, leaps to mind. So do the many reserve policemen who were horrified in the woods outside Józefów but subsequently became casual volunteers for numerous firing squads and "Jew hunts." They, like Muhsfeld, seem to have experienced the brief "instant of pity" but cannot be absolved by it. At the other boundary of the gray zone, even Lieutenant Buchmann, the most conspicuous and outspoken critic of the battalion's murderous actions, faltered at least once. Absent his protector, Major Trapp, and facing orders from the local Security Police in Łuków, he too led his men to the killing fields shortly before his transfer back to Hamburg. And at the very center of the perpetrators' gray zone stood the pathetic figure of Trapp himself, who sent his men to slaughter Jews "weeping like a child," and the bedridden Captain Hoffmann, whose body rebelled against the terrible deeds his mind willed.

The behavior of any human being is, of course, a very complex phenomenon, and the historian who attempts to "explain" it is indulging in a certain arrogance. When nearly 500 men are involved, to undertake any general explanation of their collective behavior is even more hazardous. What, then, is one to conclude? Most of all, one comes away from the story of Reserve Police Battalion 101 with great unease. This story of ordinary men is not the story of all men. The reserve policemen faced choices, and most of them committed terrible deeds. But those who killed cannot be absolved by the notion that anyone in the same situation would have done as they did. For even among them, some refused to kill and others stopped killing. Human responsibility is ultimately an individual matter.

At the same time, however, the collective behavior of Reserve

Police Battalion 101 has deeply disturbing implications. There are many societies afflicted by traditions of racism and caught in the siege mentality of war or threat of war. Everywhere society conditions people to respect and defer to authority, and indeed could scarcely function otherwise. Everywhere people seek career advancement. In every modern society, the complexity of life and the resulting bureaucratization and specialization attenuate the sense of personal responsibility of those implementing official policy. Within virtually every social collective, the peer group exerts tremendous pressures on behavior and sets moral norms. If the men of Reserve Police Battalion 101 could become killers under such circumstances, what group of men cannot?

Daniel Jonah Goldhagen

Hitler's Willing Executioners

Germans' anti-Semitic beliefs about Jews were the central causal agent of the Holocaust. They were the central causal agent not only of Hitler's decision to annihilate European Jewry (which is accepted by many) but also of the perpetrators' willingness to kill and to brutalize Jews. The conclusion of this book is that antisemitism moved many thousands of "ordinary" Germans — and would have moved millions more, had they been appropriately positioned — to slaughter Jews. Not economic hardship, not the coercive means of a totalitarian state, not social psychological pressure, not invariable psychological propensities, but ideas about Jews that were pervasive in Germany, and had been for decades, induced ordinary Germans to kill unarmed, defenseless Jewish men, women, and children by the thousands, systematically and without pity.

The conventional explanations *assume* a neutral or condemnatory attitude on the part of the perpetrators towards their actions.

They therefore premise their interpretations on the assumption that it must be shown how people can be brought to commit acts to which they would not inwardly assent, acts which they would not agree are necessary or just. They either ignore, deny, or radically minimize the importance of Nazi and perhaps the perpetrators' ideology, moral values, and conception of the victims, for engendering the perpetrators' willingness to kill. Some of these conventional explanations also caricature the perpetrators, and Germans in general. The explanations treat them as if they had been people lacking a moral sense, lacking the ability to make decisions and take stances. They do not conceive of the actors as human agents, as people with wills, but as beings moved solely by external forces or by transhistorical and invariant psychological propensities, such as the slavish following of narrow "self-interest." The conventional explanations suffer from two other major conceptual failings. They do not sufficiently recognize the extraordinary nature of the deed: the mass killing of people. They *assume* and imply that inducing people to kill human beings is fundamentally no different from getting them to do any other unwanted or distasteful task. Also, none of the conventional explanations deems the *identity* of the victims to have mattered. The conventional explanations imply that the perpetrators would have treated any other group of intended victims in exactly the same way. That the victims were Jews — according to the logic of these explanations — is irrelevant.

I maintain that any explanation that fails to acknowledge the actors' capacity to know and to judge, namely to understand and to have views about the significance and the morality of their actions, that fails to hold the actors' beliefs and values as central, that fails to emphasize the autonomous motivating force of Nazi ideology, particularly its central component of antisemitism, cannot possibly succeed in telling us much about why the perpetrators acted as they did. Any explanation that ignores either the particular nature of the perpetrators' actions — the systematic, large-scale killing and brutalizing of people — or the identity of the victims is inadequate for a host of reasons. All explanations that adopt these positions, as do the conventional explanations, suffer a mirrored, double failure of recognition of the human aspect of the Holocaust: the humanity of the perpetrators, namely their capacity to judge and to choose to act inhumanely, and the humanity of the victims, that what the perpetrators did, they did to these people with their specific identities, and not to animals or things.

My explanation — which is new to the scholarly literature on the perpetrators — is that the perpetrators, "ordinary Germans," were animated by antisemitism, by a particular *type* of antisemitism that led them to conclude that the Jews *ought to die*. The perpetrators' beliefs, their particular brand of antisemitism, though obviously not the sole source, was, I maintain, a most significant and indispensable source of the perpetrators' actions and must be at the center of any explanation of them. Simply put, the perpetrators, having consulted their own convictions and morality and having judged the mass annihilation of Jews to be right, did not *want* to say "no." . . .

One of the first slaughters of the genocidal campaign unleashed against Soviet Jewry was perpetrated by . . . Police Battalion 309. A few days after Operation Barbarossa began, the Germans of Police Battalion 309 ignited a portentous, symbolic fiery inferno in the city of Białystok.

The officers and the men of at least one company of Police Battalion 309 knew from the moment of their entry into territory taken from the Soviet Union that they were to play a role in the planned destruction of Jewry. After entering Białystok on the twenty-seventh of June, a city which the Germans had captured, like many others, without a fight, the battalion commander, Major Ernst Weis, ordered his men to round up male Jews by combing through Jewish residential areas. Although the purpose of congregating the Jews was to kill them, instructions about the manner in which the Germans would extinguish their lives were not given at that time. The entire battalion participated in the ensuing roundup, which itself proceeded with great brutality and wanton murderousness. These Germans could finally unleash themselves without restraint upon the Jews. One Jew recalls that "the unit had barely driven into the city when the soldiers swarmed out and, without any sensible cause, shot up the entire city, apparently also in order to frighten the people. The incessant shooting was utterly horrible. They shot blindly, in fact, into houses and windows, without regard for whether they hit anyone. The shooting (*Schiesserei*) lasted the entire day." The Germans of this battalion broke into people's homes who had not lifted a finger in hostility, dragged them out, kicked them, beat them with their rifle butts, and shot them. The streets were strewn with corpses. These individually, autonomously initiated brutalities and killings were by any standard of utility, unnecessary. Why did they occur? The Germans themselves, in their postwar testimony, are mute on this point. Yet some episodes are suggestive. During the roundup, one nameless Jew opened his door a crack in order to assess the unfolding, perilous scene. A lieutenant in the battalion, having noticed the slit, seized the opportunity and shot him through the small opening. In order to fulfill his orders, the German only had to bring the Jew to the assembly point. Yet he chose to shoot him. It is hard to imagine that this German felt moral qualms when the target fell to his splendid shot.

Another scene saw some of the Germans in this battalion compel old Jewish men to dance before them. In addition to the amusement that they evidently derived from their choreography, the Germans were mocking, denigrating and asserting their mastery over these Jews, particularly since the selected Jews were their elders, people of an age to whom normally regard and respect are due. Apparently, and to their great misfortune, the Jews failed to dance to a sufficiently brisk and pleasing tempo, so the Germans set the Jews' beards on fire.

Elsewhere, near the Jewish district, two desperate Jews fell to their knees begging a German general for protection. One member of Police Battalion 309, who observed these entreaties, decided to intervene with what he must have thought to be a fitting commentary: He unzipped his pants and urinated upon them. The antisemitic atmosphere and practice among the Germans was such that this man brazenly exposed himself in front of a general in order to perform a rare public act of virtually unsurpassable disdain. Indeed, the man had nothing to fear for his breach of military discipline and decorum. Neither the general nor anyone else sought to stop him. . . .

The men were bringing more Jews to the assembly points in the marketplace and the area in front of the city's main synagogue faster than they could kill them. The number of Jews was swelling. So another "solution" was improvised on the spot. . . .

The men of Police Batallion 309's First and Third Companies drove their victims into the synagogue, the less compliant Jews receiving from the Germans liberal blows of encouragement. The

Germans packed the large synagogue full. The fearful Jews began to chant and pray loudly. After spreading gasoline around the building, the Germans set it ablaze; one of the men tossed an explosive through a window, to ignite the holocaust. The Jews' prayers turned into screams. A battalion member later described the scene that he witnessed: " I saw . . . smoke, that came out of the synagogue and heard there how the incarcerated people cried louldly for help. I was about 70 meters' distance from the synagogue. I could see the building and observed that people tried to escape through windows. One shot at them. Circling the synagogue stood the police members who were apparently supposed to cordon it off, in order to ensure that no one emerged." Between 100 and 150 men of the battalion surrounded the burning synagogue. They collectively ensured that none of the appointed Jews escaped the inferno. They watched as over seven hundred people died this hideous and painful death, listening to the screams of agony. Most of the victims were men, though some women and children were among them. Not surprisingly, some of the Jews within spared themselves the fiery death by hanging themselves or severing their arteries. At least six Jews came running out of the synagogue, their clothes and bodies aflame. The Germans shot each one down, only to watch these human torches burn themselves out.

With what emotions did the men of Police Battalion 309 gaze upon this sacrificial pyre to the exterminationist creed? One exclaimed: "Let it burn, it's a nice little fire [*schönes Feuerlein*], it's great fun." Another exulted: "Splendid, the entire city should burn down."

The men of this police battalion, many of whom were not even professional policemen having opted for service with the police as a means of avoiding army service when they were called up to duty, became instantaneous *Weltanschauungskieger*, or ideological warriors, killing that day between 2,000 and 2,200 Jewish men, women, and children. The manner in which they rounded up Jews, the wanton beatings and killings, the turning of the streets of Bialystok into corpse- and blood-bestrewn pathways, and their own improvised solution of a cleansing conflagration, are indeed acts of *Weltanschauungskrieger* — more specifically, of antisemitic warriors. They carried out an order, embellished upon it, acted not with disgust and hesitation but with apparent relish and excess. . . .

[Later Goldhagen turned to the record of Police Battalion 101.]

These Germans expended no effort to spare the victims any unnecessary suffering. Moreover, the evidence does not suggest that they gave any thought to the matter. The entire course of the destruction of a Jewish community — from the brutality of the roundups, to the suffering inflicted upon the Jews at the assembly points (by forcing them to sit, crouch, or lie motionless for hours on end in the midsummer heat without water), to the manner of execution in Lomazy, for example — bespeaks a tolerance, if not a willful administration of suffering upon the victims. The roundups did not have to be such licentious affairs. The Germans did not have to instill terror in the victims and leave scores, sometimes hundreds of dead in the streets. When the Jews were waiting for the Germans to march them to the city's outskirts or to load them onto freight cars, it would have been easy for the Germans to distribute some water to them, and to let them move around a bit, rather than to shoot any who stood up. As a number of the battalion members have testified, it was evident to the Germans that the Jews suffered greatly and needlessly as they waited. Finally, the cruelty of the Germans' manner of shooting Jews or of using clubs and whips to drive them from their houses or into the freight cars speaks for itself. Because such brutality and cruelty became integral to the practice of ghetto clearings and annihilations, and also because the goal itself of mass extermination is so horrific and tends to overwhelm the consideration of "lesser" crimes, when compiling the ledger of German brutality and cruelty — in the endeavor to assess the actions and attitudes of the killers — it is easy to overlook these practices, as cruel as they were. Why did they not have "orderly" killing operations, without the public killing of children, the beatings, without the symbolic degradation?

In addition to the willfully and unnecessarily brutal manner in which the Germans and their helpers conducted the various stages of a ghetto annihilation — namely the routinized roundup and execution procedures — they also gratuitously brutalized and tortured the Jews. Sometimes the agents inflicting suffering on the Jews were the Germans' eastern European Hiwis,[1] such as during one of the

---

[1]"Hiwis," short for "Hilfswillige," refers to East European volunteers who assisted the Germans with various tasks, including actions against the Jews. — Ed.

Międzyrzec deportations, when the Hiwis, obviously influenced by the Germans' own brutality, lashed Jews with whips. Any brutality that the Hiwis publicly perpetrated upon the Jews was permitted, if not promoted, by the Germans, who had absolute control over them, and such brutality should be taken into account when evaluating the Germans' treatment of the Jews. The scene at the marketplace during the last large deportation from Międzyrzec is such an instance. The Germans forced the Jews to sit or squat huddled together. . . .

The Jews were praying and crying, and therefore making much noise. This disturbed their German masters: "Intermittently, Hiwis beat the people with their rifle-butts, in order to enforce silence. The SD men had knotted whips, similar to horse whips. They walked along the rows of the squatting people, sometimes beating them vehemently." The men of Police Battalion 101 themselves were not to be outdone by their eastern European minions. Although they also degraded and tortured Jews at Międzyrzec in the most gratuitous, willful manner, their deeds are entirely absent from their testimony. The accounts of survivors tell a different, more accurate, and revealing story. Survivors are adamant that the Germans were indeed incredibly brutal, that their cruelty that day was wanton, at times turning into sadistic sport. At the marketplace, the Jews, who had been forced to squat for hours, were "mocked" (*khoyzek gemacht*) and "kicked," and some of the Germans organized "a game" (*shpil*) of "tossing apples and whoever was struck by the apple was then killed." This sport was continued at the railway station, this time with empty liquor bottles. "Bottles were tossed over Jewish heads and whoever was struck by a bottle was dragged out of the crowd and beaten murderously amid roaring laughter. Then some of those who were thus mangled [*tseharget*] were shot." Afterwards, they loaded the dead together with the living onto freight cars bound for Treblinka. . . .

Small wonder that to the eyes of the victims — but not in the self-serving testimony of the perpetrators — these ordinary Germans appeared not as mere murderers, certainly not as reluctant killers dragged to their task against their inner opposition to the genocide, but as "two-legged beasts" filled with "bloodthirstiness."

The Germans report but rarely on their torturing of victims, on every unnecessary rifle-butt blow to a Jewish head, yet the evidence suggests that the tortures which they inflicted in Międzyrzec and

Lomazy (where they beat the bearded Jewish men whom they compelled to crawl to their execution) were not rare exceptions. Although the men of Police Battalion 101 do not tell of their cruelties in the mass deportation of Jews that they conducted from Luków, one of the *Gendarmerie* stationed in Luków recounts what he saw as he gazed out of his office window: "[The Jews] were driven on by the German policemen [*Polizeibeamter*]. It was for me a shattering sight. People who could not rise to their feet by themselves were pulled up by the policemen. The beating was constant and the driving [of the Jews] was accompanied by yelling." . . .

Members of Police Battalion 101 mocked these Jews in Luków before dispatching them and seven thousand others to the gas chambers of Treblinka. They forced them to wear prayer shawls, to kneel as if in prayer, and, perhaps, to chant prayers. The sight of Jewish religious objects and rituals evoked in the German "solvers of the Jewish Problem" derisive laughter and incited them to cruelty. In their eyes, these were undoubtedly the bizarre accouterments, the grotesque ceremonies, and the mysterious implements of a demonic brood. The Holocaust was one of the rare mass slaughters in which perpetrators, like these and other men of Police Battalion 101, routinely mocked their victims and forced them to perform antics before sending them to their deaths. These proud, joyous poses of German masters degrading men who were for them archetypical Jews wearing prayer shawls are undoubtedly representative of many such scenes of degradation and others of cruelty about which the men of Police Battalion 101 remain silent, and about which the Jews did not survive to give witness. If we relied upon the specific and precise accounts of the battalion's members themselves, then we would have a skewed portrait of their actions, grossly underestimating the gratuitous suffering that they inflicted on the Jews, not to mention the evident gusto with which they at times visited cruelties upon their defenseless victims. . . .

The conventional explanations cannot account for the findings of this study, for the evidence from the cases presented here. They are belied by the actions of the perpetrators, glaringly and irrefutably. The notions that the perpetrators contributed to genocide because they were coerced, because they were unthinking, obedient executors of state orders, because of social psychological pressure, because of the prospects of personal advancement, or because they did not comprehend or feel responsible for what they were doing, owing to the putative fragmentation of tasks, can each be demonstrated in quick order to be untenable. . . .

Regarding Germany during the Nazi period and its crimes, the argument is made, often reflexively as though it were an axiomatic truth, that Germans are particularly obedient to state authority. This argument cannot be sustained. The very people, Germans, who supposedly were slavishly devoted to the cult of the state and to obedience for obedience's sake, were the same people, Germans, who battled in the streets of Weimar in defiance of existing state authority and often in order to overthrow it. . . .

Germans should not be caricatured; like other peoples, they have regard for authority if they hold it to be legitimate, and for orders that they deem to be legitimate. They too weigh an order's source and its meaning when deciding if and how to carry it out. Orders deemed in violation of moral norms — especially of fundamental moral norms — in fact, can do much to undermine the legitimacy of the regime from which they emanate — as the order to massacre community after community, tens of thousands of defenseless men, women, and children, would have in the eyes of anyone who believed the victims' deaths to be unjust.

Indeed, Germans of all ranks, even the most Nazified, disobeyed orders that they opposed, that they deemed illegitimate. Generals who willingly contributed to the extermination of Soviet Jews conspired against Hitler. Army soldiers, on their own, participated in the killing of Jews without orders to do so, or in disobedience of orders to keep their distance from the massacres. Sometimes Germans were insubordinate in order to satisfy their lust to kill Jews. The men of Police Battalion 101 violated their commander's, indeed their beloved commander's, injunction not to be cruel. . . .

Arguments holding that Germans inflexibly obey authority — namely that they reflexively obey any order, regardless of its content — are untenable. By extension, so are the claims by Stanley Milgram and many others that humans in general are blindly obedient to authority. All "obedience," all "crimes of obedience" (and this refers only to situations in which coercion is not applied or threatened), depend upon the existence of a propitious social and political context, in which the actors deem the authority to issue commands themselves not to be a gross transgression of sacred values and the overarching moral order. Otherwise, people seek ways, granted with differential success, not to violate their deepest moral beliefs and not to undertake such grievous acts. . . .

The notion that peer pressure, namely the desire either not to let down one's comrades or not to incur their censure, could move individuals to undertake actions that they oppose, even abhor, is plausible even for the German perpetrators, but only as an account of the participation of some *individuals* in the perpetration of the Holocaust. It cannot be operative for more than a few individuals in a group, especially over a long period of time. If a large segment of a group, not to mention the vast majority of its members, opposes or abhors an act, then the social psychological pressure would work to *prevent*, not to encourage, individuals to undertake the act. If indeed Germans had disapproved of the mass slaughter, then peer pressure would not have induced people to kill against their will, but would have sustained their individual and collective resolve to avoid killing. At best, and in all probability rightly, the actions of only some small minority of the perpetrators can be accounted for by positing the existence of social psychological pressure to conform. The explanation is self-contradictory when applied to the actions of *entire groups* of Germans. Its explanatory capacity, therefore, is greatly limited. The kindred psychological argumentation of these [two] conventional lines of reasoning — that Germans in particular and humans in general are prone to obey orders, and that social psychological pressure was sufficient to induce them to kill — are untenable. As is shown, in part, by the choice of some to opt out of the genocidal killing, Germans were indeed *capable* of saying "no."

The beliefs about Jews that underlay the German people's participation and approval of the eliminationist policies of the 1930s, and that led ordinary Germans in Losice and Warsaw prior to the initiation of a formal program of genocide to act so barbarously, were the beliefs that prepared ordinary Germans — as it did the men of Police Battalion 3 — to concur with what an officer of the battalion said while addressing his men in Minsk, before the first enormous massacre that they were to perpetrate, namely that "no suffering should accrue to noble German blood in the process of destroying this subhumanity." These ordinary Germans saw the world in such a manner that the slaughter of thousands of Jews was seen as an obvious necessity that produced concern only for the well-being of "noble German blood." Their beliefs about Jews prepared these representative Germans to hear the officer's accompanying offer to be excused if they were not up to the task, yet to choose to slaughter Jewish men, women, and children willingly.

These were the beliefs that engendered in ordinary Germans the lethal racial fantasies which led them to write to loved ones and friends of the genocidal exploits of their nation and its representative men. A member of Police Battlion 105 wrote to his wife on August 7, 1941, from the Soviet Union, in explicit and approving terms, of the total annihilation of the Jews, and then added; "Dear H., don't lose sleep over it, it has to be." Having borne witness to continual, ongoing genocidal killing, and writing openly and with the obvious expectation of his wife's general understanding (whatever misgivings she might have had notwithstanding), this man could write to her again one month later that he was "proud" to be a German soldier, because "I can take part up here and have many adventures." . . .

These were the beliefs that prepared officers of Police Regiment 25 to boast, like so many other Germans engaged in the slaughter, and to believe themselves "to have accomplished feats of heroism by these killings." These were the beliefs that led so many ordinary Germans to kill for pleasure and to do so not while trying to hide their deeds but in full view of others, even of women, girlfriends and wives, some of whom, like those in Stanisławów, used to laugh as their men picked off Jews from their balconies, like so many ducks in a shooting gallery. These same beliefs moved the men of Police Battalion 61's First Company, who guarded the Warsaw ghetto and eagerly shot Jews attempting to sneak in or out of the ghetto during 1941–1942, to create a recreational shrine to their slaughter of Jews. These German reservists turned a room in their quarters into a bar, adorned its walls with antisemitic caricatures and sayings, and hung over the bar itself a large, internally illuminated Star of David. Lest some of their heroics go unnoticed, by the door to the bar was a running tabulation of the number of Jews whom the company's men shot. After successful kills, these Germans were in the habit of rewarding themselves by holding special "victory celebrations" (*Siegesfeiern*).

These beliefs about Jews that governed the German people's

assent and contributions to the eliminationist program of the 1930s were the beliefs that prepared the men of Police Battalion 101 and so many other Germans to be eager killers who volunteered again and again for their "Jew-hunts," and to call Międzyrzec, a city in which they conducted repeated roundups, killings, and deportations — playing on its name with obvious reference to its many thousands of Jews — "*Menschenschreck*," or "human horror." These were the beliefs that led Germans, in the words of Herbert Hummel, the Bureau Chief of the Warsaw District, to have "welcomed thankfully" the 1941 "shoot-to-kill order," which authorized them to kill any Jews found outside ghettos. These same beliefs moved the men of another police unit, ordinary Germans, to shoot Jews whom they found even "without express orders, completely voluntarily." One of the men explains: "I must admit that we felt a certain joy when we would seize a Jew whom one could kill. I cannot remember an instance when a policeman had to be ordered to an execution. The shootings were, to my knowledge, always carried out on a voluntary basis; one could have gained the impression that various policemen got a big kick out of it." Why the "joy," why the eager voluntarism? Obviously, because of these ordinary Germans' beliefs about the Jews, which this man summarizes definitively: "The Jew was not acknowledged by us to be a human being." With this simple observation and admission, this former executioner uncovers from below the shrouds of obfuscation the mainspring of the Holocaust.

These were the beliefs that led so many ordinary Germans who degraded, brutalized, and tortured Jews in camps and elsewhere — the cruelty in the camps having been near universal — to *choose* to do so. They did not choose (like the tiny minority who showed that restraint was possible) not to hit, or, if under supervision, to hit in a manner that would do the least damage, but instead regularly chose to terrorize, to inflict pain, and to maim. These were the beliefs that prepared the men of Police Battalion 309, ordinary Germans, not to hate, but to esteem the captain who had led them in their orgy of killing and synagogue-burning in Białystok in a manner similar to the glowing evaluations of "Papa" Trapp given by the men of Police Battalion 101, esteem which echoed the sentiments of men in many other killing institutions towards their commanders. This captain, according to his men, "was entirely humane [sic] and as a superior beyond reproach." After all, in the transvaluated world of Germany during the Nazi period, ordinary Germans deemed the killing of Jews to be a beneficent act for humanity. These were the beliefs that led Germans often to mark and celebrate Jewish holidays, such as Yom Kippur, with killing operations, and for a member of Police Battalion 9, who was attached to *Einsatzkommando IIa*, to compose two poems, one for Christmas 1941 and the other for a social evening, ten days later, that celebrated their deeds in the Soviet Union. He managed to work into his verse, for the enjoyment of all, a reference to the "skull-cracking blows" (*Nüssknacken*) that they had undoubtedly delivered with relish to their Jewish victims.

These were the beliefs that led Germans to take joy, make merry, and celebrate their genocide of the Jews, such as with the party (*Abschlussfeier*) thrown upon the closing down of the Chełmno extermination camp in April 1943 to reward its German staff for a job well done. By then, the Germans had killed over 145,000 Jews in Chełmno. The German perpetrators' rejoicing proudly in their mass annihilation of the Jews occurred also at the conclusion of the more concentrated slaughter of twelve thousand Jews on the "Bloody Sunday" of October 12, 1941, in Stanisławów, where the Germans there threw a victory celebration. Yet another such celebration was organized in August 1941, during the heady days in the midst of the Germans' campaign of extermination of Latvian Jewry. On the occasion of their slaughter of the Jews of Cēsis, the local German security police and members of the German military assembled to eat and drink at what they dubbed a "death banquet [*Totenmahl*] for the Jews." During their festivities, the celebrants drank repeated toasts to the extermination of the Jews.

While the perpetrators' routine symbolic degradation of their Jewish victims, their celebrations of their killings, and their photographic mementos of their genocidal achievements and milestones all attest to this transvaluation of values, perhaps nothing demonstrates this more sharply than the farewell given by a man who should have been a moral conscience for Germany. Like the leaders of a good portion of the Protestant Evangelical Church of Germany, who in a proclamation declared the Jews to be "born enemies of the world and the Reich," incapable of being saved by baptism, and responsible for the war, and who, having accepted the logic of their racial, demonological antisemitism, gave their explicit ecclesiastical authorization for the implementation of the "severest measures" against the Jews while the genocidal program was well under way, Cardinal Adolf Bertram of Breslau once appears to have explicitly expressed his own understanding of the extermination of Jews, except for those who had converted to Christianity. The beliefs that led the German people to support the eliminationist program and the perpetrators to carry it out were the beliefs that moved Bertram — who, like the entire Catholic and Protestant ecclesiastical leadership, was fully cognizant of the extermination of the Jews and of the antisemitic attitudes of his parishioners — to pay final homage to the man who was the mass murderer of the Jewish people and who had for twelve years served as the beacon of the German nation. Upon learning of Hitler's death, Cardinal Bertram in the first days of May 1945 ordered that in all the churches of his archdiocese a special requiem, namely "a solemn requiem mass be held in commemoration of the Führer . . ." so that his and Hitler's flock could pray to the Almighty, in accord with the requiem's liturgy, that the Almighty's son, Hitler, be admitted to paradise.

The beliefs that were already the common property of the German people upon Hitler's assumption of power and which led the German people to assent and contribute to the eliminationist measures of the 1930s were the beliefs that prepared not just the Germans who by circumstances, chance, or choice ended up as perpetrators but also the vast majority of the German people to understand, assent to, and, when possible, do their part to further the extermination, root and branch, of the Jewish people. The inescapable truth is that, regarding Jews, German political culture had evolved to the point where an enormous number of ordinary, representative Germans became — and most of the rest of their fellow Germans were fit to be — Hitler's willing executioners.

Survivors of the Warsaw ghetto uprising being deported to forced labor camps and killing centers, May 1943. (AP/Wide World Photos)

PART V

Gentiles During the Holocaust

Variety of Opinion

The over-all balance between the acts of crime and acts of help, as described in the available sources, is disproportionately negative. . . . To a significant extent, this negative balance is to be accounted for by the hostility towards the Jews on the part of large segments of the Polish underground, and, even more importantly, by the involvement of some armed units of that underground in murders of the Jews.

Yisrael Gutman and Shmuel Krakowski

[N]o reasonable student of World War II can deny that Hitler's policy toward the Poles was also genocidal. . . . If the magnitude of the Polish tragedy were objectively presented, unrealistic and unhistorical judgments about the possibilities and opportunities available to the Poles to render greater aid than they did to the Jews would not be made.

Richard C. Lukas

Very many, probably most, Germans were opposed to the Jews during the Third Reich. . . . Most would have drawn the line at physical maltreatment. . . . The very secrecy of the "Final Solution" demonstrates

199

*more clearly than anything else the fact that the Nazi leadership felt
it could not rely on popular backing for its extermination policy.*

Ian Kershaw

*It seems plain that German policy, and also the ability of the Nazis to
apply their power, were decisive in determining how far the destruction process went. . . . Only the defeat of the Reich brought the trains
to a halt.*

Michael R. Marrus and Robert O. Paxton

At least to some degree, the Jews' chances of survival depended
on getting help from their Gentile neighbors. Especially (but not
exclusively) in the killing fields of Eastern Europe it was those
neighbors who could give or withhold hiding places, food, and
even false papers and arms that sometimes made the difference
between life and death. Elsewhere the Germans were not in direct
control or else lacked sufficient numbers to manage everything,
which gave local officials room to take decisive action. That could
work for or against the Jews. For example, in Bulgaria, a German
ally, local authorities simply refused to give up Jews who were
Bulgarian citizens. The same thing happened in Hungary until the
Germans took control in March 1944, after which Hungarian officials helped send most of the country's Jews to Auschwitz. In
Hungary and other countries that collaborated with Nazi Germany, the rounding up and deportation of Jews to death camps
could not have been done efficiently without the assistance of
local authorities.

This section looks at the attitudes and actions of Gentiles in
Poland, Germany, and the countries of occupied Western Europe.
Poland deserves special attention, as most victims of the Holocaust lived there, and it was in Poland that all of the extermination
centers were located. For Germans the situation was clouded by
the obvious fact that their own leadership was carrying out
anti-Jewish measures. What is much less obvious is how much
they knew about those measures, and whether or not they
approved. Western Europe presents still different circumstances.
Like Germany, it was remote from the scene of the crime, but
there, patriotism was no impediment to opposing Nazi Jewish
policies.

Yisrael Gutman and Shmuel Krakowski examine the sensitive subject of Polish-Jewish relations during the Holocaust. They acknowledge that the Poles, too, were persecuted by the Nazis and that aiding Jews only increased the dangers to which Poles were exposed. But the authors assert that the two groups were anything but equal victims. The Jews, unlike their Gentile neighbors, were herded into ghettos and camps, and marked for mass extermination. If one group were to aid the other, it would have to be the Poles. Some did, but, the authors conclude, most did not. In the excerpts included below, Gutman and Krakowski note the persistence of popular antisemitism in Poland and the failure of the Polish underground to support the Warsaw ghetto uprising. At the same time they pay tribute to the minority of Poles that helped Jews. In their balancing of acts of kindness against those of hatred, however, the Poles come out wanting.

Richard C. Lukas assesses the evidence differently in his book on Poland under Nazi rule. A one-sided emphasis on the Jewish tragedy, he argues, leads to underestimation of the plight of the Poles and to exaggeration of their opportunities to help anyone, even themselves. Antisemitism in Poland, brought on to some degree by the Jews themselves, was qualitatively different from that of the Nazis and did not determine Polish reactions to persecution of the Jews. What did was implacable German pressure on the Poles, which was so intense that documented acts of Polish aid to Jews should be regarded as little short of miraculous. In view of the "forgotten holocaust" against Polish Gentiles, Lukas concludes, the Germans alone must be held responsible for the fate of the Jews.

Ian Kershaw examines public opinion about Jews and antisemitism in the large south German state of Bavaria during World War II. Other historians have argued that facts about the Holocaust were fairly well known in Germany despite official efforts to keep them hidden. Kershaw, however, presents evidence disputing that view on the basis of his research in the Nazis' own secret public opinion reports and the records of the anti-Nazi underground in Germany. Not only were Germans ill-informed about the Holocaust, he finds; they were preoccupied with countless problems of coping with an increasingly difficult wartime situation and the demands of a relentless totalitarian state. Hence they were largely unconcerned about the "Jewish problem." The Nazi state had not been able to turn many Germans into virulent Judeophobes, but it had created conditions that caused them to be indifferent to the fate of Jewish neighbors.

Michael R. Marrus and Robert O. Paxton are the authors of an important book showing that French acceptance of the anti-Jewish policies of the collaborationist Vichy regime was widespread until late in 1942. Here they survey the situation in all of Nazi-occupied Western Europe. Cautioning against overgeneralizing about the various countries during the Holocaust, they identify the local conditions that determined widely different Jewish losses: from 75 percent in the Netherlands to about 5 percent in Denmark. The authors note that the collaboration of government officials in several of the countries was immensely helpful to the Nazis in the early months of Jewish deportation. On the other hand, increasing resistance to deportation policies slowed the Final Solution to varying degrees in different places. In the end, however, Marrus and Paxton conclude that military defeat alone stopped the German trains from leaving for the East.

Essays such as these make it more difficult than once was the case to indulge in facile generalizations about Gentiles during the Holocaust. No one who has read them will easily fall prey to demeaning portrayals of "all" Poles or "all" Germans or "all" Europeans. Rather, our attention should be fixed on questions such as these: What conditions caused Gentiles to give or withhold aid to Jews? What role did antisemitism play in shaping Gentile behavior? (If a country such as Holland with little history of popular Judeophobia suffered one of the highest levels of Jewish losses, can it have been decisive in determining the fate of the Jews?) If ordinary Germans — and many other Europeans — were uninformed, or imperfectly informed, about the genocide of the Jews, how can they be charged with complicity in it?

Yisrael Gutman and Shmuel Krakowski

The Poles Helped Persecute the Jews

Immediately prior to the Warsaw Ghetto uprising in April 1943, the ZOB[1] had no more than five hundred fighting men at its disposal. Shortage of arms was the principal factor that prevented the organization from increasing its manpower. In fact, there were not enough arms to go around. Even if we accept the figures cited by Pelczynski as accurate, we find that the ghetto fighters had available to them only one pistol for every seven men, one rifle for every fifty men, and one machine gun for more than every hundred and fifty men. The AK's claim about the inadequacy of its own store of arms can be considered from a variety of points of view. The types and quantities of weapons and ammunition available to the AK were certainly inadequate for it to confront the German army in the field. But the claim that the few scores of pistols handed over to the ZOB represented a significant sacrifice on the part of the Polish military underground cannot be taken seriously, when we consider that the AK possessed tens of thousands of rifles and approximately one thousand light machine guns. In any event, the unsuitability of the arms made available to the ZOB was patently revealed to the Jews by the time of the ghetto rebellion. So we find Mordecai Anielewicz, commander of the Warsaw Ghetto uprising, writing to Yitzhak Zuckerman, the ZOB representative to the Poles, on April 23, 1943: ". . . and you should know that pistols are absolutely useless, we've almost not used them at all. What we need is: grenades, rifles, machine guns and explosives."

The heads of the Jewish Fighting Organization seem to have been aware of the AK leadership's reservations, even hostility, as expressed by their failure to arm the ZOB adequately during the initial

Text by Yisrael Gutman and Shmuel Krakowski from *Unequal Victims*, Holocaust Library, 1986. Reprinted by permission of Holocaust Publications.

[1]"Jewish Fighting Organization" in Poland. — Ed.

phases of its formations and preparations for battle. In March 1943, as units of the ZOB clashed with the Germans in the ghetto, a letter attributed to Anielewicz was sent to the Jewish underground representative to the Poles. The letter included the following statement: "Please inform the authorities in our name that if massive assistance does not arrive at once, it will look as if the representation and the authorities are indifferent to the fate of the Jews of Warsaw. The allocation of weapons without ammunition seems like a bitter joke and a confirmation of the suspicion that the poison of anti-Semitism still permeates the ruling circles of Poland in full force, despite the tragic and brutal experience of the past three years. We are not about to prove to anyone our readiness and ability to fight. Since January 18 the Jewish community in Warsaw has existed in a state of war with the invader and his noxious henchmen. Whoever denies or doubts this is merely an anti-Semite out of spite."

Most of the weapons the ZOB fought with had to be purchased. The Polish Communists were more magnanimous than the AK in helping the Jewish Fighting Organization; but their resources were so limited as to render their assistance nearly worthless. . . .

Polish attitudes and conduct with respect to the Jewish resistance in Warsaw [were] not as unrelievedly unsympathetic as a dry account of the events makes them appear. There were some Poles who did everything that was in their power to advance the interests of Jewish armed resistance. But the official representatives of the "military authorities in the underground" — the commanders and upper political echelons — tended on the whole to regard the catastrophe of the Jews and Jewish appeals for assistance as something remote from their immediate concerns. Only when long-range Polish interests became involved, or when the appeals of men and women of conscience became too insistent to be ignored, were they moved to act, though only hesitantly, on a small scope and without conviction. . . .

Thousands of Polish Gentiles became involved in varying degrees in efforts to save Jews. We know that many Poles — hundreds apparently — lost their lives because of their actions on behalf of Jews.

But the gallant record of those Poles who came to the assistance of Jews does not alter the fact that there also existed a malignant element in Polish society that was responsible for creating a hostile climate of opinion among broad sections of the Polish public concerning the rescue of Jews. The *shmaltsovniks* [blackmailers] were a relatively large group in Poland. They operated on an organized basis and made a profession of the betrayal of Jews.

We have already observed that the German invader found it difficult to distinguish between Jews and Gentiles in Poland, and that the fear experienced by Jews hiding out on the "Aryan side" was of being informed on by Poles. Similarly, those who worked to save Jews did so without benefit of support from the great mass of Poles; indeed, they were forced to keep their activities secret from neighbors, friends and, sometimes, even from relatives. The act of concealing or helping a Jew was distinctly unpopular; it was a cause of distress among Poles and often actively opposed by them. One Polish heroine who had taken an abandoned Jewish child under her protection tells of having constantly to change her residence because she was actually driven away by her neighbors, who knew the child was not hers and was Jewish. Many of the accounts of Jewish survivors are replete with expressions of gratitude and esteem for the devotion and courage of the Poles who had helped save them. Most of these stories also tell of the ordeals experienced by Polish benefactors and cite countless instances of Jews being blackmailed or turned over to the German police by Poles. . . .

Just who were these [extortionists and informers] and how large were their numbers? Polish writers are probably correct in claiming that most of them came from the very lowest orders of society and either lived on the fringes of the criminal underworld or were outright criminals themselves. Affiliated with the extortionist gangs, too, were persons with no criminal past but whom wartime conditions freed from all social inhibiting restraints, allowing them to indulge their overriding desire for easy money and their innate taste for debauchery. But such people were at least no more than a by-product of the war, a wild strain produced by circumstance and the times. However, we learn from the reports of many witnesses that these circles were also joined by rabid anti-Semites for whom such contemptible activities provided an opportunity to give vent to their ideological inclinations.

We have no figures concerning the number of street toughs and informers who made up the gangs that victimized Jews. But there were enough of them around to make life a constant nightmare for

Jews living as Poles or hiding in the Aryan part of Warsaw. Polish writers argue, not unreasonably, that the entire Polish nation cannot be blamed for crimes committed against the Jews by a mere handful of thugs. They are also correct in observing that under the occupation it was easier for evildoers than for decent men to flourish. Those who blackmailed and informed against Jews acted under the protection of the Polish and Nazi police, or were at least tolerated by them.

Apart from the hunters, their prey and the occupation authorities, there existed another element whose position must be explained — the Polish public, and especially that segment which made up the powerful underground organization, the so-called "underground state," which operated among the populace. The mere reluctance of most Poles to become involved or forcefully to oppose the extortionists cannot in itself account for the extraordinary confidence and freedom with which these gangs were able to carry on their activities. Naturally they were enthusiastically assisted by the anti-Semitic climate of opinion among the Polish people. In that atmosphere the extortionists were given no reason to feel that their activities in any way struck at Polish patriotism. Moreover, as we have observed elsewhere, the underground took no affirmative action against these gangs, as they routinely did in the case of other types of collaborationists. We can assume that the majority in the underground had no sympathy for extortionists and informers who were battening on Jews; but they were also reluctant to declare war against them, since they were aware that such a move would be unpopular among wide sections of the populace. We need only examine the history of the fruitless efforts by members of *Zegota*[2] to convince underground authorities to take effective reprisals against the extortionists for us to gain a fair idea of the nature of the inhibitions and hesitancies that prevented the Polish underground from taking action.

Ringelblum told in his *Polish-Jewish Relations* about the operations of the *Shmaltsovniks* (blackmailers) in Warsaw, and his personal experiences with them:

> *Extortion by* shmaltsovniks *begins the moment a Jew crosses through the gates of the ghetto, or rather while he is still inside the ghetto gates, which are watched by the swarms of* shmaltsovniks . . . *The* shmaltsovniks *walk around in the streets stopping anyone who even*

[2]"Council for Aid to Jews," an organization made up of Polish Gentiles. — Ed.

looks semitic in appearance. They frequent public squares, especially the square near the central [Railway] station, cafes and restaurants, and the hotels . . . The shmaltsovniks operate in organized bands. Bribing one of them does not mean that a second cohort will not appear a moment later, then a third and so on, a whole chain of shmaltsovniks who pass the victim on until he has lost his last penny. The shmaltsovniks collaborate with police agents, the uniformed police and in general with anyone who is looking for Jews. They are a veritable plague of locusts, descending in large numbers upon the Jews on the Aryan side and stripping them of their money and valuables and often clothing as well. . . .

It was quite common for the rural populace to take part in raids against the fugitives from liquidated ghettos who hid in the forests. Two major forms of such participation are to be distinguished: (1) Peasant participation in raids organized by the Nazi police and gendarmerie shortly after the deportations from local ghettos, in order to capture the fugitives; (2) The forest campaigns which the larger groups of local peasants organized and carried out on their own initiative, without notifying the Nazi police.

In the raids of the former type, the participating peasants would most typically serve the Nazis in the capacity of guides, pinpointing the possible sites in forest areas with which they were much more thoroughly familiar than the Germans. But it often happened that peasants themselves would murder the encountered Jews with pick-axes or scythes. The usual incentive for their participation in anti-Jewish raids was either German instigation or the hope for an opportunity to loot the belongings, clothes or valuables of captured fugitives. In some instances, the Germans would reward the peasant participants with allotments of sugar or salt. But the most common form of reward was simply the division of spoils.

The self-initiated raids of the second type would usually take place no sooner than several months after the largest mass deportations from local ghettos. Accordingly, such raids tended to be aimed at those Jewish fugitives who had already had some opportunity to establish themselves in well-concealed hiding places in the forests. Unaided by anyone, and long after the meager food rations which they could possibly bring with them to the forest had become exhausted, such fugitives for purposes of self-preservation had no alternative save to supply themselves with food stolen from peasant households or fields. Hence the common purpose of the collective raids of the villagers was to kill the Jews in hiding in forests in order to stave off the recurrent farm thefts.

The peasant participation in the anti-Jewish raids carried out by the Nazis is noted in the diary of S. Zieminski, a Polish teacher from Lukow:

> *On November 5 [1942] I stopped in the village of Siedliska. I entered the cooperative store. The peasants were buying scythes. I heard the saleswoman say: "They will be helpful during the raid today." I asked about the nature of the raid. "Against the Jews." I then asked: "And how much do you get for a captured Jew?" No one answered. I therefore went on: "For Christ they paid thirty pieces of silver; so make sure that you are paid no less." Again no one replied. But the answer came a little later. While crossing the forest, I heard salvos of machine gun fire. The raid was in progress. . . .*

Our file contains the records of participation of the local villagers in raids on the Jews in 172 localities. Here is a sample of pertinent personal accounts by the surviving witnesses of the recorded events:

Ignacy Goldstein recounts that peasants from the village of Iwanisko and its environs (Opatow county, Kielce district) were being rewarded for their participation in raids with a bag of sugar and one liter of refined alcohol. Later, however, it was the clothes of captured Jews which became the sole reward.

Gitla Kopylinska recounts that in Zambrow region there were a number of Jews hiding in the forest. The peasants were aware of this, but at the beginning showed no interest. Once the Germans announced the reward of one kilogram of sugar for every captured Jew, the local populace began raiding them. . . .

No less common were the murders of Jews usually perpetrated by rural groups of relatives or neighbors, whose general purpose was plunder. Here is a sample of cases of this category of anti-Jewish crimes from our records:

A group of villagers for [from] Lukowa, Bilgoraj county, tracked down, robbed and shot Abraham Gutherc who was sheltered by the murderer's neighbor, a farmer by the name of Machen.

In the village of Markowa near Lancut, Przeworsk county, a group of Poles led by Antoni Cyran murdered twenty-eight Jews and looted their belongings.

In the village of Dolmatowszczyzna near Wilno, Janek Achron, twenty-five, organized five persons into a gang which on November 18, 1942, murdered a hiding physician, Dr. Jehuda Barzak, his wife, mother, and son. . . .

Single-handed murders were no less common than the collective ones. The murderers who acted alone were in most cases peasants whom the Jewish fugitives approached for shelter. As in collective murders, the usual motive of the crime was the intent to ransack whatever money, valuables or clothes could be found on the bodies of the victims. Here is a sample of pertinent cases from our files:

A farmer by the name of Sienkiewicz from a village in the vicinity of Nowe Miasto murdered the parents of Nachman Segal. Sienkiewicz had previously provided the couple with shelter: he murdered them only when they ran out of money and could no longer pay him.

A farmer by the name of Kumin from the village of Smoryn near Frampol murdered and looted the body of a Jew by the name of Yitzhak, a cousin of Aharon Kislowicz.

Kapczuk from Komorowka Podlaska murdered the three year old daughter of Estera Rybak, after extorting a considerable amount of money which he had received for sheltering the child. . . .

Tracking down the Jews in hiding, capturing them, and handing them over to German police or gendarmerie, to Polish "blue" police or to Ukrainian auxiliary police was another very common form of anti-Jewish crime. As a rule, the police would in such cases shoot the Jews delivered into their hands in this way on the spot. Here is a sample of cases from our records:

A Jewish woman by the name of Maurer, with two children, completely exhausted after several months of hiding in the woods, returned to their former home in the village of Kurzyna near Ulanow, Nisko county. Maurer's Polish neighbors apprehended and escorted them to the German police post in Ulanow. All three were shot at once.

In the town of Frampol a certain Poteranski captured two children of Yakov Mordechaj Lichtfeld, and handed them over to the Germans.

On the landed estate of Starzyna near Horodlo, Hrubieszow county, Stanislaw Siemicki captured Mirela Pipler and handed her over to the Germans.

The inhabitants of the village of Potok, Bilgoraj county, captured Moshe Knoch with two children, and delivered all three to the Germans. . . .

Organized murders of Jews committed by various underground formations began toward the end of 1942, and occurred quite frequently thereafter. They did not stop entirely at the moment of termination of the Nazi occupation, but continued for some time afterwards. The largest number of such murders were perpetrated by the units of National Armed Forces; but some groups of the Home Army also shared this guilt. Obviously most of these units may have belonged to that part of the National Armed Forces which joined the Home Army.

Beginning with December 1942, some Polish underground formations undertook searches for the Jews in hiding. Whenever they discovered any, they would kill them on the spot. Beginning with the summer of 1943, crimes of this type reached a high frequency, due to the simple fact that the first major armed Polish underground formations appeared in the forests at that time. From then on, we can distinguish between the searches for the Jews hiding in village households, and the murders of accidentally encountered Jews, whatever their place of hiding. Many murders were also committed in the first days after the withdrawal of the German troops, when the Jewish survivors, finally feeling secure, were resurfacing from their places of hiding.

Our file contains cases of murder of Jewish fugitives by Polish underground groups from 120 different localities or forest ranges. Here is a sample:

Eight Jews found a hiding place in a forest bunker near the village of Kamieniec near Polaniec, Sandomierz county. After several weeks their bunker was surrounded by a local unit said to belong to the Home Army. The Jews were ordered to get out of the bunker, and then fired upon. Seven, including Moshe Gladstein, were killed; one, David Sznyper, managed to escape.

In the village of Zarki near Janow, Zawiercie county, a detachment of Jedrusie units encountered a Jewish woman disguised as a peasant girl. After checking her identity, they notified the police station in Zarki. Several days later the "Jedrusie" members learned that the girl avoided capture and was still alive. Thereupon they murdered her on their own, afterwards notifying the gendarmerie in Zarki. . . .

Of all crimes committed against the Jews, the most common and probably the most lethal was informing. It assumed epidemic proportions, and it affected as well the Poles who provided the Jews with any help. Informing incurred no risks. Ordinarily, it was sufficient to mail an unsigned postcard to the Gestapo. But many informers acted openly, appearing in person at a station of either the German or Polish auxiliary ("blue") police. This was especially true, when an informer hoped to receive a reward for a Jewish fugitive whom he delivered into German hands. Our records seldom make it possible to identify informers. In most cases they merely ascertain the fact and the identity of the informer's victims. Here is an extensive sampling of cases of informing:

Josef Zajwel and Icek Szer were hiding in an abandoned house in Lezajsk. They were aided by Tosiek Krasinski and Zygmunt Przybylski who supplied them with food. But some of the neighbors notified the Germans. The Germans came, surrounded the house, captured Zajwel and Szer, and shot them.

Ten Jews were hiding on farmland adjacent to the forest near Okrzeja, Lukow county. In the summer of 1943, they were betrayed by the farm owner's son. The Germans murdered them all.

In the town of Gorlice, Cracow district, a Polish woman turned the Meinhardt family over to the Germans: the parents and two children. All four were shot by a single SS man, whose name was Otto. As a result of her guilt feeling the informer went insane. . . .

Plunder of Jewish property and blackmail of Jews for the purpose of extortioning ransom were also quite common occurrences. Here is a sample of typical cases of such crimes:

Wicek Mincenty from the village of Zwada near Czestochowa sheltered Gabriel Horowicz's family for some time, then looted their belongings and evicted them from his premises.

The director of the KKO savings bank in Staszow, Rzadkobulski, accepted deposits of money and valuables from the Jews, then later refused to return anything.

In the vicinity of Jadow, Warsaw district, Chana Dzbanowicz left her hiding place in the forest in order to visit the Kalinski family whom she had known from before the war. Mrs. Kalinski fed her and hid her in her garret. But when Mr. Kalinski returned home, he began to scream and told Dzbanowicz to go away. On her way back to her hiding place in the forest she was assaulted by a group of Poles who stripped her of her shoes and sweater. In the same locality, Meir Dzbanowicz was stripped of his jacket during a similar assault. . . .

Obviously, we have succeeded in authenticating merely a fraction — perhaps only an infinitesimal fraction — of the crimes actually perpetrated against Jewish fugitives in hiding. Crimes such as murders, or informing, or turning Jews over to the Germans, were as a rule committed underhandedly. Seldom did the perpetrators want to have any witnesses. In very rare cases would a Jew who accidentally witnessed a crime committed against other Jews be allowed to survive. Also, the Polish witnesses of crimes against the Jews were later seldom willing to testify, if their statements would have implicated their friends or neighbors. As for the perpetrators themselves, they obviously wouldn't reveal their own crimes either. To compound matters, those directly implicated in crimes can usually rely on the solidarity of the people from within the social environment in which they operate. Actually, it is the latter who are often most helpful in covering up the traces.

The instances of participation by Poles in raids on Jewish fugitives have been authenticated as having occurred in 172 localities and the murders committed by Polish underground formations (National Armed Forces and a Part of the Home Army) as having occurred in 120 localities. Beyond any doubt these figures are incomplete: there certainly were other localities in which collective crimes against the Jews were committed, either by groups of local populace or by underground units. Unfortunately, there is absolutely no way of estimating the total number of victims of these crimes in even the roughest general terms. Some Jewish survivors recount that tens and even hundreds of Jews could be either murdered on the spot or turned over to the Germans as a result of one raid in a single locality. The accounts of Icchak Golabek and Icchak Szumowicz which describe the raids in the forests surrounding the town of Zambrow are cases in point. Golabek tells of hundreds of Jews captured by Poles and turned over to the Germans during one single raid of no more than one day's duration. Szumowicz estimates that about 150 Jews who escaped the deportation from Zambrow on January 15,

1943, were subsequently tracked down by the local villagers in a nearby forest and turned over to the Germans.

Similar facts are reported by the survivors from dozens of other localities. The existing evidence does not make it possible, however, to corroborate reliably the raid casualty estimates as given by the authors of the accounts. When totaled, these estimates would reach many thousands who fell prey to raids which Poles either organized or were involved in. Of this, the figure of over 3,000 Jews whom Poles (under varying circumstances) either murdered or turned over to the Germans can be considered reliably authenticated on the basis of the existing sources. . . .

We have studied the files concerning 2,652 Jews rescued by help obtained from the Poles. Likewise, we have identified 965 Polish individuals and families outside Warsaw who under many differing circumstances and for specific considerations sheltered Jews or helped them otherwise to hide. We have found that of the 965, eighty persons paid for their deeds with their lives. But again, the existing documentation has undoubtedly failed to record all the acts of help which the Jews received from the Poles. As in the case of the crimes, the actual number of Jews saved by the Poles and the actual number of their Polish benefactors (and of those from among them who made the ultimate sacrifice of their lives) are certainly much higher than the figures presented here. Yet there are reliable reasons to presume that the figures concerning the help to the Jews deviated from the actual realities comparatively less often than the figures concerning the crimes against the Jews. Simply put, the dead can no longer produce information, and the perpetrators of crimes prefer to remain silent. In contrast, the survivors can speak, and they have indeed recounted numerous instances of help received from the Poles. Furthermore, the Poles who did extend such help have had no reasons to be ashamed of their deeds either.

This is applicable in cases where the Poles paid for their help to the Jews with their lives. As noted, the actual number of such cases is certainly higher than the figure cited above. It is well documented that the Polish population was subjected by the Germans to brutal terror. Within the framework of that terror, particularly atrocious reprisals were meted out even for minor breaches of all conceivable rulings of the Nazi authorities. Adding the general balance sheet of anti-Polish repression, however, the reprisals for helping the Jews rank rather low in frequency. . . .

In summation, documents reviewed in our study point to a negative balance, in which instances of help to the Jews are outnumbered by instances of crimes against the Jews. To a considerable extent, this negative balance can be accounted for by the policies of the German conquest, which consciously aimed at spreading corruption within as large a fraction of the Polish society as possible. Severe penalties for even the slightest relief offered to a Jew, coupled with rewards for committing crimes against them, did exert a negative influence upon the Polish society's attitudes. Recurrently posted announcements warning of the death penalty for helping the Jews were visible at all the locations in the Government General beginning with September 1942. They were followed by the promulgation of executive ordinances in each of its counties. At the same time, the occupation authorities did everything possible to encourage the Poles to participate in raids on the Jewish fugitives in hiding, and to loot their property. . . .

The over-all balance between the acts of crime and acts of help, as described in the available sources, is disproportionately negative. The acts of crime outnumbered the acts of help. To a significant extent, this negative balance is to be accounted for by the hostility towards the Jews on the part of large segments of the Polish underground, and, even more importantly, by the involvement of some armed units of that underground in murders of the Jews. Still, several thousand Jews from our files succeeded in finding shelter and in being rescued because of Polish help. Yet for a Jewish fugitive, the chance of obtaining any help was slight under the conditions of the raging Nazi terror, of the death penalty for anyone extending such help, and of widespread hostility towards the Jews in both the Polish society and its underground organizations. Of the many who sought help, only a few found it. The overwhelming majority of Jews who approached Poles for help fell prey either to Nazi police or gendarmerie, or to rabid anti-Semites in the Polish society and in the Polish underground.

Thousands who sought help but failed to obtain it, unable to cope any longer with all the constant dangers lurking about, were returning to the ghettos already reduced after the mass deportations, or to the newly formed secondary ghettos. It meant that they would be killed eventually, during a later deportation to death camps.

Still more tragic were the instances when Jewish fugitives would come to a German police station to seek death by turning themselves in, after they lost all hope of survival in the forest or elsewhere, or of ever obtaining shelter or any other help from the Poles.

Richard C. Lukas

The Poles Were Fellow Victims

One of the most controversial aspects of the history of wartime Poland is the subject of Polish-Jewish relations. Much that has been written on this subject is badly flawed: Jewish historians tend to make sweeping claims that label most Poles anti-Semites who did little to help the Jews against the Nazis; Polish writers tend to minimize Polish anti-Semitism and sometimes exaggerate the amount of assistance Poles gave the Jews. Anti-Semitism was less a factor in Polish-Jewish wartime relations than the reality of the Nazi terror, which was so overwhelming that the opportunities to assist the Jews were more limited in Poland than anywhere else in occupied Europe. When one considers the fact that most of the three million Jews who lived in Poland were unassimilated, the task of saving Jews was even more formidable.

Anti-Semitism did exist in wartime Poland, but it did not meet with a sympathetic response among the majority of people, who were preoccupied with their own survival during the German occupation. Further, a minority of Poles from various social classes, including former anti-Semites, risked their lives to aid Jews. . . .

Reprinted from *The Forgotten Holocaust: The Poles Under German Occupation, 1939–1944*, by Richard C. Lukas. © 1986 by the University Press of Kentucky. Reproduced by permission of the publishers.

It is impossible to generalize about Polish attitudes toward the Jews during the German occupation, because there was no uniformity. Despite German persecution of the Polish people, a small minority of Poles openly approved of German policies toward the Jews, and some actively aided the Nazis in their grim mission. But even the anti-Semitic National Democrats in Poland altered some of their traditional views toward the Jews as the bizarre logic of German racial policy became apparent in the extermination campaign; and some National Democrats personally aided Jews. Other Poles showed no outward pleasure at the removal of Jews from Polish offices, professions, and businesses but were not opposed to the economic expropriation involved. These people had anti-Semitic views which were economic, not racial in character; if we can hazard any generalization at all, it is that to the extent there was anti-Semitism among some Poles, it reflected this *economic* anti-Semitic attitude. Still others quietly felt compassion for the Jewish people; they might be described, in Philip Friedman's words as "passive humanitarians." These people either feared becoming actively involved in aiding Jews because of the risk of the death penalty the Germans automatically imposed on Poles who helped Jews — Poland was the only occupied country where this was done — or were so pauperized by the war they simply could not afford to aid anyone without jeopardizing the survival of their own families. Then there was a very active group of Poles who were openly sympathetic toward the Jews, and many of these risked their lives to help Jews.

Several factors had a negative impact on Polish attitudes toward Jews. Until at least the latter part of 1941, when the Germans began to exterminate the Jews, Poles felt that their situation was far worse than the Jews who lived in ghettos. They saw a big difference in Nazi aims toward the two groups; the Germans wanted to destroy the Poles politically, while they seemed to want only to cripple the Jews economically. After all, Jews as a group were not deported or executed as the Poles were in these early years. On the other hand, Jews in the ghettos tended to see only advantages that the Poles enjoyed on the Aryan side of the walls, while they alone experienced difficulties. Before the resistance efforts of the Jews developed later in the occupation, Poles perceived the Jews as being craven in their behavior toward the Germans, accepting without defiance the restrictions and persecutions imposed on them, collaborating with the Germans, and even denouncing Poles who hid them when the Germans discovered their hiding places outside the ghettos. By contrast, the Poles saw themselves as bearing their ordeal with pride and defiance. Poles were outraged by the active business the Jews conducted with the Germans, accused them of buying food which kept prices high, and saw many Jews preferring to have the Germans confiscate their goods rather than share them with Poles. On the other hand, those Poles who had economically benefitted from the move of the Jews to the ghettos by acquiring Jewish homes and businesses opposed the Polish government-in-exile's decree declaring all such actions under German occupation as illegal. "We will not return the shops and factories" was an all-too-familiar Polish cry.

"We shall never forget their [Jewish] behavior toward the Bolsheviks" was a familiar statement heard in Poland during the war, underscoring the negative behavior of many Jews during the Soviet occupation of eastern Poland beginning in September 1939. Some of these Jews were influenced by Soviet propaganda which promised them improvement in their social and economic status. Others were known to be sympathizers with the Soviet system and welcomed the opportunity that presented itself. No doubt there were also Jews who, unhappy with some of the discrimination that had existed in prewar Poland, believed their condition would improve under new landlords, a hope that soon proved illusory.

Jews in cities and towns displayed Red flags to welcome Soviet troops, helped to disarm Polish soldiers, and filled administrative positions in Soviet-occupied Poland. . . .

Jewish collaboration with the Soviets, more than any other factor, was responsible for increasing anti-Semitism in Poland during the war. In these circumstances, many Poles did not understand and were even critical of the pro-Jewish declarations during these early years of the Polish government-in-exile. When the Germans invaded the Soviet Union in June 1941, the Polish government was understandably alarmed that once the Germans reoccupied eastern Poland, the Poles there would try to revenge themselves on the Jews.

In the midst of the mutual antagonisms shared by Poles and Jews during the German occupation, the Germans launched a massive program of anti-Semitic propaganda through the media. They installed loudspeakers on street corners and in public places and published newspapers in Polish and German which continually spewed forth anti-Semitic themes. . . .

[T]he most overt examples of anti-Semitism came during the early months of the occupation when the Germans encouraged gangs of young Polish hoodlums to attack Jews. Sometimes these criminals even attacked Poles. The pogroms against the Jews were not spontaneous; they usually were well-orchestrated by the Germans, who even conducted a course for members of anti-Semitic groups. The youngsters, often intoxicated, were paid by the Germans for their activity. One Jewish eyewitness described the scene in Warsaw during the Passover pogrom in 1940:

> *The Passover pogrom continued about eight days. It began suddenly and stopped as suddenly. The pogrom was carried out by a crowd of youths, about 1,000 of them, who arrived suddenly in the Warsaw streets. Such types have never before been seen in the Warsaw streets. Clearly these were young ruffians specially brought from the suburbs. From the characteristic scenes of the pogrom I mention here a few: On the second day of Passover, at the corner of Wspólna and Marszalkowska Streets about 30 or 40 broke into and looted Jewish hat shops. German soldiers stood in the streets and filmed the scenes. . . .*
>
> *The Polish youngsters acted alone, but there have been instances when such bands attacked the Jews with the assistance of German military. The attitude of the Polish intellectuals toward the Jews was clearly a friendly one, and against the pogrom. It is a known fact that at the corner of Nowogrodzka Street and Marszalkowska a Catholic priest attacked the youngsters participating in the pogrom, beat them and disappeared. These youngsters received two zlotys daily from the Germans.*

Of course, anti-Semitic groups rejoiced at these attacks, but moderate and socialist opinion in Poland condemned them. The Socialists joined the government press in decrying the criminal behavior of some Poles. The Socialists went so far as to label any Pole a collaborator who was involved in the least anti-Semitic incident and thus an "enemy who should be exterminated with complete ruthlessness." Even Emmanuel Ringelblum, who was often a severe critic of Polish behavior toward the Jews, admitted that the pogroms in Warsaw were limited to a small number of Poles: "No one will accuse the Polish nation of committing these constant pogroms and excesses against the Jewish population. The significant majority of the nation, its enlightened working-class, and the working intelligentsia, undoubtedly condemned these excesses, seeing in them a German instrument for weakening the unity of the Polish community and a lever to bring about collaboration with the Germans." . . .

It is not known how many Poles actually aided Jews during the German occupation. For that reason, glib generalizations on the subject must be suspect. What is known, however, is that after the Germans ordered the Jews to live in ghettos, and especially after they unleashed the so-called "Final Solution," Poles increasingly responded to the Jewish plight not only as an expression of pity for the Jews but also as an action of resistance against the hated Germans. Poles of all classes gave a variety of assistance to the persecuted Jews; food, shelter, and false documents were some of the more common types of aid. Considering the utter barbarity of German rule in Poland and the continuing persecution of the Poles by the Germans, it is remarkable that so many Poles were involved in the aid efforts. The wonder is not how few but how many Jews were saved in Poland during the German occupation.

Jewish leaders at the time made clear their praise for those Poles who fought against anti-Semitism and extended aid to the Jews. The Jewish Bund, which had especially close ties with the Polish socialists, denied charges of widespread anti-Semitism among the Poles by commenting on how a majority of Polish people — workers and peasants — resisted anti-Semitic propaganda. Szmul Zygielbojm, a respected Jewish member of the Polish National Council in London, gave a speech to the council, during which he read a statement from one of his kinsmen in Poland: "The Polish people showed the Jews much sympathy and gave considerable help in all these events." In the introduction to a pamphlet entitled *Stop Them Now: German Mass-Murders of Jews in Poland*, published in 1942, Zygielbojm wrote: "I must mention here that the Polish population gives all possible help and sympathy to the Jews. . . . The walls of the ghetto have not really separated the Jewish population from the Poles. The Polish and Jewish masses continue to fight together for common aims, just as they have fought for so many years in the past." His colleague in the Polish National Council, Schwarzbart, initiated a motion in the council in 1943 which praised Polish efforts to help save Jews and urged the Poles to continue their efforts. Adolf Berman, who was an important link between the Jewish and Polish underground, eloquently declared later: "Accounts of the martyrdom of Poland's Jews tend to emphasize their suffering at the hands of blackmailers and informers, the 'blue' police and other scum. Less is written, on the other hand, about the thousands of Poles who risked their lives to save the Jews. The flotsam and jetsam on the surface of a turbulent river is more visible than the pure stream running deep underneath, but that stream existed."

Even Emmanuel Ringelblum, who often caustically criticized the Poles for not doing enough to help his kinsmen, said: "There are thousands [of idealists] like these in Warsaw and the whole country. . . . The names of the people who do this, and whom the Poland which shall be established should decorate with the 'Order of Humanitarianism,' will remain in our memory as the names of heroes who saved thousands of human beings from certain death by fighting against the greatest enemy the human race has ever known." His own journal entries at the time confirm how Poles drew closer to the Jews after the September campaign. On September 9, 1940, he recorded how Poles voluntarily taxed themselves for Jewish causes. A month later, he noted "frequent occurrences where Christians take the side of Jews against attacks by hoodlums. That wasn't so before the war." About the same time, he wrote how he "heard many stories" of Polish customers who sent packages to Jewish merchants confined in the Lódź Ghetto. On November 19, 1940, he made this diary entry: "A Christian was killed today . . . for throwing a sack of bread over the wall." In May 1941, he recorded how "Catholics displayed a far-reaching tolerance" and how a Passover program "evoked great respect among the Polish populace." And on July 11, 1941, he wrote: "This was a widespread phenomenon a month ago. Hundreds of beggars, including women and children, smuggled themselves out of the Ghetto to beg on the Other Side, where they were well received, well fed, and often given food to take back to the Ghetto with them. Although universally recognized as Jews from the Ghetto, perhaps they were given alms for that very reason. This was an interesting symptom of a deep transformation in Polish society." In the latter part of 1942, Ringelblum recorded: "Polish organizations combatted and did away with blackmail."

Adam Czerniaków, who headed the Warsaw *Judenrat* until his suicide in 1942, also kept a diary which reflected Polish sympathy for the Jews. On January 29, 1942, he revealed that a Polish Christian had financed repairs on one of the synagogues in the ghetto. On July 18, 1942, he recorded that a young Polish girl had been hiding a Jewish woman in her home. Even extremely critical accounts of Poles by Jews who experienced the German occupation of Poland point up the complexity of Polish-Jewish wartime relations and the difficulty of making generalizations on the subject.

In October, 1942, the *Rzeczpospolita Polska* claimed with some justification that Polish aid to the Jews was so conspicuous and spontaneous that the Germans felt compelled to order the imposition of the death penalty on all Poles who helped Jews, a sentence which was not typical of Nazi policy elsewhere in Europe. And the fact that the Germans continually repeated warnings to the Poles that they would be executed for helping Jews suggests that Polish people ignored the risks and continued to aid them.

Perhaps the best evidence of the response of Poles to the plight of the Jews is revealed by the large number of Polish anti-Semites who, in Ringelblum's words, "grasped that . . . the Poles and Jews had a common enemy and that the Jews were excellent allies who would do all they possibly could to bring destruction on the Jews' greatest enemies." Even unreconstructed anti-Semites who had Jewish relatives helped them. "Polish anti-Semites did not apply racialism where relatives or friends were concerned," Ringelblum admitted. Many anti-Semitic Poles disliked Jews as abstractions. Once they got to know Jews, they had no personal animosity toward them and even developed genuine affection for them. Thus the truth of the old Polish maxim was confirmed: "Every Pole has his Jew." . . .

Poles who dared aid a Jew assumed risks that were largely unknown to western Europeans. As has been pointed out, the Poles automatically risked death. Since rescuing a Jew usually meant that more than one individual was involved in the effort, apprehension by the Germans often meant the execution of entire families or circles of people. A Polish historian estimated that to hide one Jew the cooperation of about ten people was required. Based on testimonies made to me, I conclude that sometimes the number was even more than that. The Germans, in their zealous efforts to uncover Jews, constantly warned the Poles of retribution for hiding them and held committees responsible in each apartment complex for ferreting them out. It was not unusual for Jews to leave the home of their Polish protectors for fear of jeopardizing their lives; sometimes they chose suicide.

Occasionally, there were Poles who hid a number of Jews and were reluctant for obvious reasons to take in any more but were forced to do so under the threat of blackmail from those who desperately needed shelter. The dangers were so great for the Poles that even the Polish Socialists were reluctant to aid their friends and colleagues in the ghetto. Poles were understandably reluctant to enter the Warsaw Ghetto, because it was not uncommon for them to be mistreated or even shot, even though they had legal passes. Thus to save a Jew in the conditions in Poland at that time represented the highest degree of heroism.

Since the Poles had experienced progressive pauperization during the German occupation and lived in conditions of bare subsistence, most Poles could not offer assistance to Jewish refugees even if they wanted to. Therefore, when Jews gave money to Poles to keep them, it was not out of greed but out of poverty that it was accepted. "There are poor families who base their subsistence on the funds paid daily by the Jews to their Aryan landlords," Ringelblum wrote. "But is there enough money in the world to make up for the constant fear of exposure, fear of the neighbors, the porter and the manager of the block of flats, etc.?"

One of the chief obstacles in rescuing Jews was the fact that the overwhelming majority of them were unassimilated. They did not know the Polish language, had few if any Polish friends, wore distinctive dress, and had been brought up in a pacifist tradition. Wladyslawa Homsowa, who played an active role in saving Jews in the Lwów area, declared, "The greatest difficulty was the passivity of the Jews themselves."

Prewar separation of the Polish and Jewish communities, along with earlier mutual animosities, sometimes got in the way of developing close relationships during the war. As one former Polish underground soldier remarked, "Before the war, they called me *goy, goy!* Now they wanted my help." He added, "Poles helped Jews, but do you realize how difficult it was to save a person who obviously looked Semitic? They had to be hidden all the time, because if they dared to venture out the Germans would pounce on them."

According to one recent sociological study of rescuers throughout occupied Europe, people who knew Jews before the war were more likely to help them than if the Jew was a stranger: "In many cases, perhaps over 75 [percent], the rescued individuals reported that they were saved by some one whom they personally knew or by members of their respective families who knew each other." In the case of Poland, it is important to understand that early in the war much of the Jewish intelligentsia, the most assimilated class of Polish Jews, had been executed along with their Polish counterparts. The Jews who remained came, for the most part, from the lower classes, were unassimilated, and had the fewest contacts with Polish Gentiles.

Finally, there was the enormous number of problems and difficulties involved in hiding a Jew — how to supply food, provide decent sanitary conditions, assure the person's security. It was difficult enough to provide these things for one refugee, let alone twenty-six Jews as Feliks Cywiński did:

> *In a flat where Jews were hiding, suitable hiding places had to be secured. Sometimes, we would set up a new wall in one of the rooms — so that people could hide behind it in case of danger; then I brought bricks home in my briefcase — not more than four at a time lest the neighbours suspect something; in the same way I brought lime and sand; other times we would conceal the last room in a large flat by covering the door with a wardrobe with a movable back wall.*
>
> *The most difficult task was to procure food. Twenty-six people is quite a lot! Food had to be brought in small quantities so that no one should wonder why a single person needed so much food. I carried it in my briefcase, in small parcels, in pockets. In one day, I had to bring successive portions many times. The purchase and transport of food consumed much of my time.*
>
> *Once it turned out that one of the women became ill. Later, the others got typhus. I contacted Dr. Ian Mocallo and asked him for assistance. The doctor came every day; he brought medicaments. Unfortunately, one of the women died. This is hard to understand today — but her death made the chances of survival very doubtful for all of us: the people under my care and myself who was giving help to Jews. We had no other way but to tie up the woman's corpse, put it in a sack and thus carry it out as a parcel containing food or, say, papers. One of my friends drove up with a car; we crammed the body into the car and started towards the Jewish cemetery. I feared all the way that*

> we might be stopped by a German patrol suspecting that the big parcel
> contained smuggled food. We reached the cemetery without any trou-
> ble, though. I attached a piece of paper to the sack with the name of
> the deceased and we threw the body over the wall. There was nothing
> more we could do.

One Polish peasant, who had saved many Jews, remarked candidly
that the penalty for hiding one or ten Jews, was the same: death. He
bluntly added, "The only difference being that it was harder to feed
so many and clean away after them."

As Jewish refugees themselves have observed, it was more difficult to hide Jewish people in the countryside than in towns and cities
because everyone knew one another, and any unusual thing — such
as large purchases of food by a Pole — could give away the rescuer to
an informer or to a loquacious friend whose remarks sometimes
found their way back to the police. There were, of course, other
major problems that made it difficult to hide a Jew — German house
searches for grain and cattle not delivered by the peasant under the
enforced quota system, frequent pacification operations by German
police and regular troops, periodic roundups of young Poles trying to
avoid deportation to forced labor in Germany.

Although this discussion has dwelt on Poles who provided Jews
with shelter and security, there were thousands of Polish humanitarians who did a plethora of lesser but no less risky things that aided the
Jews — smuggling food into the ghettos, conveying warnings about
the death camps, providing false documents to enable especially
non-Semitic-looking Jews to pass for Gentiles. . . .

The Poles were unique among the people under German
occupation to form an underground organization which specifically
aided Jews. In late September 1942, Zofia Kossak, chairman of the
Front for Reborn Poland, and Wanda Krahelska-Filipowicz, an
activist in the Socialist Party, had a major role in forming the Provisional Committee for Assistance to the Jews. During its brief existence, the committee helped hundreds of Jews in the Warsaw area.
Three months later, it was replaced by the Council for Aid to Jews
(*Rada Pomocy Żydom*), or Żegota, a cryptonym derived from the Polish word for Jew, Żyd. . . .

Żegota carried out an impressive program of aid that webbed the
entire country. It was involved in trying to find shelter, provide food
and medical assistance, and give proper documents to Jews under its

care. It also carried out an active campaign against blackmailers, informers, and the anti-Semitic propaganda of the Nazis. Żegota never seemed to lack for personnel, including members of the AK, in its activities.

One of the most critical aspects of Żegota's activities was the forging of documents which Jewish refugees needed. Using the printing presses of the Democratic Party, Żegota produced in time an average of 100 forged documents every day. In less than two years, Żegota was responsible for making available 50,000 documents, 80 percent of which reached Jews without any cost to them. . . .

German determination to kill the Jews with the apparatus of terror at their disposal was still the dominant factor that Jews themselves recognized in limiting Jewish survival. As top Jewish leaders of the Jewish underground told Jan Karski, a Polish emissary who in 1942 gave an eyewitness account to western statesmen concerning the plight of the Jews: "We want you to tell the Polish government, the Allied governments and great leaders of the Allies that we are helpless in the face of the German criminals. We cannot defend ourselves, and no one in Poland can defend us. The Polish underground authorities can save some of us, but they cannot save the masses. . . . We are being systematically murdered. . . . Our entire people will be destroyed. . . . This cannot be prevented by any force in Poland, neither the Polish nor the Jewish Underground. Place this responsibility on the shoulders of the Allies." Dr. Emmanuel Scherer, who represented the Bund on the Polish National Council after the suicide of Zygielbojm, echoed the same sentiments: "I fully realize that the main part of the work is beyond the limited possibilities of the Polish state." Żegota officials recognized this and called for a general international effort to help save the remnants of European Jewry in 1943. "The needs are enormous," Żegota declared. But there was, as is well known, no international action along the lines Żegota suggested.

Most of the Jews who survived the German occupation of Poland were saved by Poles who were not connected with Żegota. Recent estimates of the number of Jewish survivors range from 40,000–50,000 to 100,000–120,000, though one estimate of the Polish underground at the time placed the figure at 200,000. Tadeusz Bednarczyk, who was active in the Polish underground and had close contact with the Warsaw Ghetto, estimated that 300,000 Jews survived the Nazis in Poland. Władysław Zarski-Zajdler stated that at one point during the German occupation there were as many as 450,000 Jews sheltered by Poles, but not all of them survived the war. As for Warsaw itself, it is speculated that there were 15,000 to 30,000 Jews hiding in Warsaw during the period 1942–1944 and that 4,000 of them were beneficiaries of the work of Żegota. Żegota officials boasted aiding 40,000 to 50,000 Jews throughout Poland. As this study has suggested, it was the degree of Nazi control over Poland, not anti-Semitism, which was the decisive factor in influencing the number of Jews who survived the war. The Netherlands, which had few Jews and less anti-Semitism than Poland, experienced about the same percentage of Jewish losses as Poland. On the other hand, Romania, which had an anti-Semitic history, had a relatively low rate of Jewish losses.

It is equally difficult to draw precise conclusions concerning the number of Poles actively involved in aiding Jews. Ringelblum estimated that in Warsaw alone 40,000 to 60,000 Poles were involved in hiding Jews. As Polish scholar Wladyslaw Bartoszewski has pointed out, however, there were thousands of Poles who had been engaged in aiding Jews but, despite their best efforts, had been unable to save them. These people are not included in Ringelblum's guess. He estimates that "at least several hundred thousand Poles of either sex and of various ages participated in various ways and form in the rescue action." More recent research on the subject suggests that 1,000,000 Poles were involved in sheltering Jews, but some authors are inclined to go as high as 3,000,000. Thus a significant minority of Poles helped the Jews during the German occupation. Poles were no different from western Europeans, where only minorities — in much less threatening circumstances — aided Jewish refugees. The Polish record of aid to Jews was better than many Eastern Europeans — Romanians, Ukrainians, Lithuanians, Latvians — and, as Jewish historian Walter Laqueur has stated, "a comparison with France would be by no means unfavorable for Poland." . . . Estimates of the number of Poles who perished for aiding Jews run the gamut from a few thousand to 50,000. . . .

One of the most controversial aspects of Polish-Jewish relations during World War II concerns the role of the AK prior to and during the Warsaw Ghetto uprising in April 1943. Prevailing historiography depicts the AK as a nest of anti-Semites reluctant to help the Jews and implies that had the AK given substantial assistance to them, the outcome of the struggle would have been different. As has been seen, the AK was a large umbrella organization housing numerous military organizations, reflecting, in political terms, a variety of attitudes. The extreme right-wing anti-Semites, the NSZ[1], were not members of the AK during the greater part of the war. The leadership of the AK, like the Polish government in London, was not anti-Semitic, and its decisions concerning the Jews of the Warsaw Ghetto were influenced by considerations that, unfortunately, have not been given the emphasis they deserve. . . .

In comparison to the existing supply of arms in the AK, the amount of arms and ammunition given by the AK to the ZOB was small. In the city of Warsaw, the AK had immediately prior to the Ghetto Uprising 25 heavy machine guns, 62 light machine guns, 1,182 rifles, 1,099 pistols, and 51 submachine guns. But the AK had only a few anti-tank rifles and anti-tank guns in its arsenal in Warsaw, and these were the types of weapons the Jews needed in order to prolong their struggle. Even Schwarzbart saw clearly that it was not merely a matter of giving the Jewish resistance more weapons. The critical problem for the Jews and the AK was the lack of heavy arms: "It is obvious that whatever the quantity of arms at their disposal, the Jewish fighters were doomed to be defeated eventually by the formidable war machine of the Germans. The only thing which could have been achieved by the possession of more and particularly of heavy arms would have been the inflicting of greater losses upon the German forces in the ghetto."

It would have been unreasonable to have expected the AK to divest itself entirely of these few heavy weapons that it would obviously need for launching the long-planned general uprising when the Germans were at the point of military collapse. To be sure, the Poles could have given more pistols and rifles to the Jews, but smaller weapons of this type would not have altered the military situation in Jewish favor against the Germans. Moreover, it is not entirely clear how many of these guns were the personal weapons of members of the AK who, like soldiers anywhere, would have been reluctant to part with them. . . .

---

[1]"National Armed Forces," an extreme right-wing faction of the Polish underground. — Ed.

At no time did responsible Jewish leaders of the Warsaw Ghetto except perhaps Anielewicz, expect the AK to squander its strength and join the Jews in a suicidal uprising. Nor did they have the right to do so. . . . [A]ny uprising by the AK at the time would have been "pointless." This view was obviously shared by Sikorski, because as Poland's commander in chief he did not order major AK involvement in the Jewish insurgency. The only reasonable option open to the AK was to initiate diversionary attacks when the Jewish uprising began. Before the uprising began, the AK apprised the Jews of what it would do in this regard. To have attempted to do anything more would have unnecessarily eroded AK strength, depriving it of the men and resources they needed to take power in Poland at the time of German military collapse and before the Soviets took possession of the country. After all, the purpose of the Polish underground was not only to engage in anti-German conspiracy but also to help the Polish people survive the occupation into the postwar era. . . .

The word Holocaust suggests to most people the tragedy the Jews experienced under the Germans during World War II. From a psychological point of view, it is understandable why Jews today prefer that the term refer exclusively to the Jewish experience, thus emphasizing the distinctiveness of the wartime fate of the Jews. Yet, by excluding others from inclusion in the Holocaust, the horrors that Poles, other Slavs, and Gypsies endured at the hands of the Nazis are often ignored, if not forgotten.

From a historical point of view, no reasonable student of World War II can deny that Hitler's policy toward the Poles was also genocidal and that about as many Polish Christians as Polish Jews died as a result of Nazi terror. Without detracting from the particularity of the Jewish tragedy in which all Jews were victimized because they were Jews, it is time to speak about the forgotten Holocausts of World War II. By failing to broaden the scope of research on the Holocaust, we have allowed our perspective on it to become distorted, and this has led to simplistic and false conclusions about the subject. . . .

If novelists and publicists perpetuate distortions of the Poles and their history, one would at least hope for better in the writings of historians. Unfortunately, it is disquieting to read most writings on the Holocaust, because the subject of Polish-Jewish relations is treated so polemically. Preoccupied with the overwhelming tragedy of the Jews,

Jewish historians, who are the major writers on the subject, rarely if ever attempt to qualify their condemnations of the Poles and their defense of the Jews. The result is tendentious writing that is often more reminiscent of propaganda than of history. Despite the scholarly pretensions of many of these works — and there is genuine scholarship in some of these books — they have contributed little to a better understanding of the complexity and paradox of Polish-Jewish wartime relations.

If a more objective and balanced view prevailed in the historiography on the Holocaust, there would be less said about Polish anti-Semitism and more about the problems that faced the Poles and their military and political leadership in dealing with the Germans. If the magnitude of the Polish tragedy were objectively presented, unrealistic and unhistorical judgments about the possibilities and opportunities available to the Poles to render greater aid than they did to the Jews would not be made.

Ian Kershaw

The German People and Genocide

The fate of Bavarian Jews after "Crystal Night" mirrors closely that of Jews from other parts of the Reich. By the beginning of the war, following the massively accelerated emigration after the pogrom, some 10,000 Jews — less than a third of the Jewish population of 1933 — remained in Bavaria (excluding the Palatinate). The social isolation of these Jews was all but completed during the first war years. The physical presence of the Jew in the countryside or in small towns was now — except for certain parts of Swabia and Lower Franconia — largely a memory of the past, as the persecuted outcasts found their way to the slightly greater security of Jewish com-

© Ian Kershaw 1983. Reprinted from *Popular Opinion and Political Dissent in the Third Reich* by Ian Kershaw (1983) by permission of Oxford University Press.

munities in the big cities of Munich, Nuremberg, Augsburg, and Würzburg. Following the law of 30 April 1939, preventing Jews and non-Jews from living in the same tenement blocks, the social isolation was increased by the creation of "Jew houses" and the formation of ghettos in the large cities. Munich provides an example of what was happening. Between May and December 1939 some 900 Jewish dwellings were confiscated, the best of which were given over to Party functionaries, civil servants, or officers. At the start of the war, the city's Jews (numbering about 4,000) had to make room in their increasingly cramped accommodation for several hundred Jews moved to Munich from Baden. From 1939, too, Munich's Jews, like Jews elsewhere, were compelled to perform hard labour in a variety of degrading jobs, frequently as quasi-slave work-parties in armaments factories. By early 1941 many were put to work constructing ghetto barracks for the "Jewish settlement" in the north of the city. By October that year the barracks were accommodating 412 of Munich's Jews, eventually holding 1,376 persons although it was only meant to house a maximum of 1,100. The Milbertshofen Jewish settlement served from November 1941 as a collecting point for the deportation of Munich's Jews to the death-camps of the east.

The depiction of Jews as the pariahs of the "National Community" found its symbolic expression in the introduction of the compulsory wearing of the yellow "Star of David" in September 1941. Only the actual physical removal of the Jews from the sight of Germans now remained. This was not long delayed. The first deportations of 1,820 Jews to Riga from collection points in Munich, Nuremberg, and Würzburg took place in late November 1941. In Spring 1942 further deportations of almost 3,000 Jews to the Lublin area of Poland followed, and during the remainder of 1942 and the first half of 1943 another three-and-a-half thousand Jews were transported to Auschwitz and (the larger majority) to Theresienstadt. In all, 8,376 Jews were deported from Bavaria, almost all of them by September 1943. Their fate in the camps of the east merged with that of the other Jewish victims of the Nazis from within and outside Germany. Those deported to Riga were most likely among the vast numbers shot by the *Einsatzkommandos* of the *Sicherheitspolizei* between February and August 1942; those sent to Lublin probably perished in the gas-chambers of Sobibor and Belzec; very few survived the war. The post-war Jewish communities in Bavaria (numbering 5,017 Jews in 1971) have no direct line of continuity with the historic communities extinguished by Nazi terror.

How did the Bavarian population, which as we have seen was capable in the war years of significant expressions of popular feeling and opposition to Nazi measures, react to the persecution and deportation of the Jews? What did they know of the horrors taking place in the occupied territories of Poland and the Soviet Union?

Remarkable as it may sound, the Jewish Question was of no more than minimal interest to the vast majority of Germans during the war years in which the mass slaughter of Jews was taking place in the occupied territories. The evidence, though surviving much more thinly for the war years than for the pre-war period, allows no other conclusion.

Above all, the war seems to have encouraged a "retreat into the private sphere" as regards political opinion in general and the Jewish issue in particular. Such a retreat into concerns of private interest and welfare to the exclusion of all else in conditions of crisis and danger is neither specific to Germany nor to societies under dictatorial rule, but the level of repression and the increasingly draconian punishment for politically nonconformist behaviour enhanced this trend in the German population during the war. Under the growing pressures of war, the worries about relatives at the Front, fears about bombing raids, and the intensified strain of daily existence, great concern for or interest in a minority social group was unlikely to be high. Moreover, the Jews, a generally unloved minority, had become, as we have just seen, almost totally isolated from the rest of German society. For most people, "the Jew" was now a completely depersonalized image. The abstraction of the Jew had taken over more and more from the "real" Jew who, whatever animosity he had caused, had been a flesh-and-blood person. The depersonalization of the Jew had been the real area of success of Nazi policy and propaganda on the Jewish Question. Coupled with the inevitable concern for matters only of immediate and personal importance, mainly the routine day-to-day economic worries, and the undoubted further weakening that the war brought in questions of moral principle, it ensured that the fate of the Jews would be far from the forefront of people's minds during the war years.

During the first two years of the war mention of the Jewish

Question hardly occurs in the opinion reports of the Nazi authorities. SD informants in Bad Kissingen overheard conversations after the Polish campaign in late 1939 about the planned "settlement" of Polish, Czech, and Austrian Jews in the Lublin area "from which there would be no return," and from where it was presumed that the Jews concerned would go or be sent to Russia. This was said to have been "welcomed by Party comrades and by a great proportion of the national comrades, and suggestions were heard that the Jews who still live in Germany should also set out on their march into this territory." Such comments clearly emanated from Party circles. They are practically the sole recorded comments about the Jews from Bavarian sources during the first phase of the war. A more positive account, though from a non-Bavarian source, of a Rabbi written towards the end of 1940, went so far as to claim that the Jewish Question had become less important during the war, and that anti-Jewish feeling among the ordinary population had declined. He pointed to the active clandestine help which thousands of Jews living in their ghetto-like conditions still received daily from ordinary Germans.

Whether or not this account was over-generous to the state of opinion towards the Jews, there is no doubt that conditions for the tiny Jewish minority deteriorated drastically following the invasion of Russia in June 1941. Apart from the introduction of the "Yellow Star" in September, a whole series of new restrictions in the autumn deprived Jews of telephones, newspapers, and ration cards for meat, milk, fish, white bread, and many other consumer items. Jewish living conditions were reduced to a level far beyond the tolerable in the same months that the first mass deportations to the east got under way. This combination of anti-Jewish measures occurred in one of the few short periods in the war when public reactions found a muted and distorted echo in the reports of the authorities.

According to a report of the Mayor of Augsburg, the decree ordering the wearing of the "Yellow Star" brought expressions of "great satisfaction among all national comrades." A ban imposed in December on Jews attending Augsburg's weekly market was, it was claimed, equally welcomed. Similar reactions to the introduction of the "Yellow Star" were recounted in the central SD report of 9 October 1941. Summarizing responses, a later SD report emphasized that the decree had met a long-cherished wish of large sections of the population, especially where Jews were numerous, and that many were critical of the exceptions made for Jewish wives of "aryans,"saying this was not more than a "half-measure." The SD added that "for most people a radical solution of the Jewish problem finds more understanding than any compromise, and that there existed in the widest circles the wish for a clear external separation between Jewry and German national comrades." It was significant, it concluded, that the decree was not seen as a final measure, but as the signal for more incisive decrees with the aim of a final settlement of the Jewish Question. It seems difficult to accept such comments as they stand. The tone is redolent only of the overtly Nazi element of the population, and it is more than likely that the SD was in this case as in other instances repeating comments made by Party members as general popular opinion. Understandably, those critical of the measure were far less open in their comments, though the SD reports themselves point out that "isolated comments of sympathy" could be heard among the bourgeoisie and Catholics — the two groups most vociferous in their condemnation of earlier anti-Jewish measures — and "medieval methods" were spoken of. Almost certainly, those condemning the "Yellow Star" decree were in a minority, as were those openly lauding the public branding of Jews. For the majority of the population, the decree passed without comment, and very likely without much notice.

The deportations, beginning in autumn 1941, were also apparently accompanied by remarkably little attention of the non-Jewish population. Most reports fail to mention any reactions, confining their comments to a cold, factual account of the "evacuations." In one or two instances stereotyped "approval," "satisfaction," or "interest" of the local population is mentioned. The Nuremberg population was said to have "noted approvingly" the first deportations from the city on 15 November 1941, and "a great number" of Forchheim's inhabitants allegedly followed the departure of eight Jews from the town "with interest and great satisfaction." Such generalized statements of approval, skeptical though one must be of their representative value, practically exhaust the Bavarian evidence on reactions to the deportations. For the rest, the silence is evocative. The absence of registered reactions in the sources is probably not a grotesque distortion of popular attitudes. Not only intimidation but widespread indifference towards the remaining tiny Jewish minority explains the lack of involvement in their deportation. And where real interest was awakened on the part of the non-Jewish population it was less a product of human concern or moral principle than self-interest and the hope of material advantage. Such was the case when a complainant in Fürth near Nuremberg wrote to the Reich Governor of Bavaria in 1942 on behalf of the co-tenants of her apartment block protesting at the sequestration of Jewish property by the local Finance Office when so many were crying out for it. "Where is the justice and *Volksgemeinschaft* in that?" she lamented.

Such blatant self-interest existed alongside the widespread passivity and emotionless acceptance of the deportations. There can be little doubt that strong reactions would have left their mark in the reports of the authorities. Such reports contain a mass of comment critical of the regime. And at the very same time as the deportations were proceeding with minimal response from the population, the force of angry and concerned popular opinion was, as we have seen, bringing to a halt the removal of crucifixes from Bavarian schools and — of incomparably greater importance — the gassing of thousands of mentally defective persons in the "euthanasia action." Compared with the popular interest in the film *I Accuse*, which attempted a justification of euthanasia, the obnoxious "documentary" film *The Eternal Jew* was apparently badly attended. A second disguised private survey of opinion by Michael Müller-Claudius in 1942 revealed that whereas just under a third of his selected group of Party members had been indifferent or non-commital about the Jewish Question following the November pogrom of 1938, the figure was now 69 percent.

Though people often knew about the deportations before they took place, their knowledge of the fate of the Jews in the east has inevitably been the subject of much speculation and debate. Documentary evidence can hardly provide an adequate answer to the question: "how much did the Germans know?" and given the generally prevailing silence and the difficulties of interpretation only tentative suggestions can be made. Undoubtedly, however, the generalization of one historian that "people were acquainted with the ultimate fate of the deported Jews" is far too sweeping. Most people in fact probably thought little and asked less about what was happening to the Jews in the east. The Jews were out of sight and literally out of mind for most. But there is incontrovertible evidence that knowledge of atrocities and mass shootings of Jews in the east was fairly widespread, mostly in the nature of rumour brought home by soldiers on leave. If most rumour was unspecific, eye-witness accounts of shootings and also broadcasts from foreign radios provided material which was sufficiently widely circulated for Bormann to feel obliged in autumn 1942 to give new propaganda directives for countering the rumours of "very sharp measures" taken against Jews in the east. Concrete details were seldom known, but an awareness that dire things were happening to the Jews was sufficient to make people . . . worried about possible retaliatory measures of the enemy should Germany lose the war, as the Government President of Swabia pointed out in November 1942 in the light of "a further rumour about the fate of the Jews taken to the east." A month later an SD report from Middle Franconia stated:

> One of the strongest causes of unease among circles attached to the Church and in the rural population at the present time is formed by news from Russia in which shooting and extermination (Ausrottung) of the Jews is spoken about. This communication frequently leaves great anxiety, care, and worry in those sections of the population. According to widely held opinion among the rural population, it is not at all certain now that we will win the war and if the Jews come to Germany again they will exact dreadful revenge on us.

A Catholic priest in the same locality also referred directly to the extermination of the Jews in a sermon in February 1943. He was reported as saying that Jesus was descended from the Jews and that it was therefore "not right if Jewry was persecuted or exterminated (ausgerottet) since the Catholic faith was based upon the same."

It was, however, above all the attempts by Goebbels to exploit the discovery of mass graves of Polish officers at Katyn in April 1943 which suddenly cast a ray of light on knowledge among the German people of the murder of Jews in the eastern territories. The regional headquarters of the SD in Würzburg reported in mid-April:

> The thorough and detailed reportage about the murder of 12,000 Polish officers by the GPU [Soviet secret police] had a mixed reception. Especially among sections of the intelligentsia, the propaganda put out by radio and press was rejected. Such reportage was regarded as exaggerated. Among those associated with the Churches the view was put forward that it could be a matter of mass graves laid out by Germans for the murdered Polish and Russian Jews.

The Government President of Swabia also noted that, according to one report he had received, the Katyn propaganda had provoked "discussion about the treatment of the Jews in Germany and in the eastern territories." Such comments were typical of remarks being noted in many parts of Germany. According to the SD's central digest, people were saying that Germans "had no right to get worked up about this action of the Soviets because from the German side Poles and Jews have been done away with in much greater numbers." Party reports reaching Bormann spoke also of comments of clergy referring to the "terrible and inhumane treatment meted out to the Jews by the SS" and to the "blood guilt of the German people." Similar comments were heard after the uncovering at Winniza in July 1943 of mass graves of Ukrainian victims of the Russian secret police. Soon afterwards, Bormann, commissioned directly by Hitler, provided new directives about treatment of the Jewish Question, stating now that in public "all discussion of a future complete solution (*Gesamtlösung*)" had to cease, and it could only be said "that Jews had been conscripted *en bloc* for appropriate deployment of labour." The Nazi leadership was clearly aware that public feeling in Germany was not ready for frank disclosures on the extermination of the Jews.

Recorded comments about the murder of Jews refer almost invariably to mass shootings by the *Einsatzgruppen*, which in many cases were directly witnessed by members of the *Wehrmacht*. The gassing, both in mobile gas-units and then in the extermination camps, was carried out much more secretly, and found little echo inside Germany to go by the almost complete absence of documentary sources relating to it. Even so, the silence was not total. Rumours did circulate, as two cases from the Munich "Special Court" dating from 1943 and 1944 and referring to the gassing of Jews in mobile gas-vans, prove. In the first case a middle-aged Munich woman admitted having said in autumn 1943: "Do you think then that nobody listens to the foreign broadcasts? They have loaded Jewish women and children into a wagon, driven out of the town, and exterminated (*vernichtet*) them with gas." For these remarks, made to her neighbour's mother, and for derogatory comments about Hitler she was sentenced to three years in prison. In the other case, an Augsburg furniture removal man was indicted of having declared in September 1944 that the Führer was a mass-murderer who had Jews loaded into a wagon and exterminated by gas.

These appear to be the only instances in the Munich "Special Court" files which touch upon the gassing of Jews in the occupied territories. They were presumably the tip of the iceberg, but on the available evidence one can take it no further. Whether there was anything like hard information circulating about the extermination camps in Poland is again a question which cannot be satisfactorily answered on the basis of available sources. The silence of the documents on this point has to be viewed critically. One might assume that knowledge — or at very least highly suggestive rumour — of the systematic extermination of the Jews in the camps was more widely circulating than is apparent from surviving documentation. On the other hand, many people genuinely first learnt about the nature and purpose of the camps in the horrifying disclosures at the Nuremberg Trials. It is quite likely, in fact, that there were differences in the degree of knowledge or surmise between the eastern regions bordering on Poland and areas in the west and south of the Reich. At any rate, according to a report of the *Gauleitung* of Upper Silesia in May 1943, following the Katyn disclosures, the Polish resistance movement had daubed up the slogan "Russia-Katyn, Germany-Auschwitz" in public places of the industrial region of Upper Silesia. "The concentration camp Auschwitz, generally known in the east, is meant," added the report. An exhaustive search of the extensive Bavarian materials, on the other hand, reveals no mention of the name Auschwitz, or of the name of any other extermination camp in the east. There was some knowledge of the camps among leading members of the group which plotted the attempt on Hitler's life in 1944 and among Church leaders, and the extent of auxiliary services to the camps meant that total secrecy was a practical impossibility. The extent of knowledge will never be known. The judicious, if inconclusive, assessment of one historian that "it may be doubted . . . whether even rumours of Auschwitz as a Jewish extermination centre had circulated widely throughout Germany — and if they had, whether they were believed," is probably as far as one can take it.

All the evidence points towards the conclusion that for the people of Bavaria, as for the German population as a whole, the Jewish Question was hardly a central topic of concern during the war years. And most of what few comments survive from this period touch mainly upon the imagined connection between the persecution of the Jews and the war itself. A Munich waiter, for instance, was denounced for allegedly having said in May 1940 with typically Bavarian finesse: "If they had left the Jews here and not chucked them out this bloody war would not have happened." A hairdresser, also from Munich, sentenced to four years in a penitentiary for repeatedly "malicious, hateful, agitatory, and base-minded comments" about Führer, Party, and State in spring 1942 was said to have called Hitler "a crazy mass-murderer" and blamed him for the war "because if he had left the Catholic Church and the Jews alone things would not have come to this pitch." She added for good measure "that she preferred Jewish women as customers to the wives of the SS men. In the course of time she had become sick to death of the latter." A number of comments betray the fact that many people regarded the allied bombing-raids as revenge and retaliation for the treatment of the Jews. A labourer in Weissenburg was condemned by the Munich "Special Court" to eighteen months in prison for allegedly saying:

> You will see alright. Weissenburg will have to put up with the flyers in good measure. The English haven't forgotten that so many from Weissenburg were in Dachau. In fact there were hardly any others in Dachau apart from those from Weissenburg. If only they had let the Jews go. They don't fly into the bishopric [of Eichstätt] because they [the people of Eichstätt] haven't done anything.

In Lower Franconia, too, comments could be heard in the summer of 1943 relating the allied terror-bombing to retaliation for the November pogrom of 1938. People were asking whether the Jews would return to their former homes if Germany lost the war and pointed to the absence of air-raids on "outright Jewish cities" like Fürth and Frankfurt. The raids on Schweinfurt gave the inhabitants of Bad Brückenau renewed occasion in May 1944 to relate the bombing to Nazi anti-Jewish policies. Contrasts were drawn with the handling of the Jewish Question in Hungary, whose government had not followed the Nazi pattern of persecution of the Jews until March 1944:

> Many national comrades are of the opinion that the Jewish Question has been solved by us in the most clumsy way possible. They say quite openly that Hungary has learnt from our failure in this matter. And certainly our cities would still be intact if we had only brought the Jews together in ghettos. In that way we would have today a very effective means of threat and counter-measure at our disposal.

Similar sentiments also found expression in the files of unbelievably inhumane letters sent to Goebbels from all over Germany, themselves a witness of the success of years of propaganda, suggesting for example that Jews should not be allowed in air-raid shelters but should be herded together in the cities threatened by bombing and the numbers of their dead published immediately after each air-raid; or that the Americans and British should be told that ten Jews would be shot for each civilian killed in a bomb-attack.

Comments about the relationship between the Jews and the war demonstrate — and . . . this was a feature of the pre-war period too — that the methods of the persecution of the Jews were often criticized at the same time as the basic principles behind the persecution were found acceptable. Furthermore, talk of "retaliatory" air-raids, or the "revenge of the Jews" descending upon Germany if the war were lost, all point unmistakably towards the traces of belief in a "Jewish World Conspiracy" theory, present before the Third Reich and massively boosted by Nazi propaganda.

The last two years of the war saw the "broad mass" of "ordinary" Germans preoccupied less than ever with the Jewish Question, despite an unceasing barrage of propaganda on the issue. By mid-1944 there were a mere 1,084 Jews left in Bavaria, in Germany as a whole fewer than 15,000. Though slogans about the Jew being the world enemy continued to be pumped into young Germans, Party propagandists reckoned that hundreds of thousands of them were now hardly in a position to know "what the Jew is." Whereas the elder generation knew "it" from their own experience, the Jew was for the young only a "museum-piece," something to look at with curiosity, "a fossil wonder-animal (*fossiles Wundertier*) with the yellow star on its breast, a witness to bygone times but not belonging to the present," something one had to journey far to see. This remarkable admission is testimony at one and the same time to the progress of abstract anti-Semitism, and to the difficulty of keeping alive the hatred of an abstraction. To be anti-Semitic in Hitler's Germany was so commonplace as to go practically unnoticed. And the hallmarks of anti-Semitic attitudes outlasted the Third Reich, to be detected in varying degrees of intensity in three-fifths of those Germans in the American Zone tested by public opinion researchers of the occupying forces in 1946.

Very many, probably most, Germans were opposed to the Jews

during the Third Reich, welcomed their exclusion from economy and society, saw them as natural outsiders to the German "National Community," a dangerous minority against whom it was legitimate to discriminate. Most would have drawn the line at physical maltreatment. The Nazi Mayor of Mainstockheim near Kitzingen in Lower Franconia no doubt spoke for many when, in preventing violence and destruction by SA and Party fanatics during the pogrom of November 1938, he reportedly said: "You don't have to have anything to do with the Jews. But you have got to leave them in peace." Such an attitude was not violent. But it was discriminatory. And such "mild" anti-Semitism was clearly quite incapable of containing the progressive radical dynamism of the racial fanatics and the deadly bureaucratization of the doctrine of race-hatred. Our examination of popular opinion on the Jewish Question has shown that in its anti-Jewish policies the Nazi regime acted not in plebiscitary fashion, but with increasing autonomy from popular opinion until the extermination policy in the east was carried out by the SS and SD as a "never to be written glorious page of our history," as Himmler put it, whose secret it was better to carry to the grave. The very secrecy of the "Final Solution" demonstrates more clearly than anything else the fact that the Nazi leadership felt it could not rely on popular backing for its extermination policy.

And yet it would be a crass over-simplification to attribute simply and solely to the criminal ideological paranoia of Hitler, Heydrich, and a few other leading personalities of the Third Reich the implementation of policies which led to the death-camps. The "Final Solution" would not have been possible without the progressive steps to exclude the Jews from German society which took place in full view of the public, in their legal form met with widespread approval, and resulted in the depersonalization and debasement of the figure of the Jew. It would not have been possible without the apathy and widespread indifference which was the common response to the propaganda of hate. And it would not have been possible, finally, without the silence of the Church hierarchies, who failed to articulate what opposition there was to Nazi racial policies, and without the consent ranging to active complicity of other prominent sections of the German élites — the civil service bureaucracy, the armed forces, and not least leading sectors of industry. Ultimately, therefore, dynamic hatred of the masses was unnecessary. Their latent anti-Semitism and apathy sufficed to allow the increasingly criminal "dynamic" hatred of the Nazi regime the autonomy it needed to set in motion the Holocaust.

Michael R. Marrus and Robert O. Paxton

Western Europeans and the Jews

Nazi policy toward the Jews of occupied western Europe evolved in three phases, determined by far-flung strategic concerns of the Third Reich. In the first, from the outbreak of war in the west in April 1940 until the autumn of 1941, all was provisional: Nazi leaders looked forward to a "final solution of the Jewish question in Europe," but that final solution was to await the cessation of hostilities and an ultimate peace settlement. No one defined the Final Solution with precision, but all signs pointed toward some vast and as yet unspecified project of mass emigration. When the war was over, the Jews would leave Europe and the question would be resolved. Until that time the various German occupation authorities would pursue anti-Jewish objectives by controlling the movements and organizations of Jews, confiscating their property, enumerating them, and sometimes concentrating them in certain regions. Throughout this phase, the circumstances of Jews varied importantly according to various occupation arrangements worked out by Germany following the spectacular blitzkrieg of 1940.

In the second phase, from the autumn of 1941 until the summer of 1942, Hitler drew implications from a gradually faltering campaign in Russia: the war was to last longer than he had planned, and the increasingly desperate struggle against the Bolsheviks prompted

Excerpted from Michael R. Marrus and Robert O. Paxton, "The Nazis and the Jews in Occupied Western Europe, 1940–1944," *Journal of Modern History*, 54:4 (1982), pp. 687–714. Copyright © 1982 by the University of Chicago Press. Reprinted by permission.

a revision of the previous timetable and general approach to the Jewish problem. Now Nazi leaders were told to prepare for the Final
Solution itself, which could not be postponed. The Jewish question
had to be solved quickly, *before* the end of the war. Nazi Jewish
experts soon adopted the new rhythm, and began urgent preparations. Henceforth, mass resettlement was taken to be impractical,
and Jewish emigration was indeed forbidden. By the end of 1941, in a
dramatic reversal of policy, Jews were no longer permitted to leave
German-controlled Europe. With the exception of Norway and Denmark, where the numbers of Jews were unimportant, the Jews were
subjected to a concerted series of new harassments, beginning with
segregation by means of a yellow star. More Jews were interned in
camps, made ready for deportation to the east.

The third phase began in the summer of 1942, and continued to
the end of the war in the west. . . .

The Final Solution was launched in the west in the summer of
1942, at a high point in the history of Hitler's continental empire.
But one should not assume from the outstanding fact of German
hegemony from the Atlantic to the outskirts of Moscow and Stalingrad that the Nazis had unlimited power everywhere in Europe. On
the contrary, German forces were stretched thin, and nowhere more
so than in western Europe. There were enormous new demands upon
German manpower. After the blitzkrieg stalled in Russia at the end
of 1941, Hitler ordered a transformation of the wartime economy of
the Reich, building for a longer war which would require a vastly
greater production of arms and equipment. Together with increasing
calls for men by the armed forces, this meant a growing reliance upon
foreign workers in Germany. By the end of 1941 there were close to 4
million of these, eventually to reach more than 7 million by
mid-1944 — 20 percent of the German work force — when 7 million
more were working in their own countries for the German war effort.
Despite this heavy reliance on foreign labor, there were few Nazi
police and troops available in the west to handle the deportations of
Jews. Without the extensive cooperation of indigenous police forces
and other officials, the Germans were therefore incapable of realizing
their plans for the murder of west European Jews.

Help came easily to the Nazis during the early stages of deportation. Participation by the Belgian police was extremely limited, but
both the French and the Dutch police rounded up Jews, held them

in camps, and saw the convoys off to the east. Frequently, the mere presence of the local gendarmerie helped lull the Jews who were taken away; certainly, their participation reduced apprehensions among the surrounding population by making the arrests seem as normal as possible. In addition to the police, who were the most directly involved, there were countless others — prefects and their subordinates, judicial officials, mayors, railwaymen, concierges — who had a part to play. The French government at Vichy authorized their involvement, and indeed welcomed a situation in which French and not German personnel exercised authority in the country. In Belgium and Holland the captive administrations, with each ministry headed by a secretary-general, carried on in a similar fashion, although municipal officials in Brussels took a clear stand against persecution after the yellow star was imposed in June. In all west European states there were local, homegrown fascists to join domestic or German police from the beginning in rounding up Jews — Jacques Doriot's Parti Populaire Français in France, Rexist and Flemish bands in Belgium, Anton Mussert's National Socialist movement in the Netherlands, and Quisling's Nasjonal Samling in Norway.

Such collaboration, especially that of ordinary officials who were not particularly sympathetic to nazism, reflected in part the momentum generated by two years of working with the Germans. During these two years officials had acquired the habits of a new chain of command, sometimes involving unpleasant tasks. Many could not conceive deporting Jews in any other context. Collaboration also reflected the disposition on the part of local authorities to view refugees harshly, particularly Jewish refugees. Since the Germans encouraged the rounding up of foreign Jews at the start, many bureaucrats lent a hand to what might simply be considered a long-standing national effort to rid their countries of unwanted outsiders. The proportion of foreign Jews was by far the highest in Belgium, where only 6.5 percent of the over 57,000 Jews enumerated by the Gestapo had Belgian citizenship. About half of the 350,000 Jews in France were noncitizens, as were 19 percent of Denmark's 8,000 Jews, and almost 16 percent of Holland's 140,000. In this regard, French authorities outdid any in Europe except the Bulgarians and possibly the Slovaks, by actually volunteering to hand over such unwanted Jews from *un*occupied territory.

Collaboration was never complete, and in France, Belgium, and the Netherlands various officials showed signs of reluctance by the beginning of 1943. Only in Norway did this not pose a serious problem. There were almost twice as many German police in that country (3,300) than there were Jews, and so even when some of Quisling's men turned unreliable for the deportations, it was possible to send more than a quarter of the Jews from the port of Bergen to Auschwitz by the end of 1942. Proportionately, deportations went furthest in Belgium during the first three months of convoys, when close to 30 percent of the Jews were taken from that country. Yet many Jews fled successfully from Belgium into France or Switzerland, found hiding places provided by non-Jews, or procured false identity papers with which they could evade capture. Already in December 1942 Martin Luther was pressing for the inclusion of Belgian citizens, a sign that all was not quite going in Belgium as he had hoped. Thanks to the intervention of von Falkenhausen, responding to local appeals, Belgian citizens were not deported for about a year. In September 1943, when the first and only mass roundup of Jews of Belgian nationality occurred, there was once again a loud protest, and General Reeder ordered their release from the assembly camp of Malines. Once native French Jews were included in the shipments, the police in France proved less and less reliable; much the same was true in the Netherlands. Of course, the Germans were able to continue their work despite these problems with local authorities. Yet the job required more German effort than at the beginning, and the momentum of the first months of the Final Solution in the west could not be sustained.

The Germans encountered a very serious obstacle in 1943 owing to the position of the Italian government. Anti-Semitism had never struck deep roots among the Italian people, or even the Fascist Party, which had considerable Jewish support and membership during the 1920s and early 1930s. Mussolini himself did not particularly like Jews, but shared the indifference of most of his countrymen to a "problem" which did not exist in their society. In 1938, to bring Italy into ideological tune with the Reich, Mussolini opportunistically adopted a racist posture, and issued laws against the 50,000 Italian Jews. But persecution was mild in comparison with the Hitlerian version, involved many exceptions, and did not have the enthusiastic support of the Italian population. When in November 1942, in response to the Allied landings in North Africa, the Germans swept south across the demarcation line in France, the Italians moved west to the Rhone River and occupied eight French departments. To the Nazis it was bad enough that the duce had seemed unwilling to contribute his Jews to the contingents deported from western Europe since the summer of 1942; by the beginning of 1943 it became apparent that the Italians were also shielding French Jews as well. The Italian troops shared much of the anti-German sentiment of the increasingly war-weary Italian population, and in this climate the idea of a racialist crusade on behalf of Aryan civilization seemed even more alien and absurd than before. Italian occupation officers not only refused to turn Jews over to Vichy or the Germans, they also blocked the application of French anti-Semitic legislation. As with their occupation policy for Croatia and part of Greece, the Italians held firm, and by one means or another resisted every effort to bring them into line. Ribbentrop failed to convince Mussolini to change his policy when he visited Rome in March 1943, and the SS ground their teeth over the obstruction they encountered. The Italian zone of France became a haven for some 50,000 Jews, protected by *carabinieri* against both the Germans and the French police.

Unfortunately, this protection was not to last. It continued after the fall of Mussolini in July 1943, but could not survive the surrender of Italy to the Allies early in the autumn. The Italians evacuated their zone of France suddenly when the armistice was announced prematurely on September 8, too quickly to implement an evacuation scheme which had been negotiated by an Italian Jew, Angelo Donati. As the Italians left, the Germans moved in, and the Jews were caught. Very few escaped, and most were sent to Auschwitz in a matter of days.

Only now did the deportation of Italian Jews begin. Despite Hitler's restoration of an Italian fascist regime, the phantom Republic of Salo, the renewed persecution and the deportation of Jews from the parts of Italy outside Allied hands was entirely a German operation. Himmler pressed for the application of the Final Solution, and neither the severe difficulties associated with the worsening war situation in the peninsula nor the widespread opposition to the deportations among Italians, and even some Germans on the spot, prevented the dispatch of more than 8,000 Jews to the east.

As in Italy, the Germans knew that the Final Solution could be extended to Denmark only through their own efforts. Anti-Semitism had flared briefly in Denmark in the wake of surrender, as elsewhere in western Europe, but the Danish political leadership, continuing in place from before the war, remained adamantly opposed to all manifestations of anti-Jewish feeling. Danish Nazis were hopelessly divided among themselves, and politically incompetent. Nazism and anti-Semitism remained unpopular. For three years the Danes collaborated economically with the Reich, in exchange for which the Germans did not interfere in internal Danish affairs. When the German representative in Copenhagen, the traditionalist Cecil von Renthe-Fink, was replaced by the former police and military administrator Werner Best in November 1942, the latter searched imaginatively for some means to move against the Jews without unduly disturbing relations with a cooperative Danish government. No real opportunities appeared, however. Even the ambitious Martin Luther at the Foreign Office, never one to neglect an opportunity for pressing forward with Jewish persecution, felt unable to recommend a change in policy.

Until the summer of 1943, therefore, the Germans left the Danes alone with their Jews. The Jewish issue suddenly came to a head, however, with the general crisis in Danish-German relations that arose in August 1943. As political and social conditions worsened dramatically throughout the country, due largely to Danish protests against mounting German exactions, the occupation imposed a state of emergency. The government of Erik Scavenius resigned, leaving internal control of Denmark in the hands of its civil service. Taking advantage of the upheaval, Ministerialdirigent Werner Best triggered the persecution of local Jews, with the object of deporting them by sea, from Copenhagen.

This operation failed utterly, as is well known, and in the end the Nazis were able to lay their hands on only 475 of the close to 8,000 Jews in Denmark. During the first week of October 1943, within a matter of days, thousands of Danes organized a rescue expedition unprecedented in the history of the Final Solution, which transferred nearly the entire community of Jews across the Sund to Sweden in small boats. In part the impotence of the Germans flowed from internal divisions among the occupation authorities. Best failed to obtain the cooperation of the Wehrmacht in Denmark because of his rivalry with its commander, General Hermann von Hannecken, who opposed the deportations, and he failed also to win full authority to seize control of the Danish civil service because he was so distrusted in Berlin, particularly by Himmler, who seems for the moment to have had other priorities in mind than the deportation of a small number of Danish Jews. But most importantly, Best failed to get the support of the Danish administration and public opinion, without which the deportation could not succeed.

The source of this failure has often been pondered by those concerned with drawing some moral lesson from the terrible events we have been considering. The most important study of the rescue, by the Israeli historian Leni Yahil, discusses several explanations, but judges the decisive factor to have been "the special character and moral stature of the Danish people and their love of democracy and freedom." Hannah Arendt saw in the Danish response an exemplary demonstration of the efficacy of nonviolent resistance to tyranny. The Nazis, she wrote in *Eichmann in Jerusalem*, changed their entire posture when faced with open native opposition. "They had met resistance based on principle, and their 'toughness' had melted like butter in the sun." While not wishing to depreciate the significance and moral import of the rescue or strategies of nonviolence, it is well to remember that the community of Jews in that country was small, that the haven of Sweden was close (between five and fifteen miles across open water), that the Swedes were willing to accept all the Jews, and that the persecutions occurred in a country already seething with opposition to nazism. These conditions greatly facilitated the rescue operation, which would, indeed, have been impossible without them.

It is also worth considering how the timing of the Nazi attempt to implement the Final Solution in Denmark differed so sharply from the other cases in western Europe we have been discussing. The attack upon the Danish Jews coincided with a sharp reversal of occupation policy which, after three years of encouraging a model protectorate, suddenly subjected the entire state to humiliating subservience and oppression. The contrast is obvious with other west European countries, where deportations of Jews followed two years of habituation to anti-Jewish laws and policies, introduced at a time of national prostration and soul-searching following an overwhelming military collapse. Defenders of Jews everywhere in Europe claimed that the Jewish fate was part of the general fate of people conquered by nazism. Unfortunately, it was not always easy to demonstrate how this was so, when the Jews were so sharply singled out. But in Denmark, as Yahil suggests, the victimization of Jews coincided exactly with a sudden political assault upon the entire Danish people.

Notably, all this happened when the Reich was in retreat, following the German defeats at El Alamein, Stalingrad, and Kursk, and the Allied landings in Italy. By the autumn of 1943, as the British and American air offensive against the Reich reached spectacular proportions, Hitler no longer seemed invincible — a sharp contrast with the beginning of the occupation in 1940, or the launching of the Final Solution in the summer of 1942. The implication is clear: because of the delay in preparing deportations in Denmark, it was easier for Danes to perceive the attack on Jews as an attack upon themselves and hence to rally to their defense; it was also morally easier to challenge the power of the Reich, which by late 1943 showed signs of its eventual collapse.

Proper timing was obviously crucial to the success of opposition to Nazi Jewish policy. On one rare occasion in western Europe public protest came too soon — the Dutch workers' strike of February 1941, in solidarity with persecuted Jews. This was the first massive, open opposition anywhere in occupied Europe to Nazi anti-Semitism. The strike was crushed by overwhelming force, and to an important degree the courageous Dutch opposition continued for years to be demoralized by the brutally effective display of German power so early in the occupation. And the strike had no effect whatever on the substance of Nazi anti-Jewish activity in Holland, except perhaps to worsen the plight of native Jews. This resistance therefore seems to have come prematurely; on the other hand, resistance more often came too late to help at all. By the latter part of 1943 the unpopularity of the deportations of Jews caused problems for the Nazis in France, Belgium, and the Netherlands, precisely at the moment when protests against the conscription of the indigenous labor force to work in the Reich made local police less reliable. But by that time it was not possible to do more than slow the deportation machinery, and even then the rescue of Jews does not seem to have ranked high for resistance strategists in selecting targets. In any event, by late 1943 the great majority of Jewish deportees were already dead.

Assessment: The Holocaust in Western Europe

The Final Solution did not succeed in western Europe because the war ended too soon and the Nazis did not have time to complete their task. Nevertheless, the scale of destruction was staggering — some 40 percent of west European Jews killed. With 105,000 deported, or 75 percent of its Jews, the Netherlands suffered the greatest losses, both in absolute and relative terms. Belgium came next, with the murder of over 24,000, more than 40 percent of its Jewish population of late May 1940. Norway lost about the same proportion — 760 Jews. In France 20 percent of the Jews — about 75,000 — were murdered. Italy lost about 8,000, or 16 percent.

What accounts for these variations? Let it be clear at the outset that these figures do not reflect any absolute measure of Nazi capability, but rather the results of a program interrupted prematurely by the military reverses suffered by the Reich in the latter part of 1944. For the Nazis' will to destroy the Jews weakened only at the end of that year, among certain top leaders, in the face of impending defeat. So what we are really considering is the relative pace of deportations from west European countries.

We hope that enough has been said to caution against relying on any single factor to explain this. A recent effort by a sociologist to isolate, quantify, and assess the significance of variables which would account for the incidence of genocide in European countries failed notably to produce a clear answer because the work ignored the evolution of German strategy and certain basic problems associated with comparison. None of these variables makes sense outside of the particular experiences of individual states. The availability of a haven to which Jews could flee, for example, was unquestionably crucial in the rescue of Danish Jews, but did not prevent the proportionately high level of destruction in Norway, despite the existence of a thousand miles of frontier with Sweden. Concentration of Jews in one place clearly could be dangerous, as in the cases of Amsterdam and also Oslo, where the Jews could easily be identified and rounded up. But concentration in the port of Copenhagen, only a few miles from freedom, helped save the Danish Jews. Without it, the rescue could not have succeeded. Sheer numbers could be important. Clearly, the Nazis felt that Denmark, with a mere 8,000 Jews, could wait for the implementation of the Final Solution, whereas France, with the largest Jewish population in the west, received a high priority. But in France, owing to the circumstances of the military defeat in 1940 and the peculiar armistice arrangement with the Germans, the Jews remained scattered across a large and, relatively speaking, sparsely settled country. In view of the thin screen of German troops and police available for the job, it is not surprising that the proportion of deported Jews from France was relatively low, despite the valuable aid given the Germans by the Vichy government.

Generalizations break apart on the stubborn particularity of each of our countries. Nowhere is this more obvious than in considering the dominant religious traditions in western European states. Catholic Italy and Protestant Denmark provide the two outstanding cases of consistent popular resistance to the persecution of the Jews. Lutheran theologians made the earliest and most forceful denunciation of anti-Semitism in Denmark, which was decidedly not the case among their coreligionists in Germany. The notable lack of public protest against Jewish deportations from the Vatican, about which there has been so much discussion, does not seem to have affected the deep antipathy toward anti-Semitism among the Italian population, including the Catholic clergy. In the Netherlands, the Catholics and the Protestant Dutch Reformed Church were about equally divided in their numbers of adherents. When they were about to issue a joint public denunciation of the deportations in the summer of 1942, the Germans threatened reprisals unless they desisted. The Synod of the Dutch Reformed Church complied, but the Catholics did not, immediately resulting in the inclusion of Catholic Jews in shipments to the gas chambers. There has been anguished discussion about this episode ever since it occurred, but it seems unlikely that one can draw from it any useful generalization about how the behavior of particular denominations might have influenced the Final Solution.

Each case was different. It makes little sense to attempt to deduce laws about victimization from an examination of so few cases, in which the degree of particularity was so high. Our conclusion is more modest. It seems plain that German policy, and also the ability of the Nazis to apply their power, were decisive in determining how far the destruction process went by the time of liberation. Nazi policy in the first phase, when the European war was going well for the Germans, was governed by pragmatic considerations. During this period some groundwork was laid for a final solution, the outlines of which remained unclear and the timing obscure. Because conditions for occupation differed, and because of the lack of urgency, the degree to which the Jews were isolated from the surrounding population differed considerably, and remained incomplete. Then, in response to the changed war situation in the east, policy changed: the Final Solution was defined, and declared a compelling necessity. The second phase involved adjustment to these new circumstances, by sometimes feverish planning and preparations. In the third phase, from the summer of 1942, the plans were implemented. For a time all went according to projection. But by 1943 serious military setbacks suffered elsewhere by the Reich took their toll: the Germans were unable to supply sufficient men and railway transport to keep up the pace of the first deportations and to finish the job quickly. Geography, administrative difficulties, conflicts among German agencies, Jewish resistance, and the actions of some west Europeans all helped to slow the process of deportation at various points. But only the outcome of the military conflict itself could have a decisive effect upon the Final Solution.

Only the defeat of the Reich brought the trains to a halt. This is especially clear when one observes how long the shipments of Jews continued. The last regular deportation from Drancy, outside of Paris, left France for Auschwitz on July 31, 1944, almost two months after the Allied landings in Normandy; two more smaller convoys followed from France, the last departing on August 17, only a week before the first tanks of General Leclerc arrived to liberate Paris. The last convoy from Belgium left Malines for Auschwitz on July 31, with 554 Jews. The last convoy from Holland went to Auschwitz on September 3, with over 1,000 Jews. Deportations from northern Italy continued the longest of all, due to the tenacious and successful German resistance against the Allies: trains went to Auschwitz until October 24, when the death factory in Poland had only days left to function; and on December 14 to Ravensbrück and Flossenbürg; a final convoy of Jews went from Trieste to Bergen-Belsen on February 24, 1945.

Prisoners behind barbed wire in Auschwitz, 1945. (Institute of Contemporary History and Weiner Library, London)

Possibilities of Rescue

Variety of Opinion

A substantial commitment to rescue almost certainly could have saved several hundred thousand. . . . But America did not act at all until late in the war, and even then, though it had some success, the effort was a very limited one.

David S. Wyman

Although the possibility of murder was inherent in Nazi ideology, there were, apparently, alternatives. To realize these alternatives, the West needed different priorities: the preservation of human lives required a higher priority than military considerations.

Yehuda Bauer

It is very easy to claim that everyone should have known what would happen once Fascism came to power. But such an approach is ahistorical. . . . There was no precedent in recent European history for the murderous character of German National Socialism and for this reason most contemporaries were caught unprepared.

Walter Laqueur

Finally, we turn to reactions to the Holocaust by foreign governments and institutions. Word about the genocide of the Jews leaked to the outside world within months of its start. We will inquire into the policies of the United States and examine prospects of rescuing the Jews or slowing the Final Solution through negotiations or other outside action. Why was so little done and still less accomplished?

David S. Wyman delivers a scathing rebuke of American leaders for "abandoning" the Jews during the Holocaust. Convinced that hundreds of thousands of them could have been saved from the Final Solution, Wyman attacks the American State Department and the British Foreign Office for obstructing and sabotaging proposals that might have achieved that end. He faults the American president, Franklin Delano Roosevelt, for indifference to the Jews that, among other things, caused him to delay establishing the War Refugee Board, an official relief and rescue office, for fourteen critical months. In evaluating Wyman's points, it would be well to consider whether the Nazis and their allies might have been susceptible to outside pressures to release the Jews and whether alternative means of extermination could have been found had Auschwitz been bombed.

Yehuda Bauer cautiously explores possibilities of ransoming the Jews. Noting German willingness to negotiate for Jewish lives in Slovakia in 1942 and Hungary in 1944, he opens the door to such rescue by suggesting that the Nazis may not have been single-mindedly committed to genocide after all. Always exaggerating the power of "world Jewry," they may have hoped to secure a negotiated end to the war on terms favorable to Germany in return for Jewish lives. Other historians have pointed out that Western negotiations with Nazi Germany, especially in 1944, would have risked disrupting the anti-German alliance by increasing Stalin's suspicions of his wartime partners. That would have played directly into the hands of Hitler, who hoped to save himself by making a separate peace with the Soviet Union or the West. Bauer acknowledges that wartime priorities made such negotiations problematic, but he regrets that precedence was not given to saving Jewish lives.

Walter Laqueur questions people's ability to comprehend the Holocaust at the time it was happening. The Jews in Nazi hands, terrified and helpless, could not surmount the psychological obstacles to confronting their own extermination. Jews in the free world often denied the evidence before them out of vicarious participation in the horror of their coreligionists. Among the Allies, skepticism about stories that seemed inherently incredible and preoccupation with purely military objectives led to the same result. Perhaps nothing better illustrates this than the astonishment of American and British officers and newsmen upon the liberation of concentration camps in 1945. All had read and heard about Nazi atrocities, but they had not registered. Laqueur concentrates on the first year of the Holocaust, during which most of the victims died; however, the implications of his analysis apply to the entire period. They place issues of Jewish resistance and outside responses in arguably less moralistic light.

It should be clear from these essays that assessing prospects of rescue during the Holocaust depends on our understanding of several issues. Were the Nazis determined to kill all the Jews of Europe, or prepared to negotiate for their release? Were Allied leaders antisemitic, indifferent to the fate of the Jews, or lacking in imagination about how to help them? Or were these leaders helpless to act? If helpless, was that because of psychological impediments to comprehending the Holocaust, or because there was literally nothing they could do to save the Jews except defeat the Third Reich as quickly as possible?

David S. Wyman

The Abandonment of the Jews

Between June 1941 and May 1945, five to six million Jews perished at the hands of the Nazis and their collaborators. Germany's control over most of Europe meant that even a determined Allied rescue campaign probably could not have saved as many as a third of those who died. But a substantial commitment to rescue almost certainly could have saved several hundred thousand of them, and done so without compromising the war effort. The record clearly shows, though, that such a campaign would have taken place only if the United States had seized the initiative for it. But America did not act at all until late in the war, and even then, though it had some success, the effort was a very limited one. . . . Why did America fail to carry out the kind of rescue effort that it could have?

In summary form, these are the findings that I regard as most significant:

1. The American State Department and the British Foreign Office had no intention of rescuing large numbers of European Jews. On the contrary, they continually feared that Germany or other Axis nations might release tens of thousands of Jews into Allied hands. Any such exodus would have placed intense pressure on Britain to open Palestine and on the United States to take in more Jewish refugees, a situation the two great powers did not want to face. Consequently, their policies aimed at obstructing rescue possibilities and dampening public pressures for government action.

2. Authenticated information that the Nazis were systematically exterminating European Jewry was made public in the United States in November 1942. President Roosevelt did nothing about

From *The Abandonment of the Jews: America and the Holocaust, 1941–1945*, by David S. Wyman. Copyright © 1984 by David S. Wyman. Reprinted by permission of Pantheon Books, a division of Random House, Inc.

the mass murder for fourteen months, then moved only because he was confronted with political pressures he could not avoid and because his administration stood on the brink of a nasty scandal over its rescue policies.

3. The War Refugee Board, which the President then established to save Jews and other victims of the Nazis, received little power, almost no cooperation from Roosevelt or his administration, and grossly inadequate government funding. (Contributions from Jewish organizations, which were necessarily limited, covered 90 percent of the WRB's costs.) Through dedicated work by a relatively small number of people, the WRB managed to help save approximately 200,000 Jews and at least 20,000 non-Jews.

4. Because of State Department administrative policies, only 21,000 refugees were allowed to enter the United States during the three and one-half years the nation was at war with Germany. That amounted to 10 percent of the number who could have been legally admitted under the immigration quotas during that period.

5. Strong popular pressure for action would have brought a much fuller government commitment to rescue and would have produced it sooner. Several factors hampered the growth of public pressure. Among them were anti-Semitism and anti-immigration attitudes, both widespread in American society in that era and both entrenched in Congress; the mass media's failure to publicize Holocaust news, even though the wire services and other news sources made most of the information available to them; the near silence of the Christian churches and almost all of their leadership; the indifference of most of the nation's political and intellectual leaders; and the President's failure to speak out on the issue.

6. American Jewish leaders worked to publicize the European Jewish situation and pressed for government rescue steps. But their effectiveness was importantly diminished by their inability to mount a sustained or unified drive for government action, by diversion of energies into fighting among the several organizations, and by failure to assign top priority to the rescue issue.

7. In 1944 the United States War Department rejected several appeals to bomb the Auschwitz gas chambers and the railroads leading to Auschwitz, claiming that such actions would divert

essential airpower from decisive operations elsewhere. Yet in the very months that it was turning down the pleas, numerous massive American bombing raids were taking place within fifty miles of Auschwitz. Twice during that time large fleets of American heavy bombers struck industrial targets in the Auschwitz complex itself, not five miles from the gas chambers.

8. Analysis of the main rescue proposals put forward at the time, but brushed aside by government officials, yields convincing evidence that much more could have been done to rescue Jews, if a real effort had been made. The record also reveals that the reasons repeatedly invoked by government officials for not being able to rescue Jews could be put aside when it came to other Europeans who needed help.

9. Franklin Roosevelt's indifference to so momentous an historical event as the systematic annihilation of European Jewry emerges as the worst failure of his presidency.

10. Poor though it was, the American rescue record was better than that of Great Britain, Russia, or the other Allied nations. This was the case because of the work of the War Refugee Board, the fact that American Jewish organizations were willing to provide most of the WRB's funding, and the overseas rescue operations of several Jewish organizations. . . .

What could the American government have achieved if it had really committed itself to rescue? The possibilities were narrowed by the Nazis' determination to wipe out the Jews. War conditions themselves also made rescue difficult. And by mid-1942, when clear news of the systematic murder reached the West, two million Jews had already been massacred and the killing was going forward at a rapid rate. Most likely, it would not have been possible to rescue millions. But without impeding the war effort, additional tens of thousands — probably hundreds of thousands — could have been saved. What follows is a selection of twelve programs that could have been tried. All of them, and others, were proposed during the Holocaust.

1. Most important, the War Refugee Board should have been established in 1942. And it should have received adequate government funding and much broader powers.

2. The U.S. government, working through neutral governments or the Vatican, could have pressed Germany to release the Jews. If

nothing else, this would have demonstrated to the Nazis — and to the world — that America was committed to saving the European Jews. It is worth recalling that until late summer 1944, when the Germans blocked the Horthy offer, it was far from clear to the Allies that Germany would not let the Jews out. On the contrary, until then the State Department and the British Foreign Office feared that Hitler might confront the Allies with an exodus of Jews, a possibility that they assiduously sought to avoid.

In a related area, ransom overtures might have been much more thoroughly investigated. The use of blocked funds for this purpose would not have compromised the war effort. Nor, by early 1944, would payments of limited amounts of currency have hurt the progress of the war. . . .

3. The United States could have applied constant pressure on Axis satellites to release their Jews. By spring 1943, the State Department knew that some satellites, convinced that the war was lost, were seeking favorable peace terms. Stern threats of punishment for mistreating Jews or allowing their deportation, coupled with indications that permitting them to leave for safety would earn Allied goodwill, could have opened the way to the rescue of large numbers from Rumania, Bulgaria, Hungary, and perhaps Slovakia. Before the Germans took control of Italy, in September 1943, similar pressures might have persuaded the Italian government to allow its Jews to flee, as well as those in Italian-occupied areas of Greece, Yugoslavia, and France.

4. Success in setting off an exodus of Jews would have posed the problem of where they could go. Strong pressure needed to be applied to neutral countries near the Axis (Spain, Portugal, Turkey, Switzerland, and Sweden) to take Jews in. To bypass time-consuming immigration procedures, these nations could have been urged to set up reception camps near the borders. In return, the Allies should have offered to fund the operations, supply food, and guarantee removal of the refugees. At the same time, havens of refuge outside Europe were essential to accommodate a steady movement of Jews out of the neutral countries. Thus the routes would have remained open and a continuing flow of fugitives could have left Axis territory.

5. Locating enough outside havens, places beyond continental Eu-

rope where refugees could safely await postwar resettlement, would have presented difficulties. The problems encountered in finding havens for the limited numbers of Jews who did get out during the war pointed up the callousness of the Western world. But an American government deeply concerned about the Jews and willing to share the burden could have used its prestige and power to open doors. If a camp existence was all that was offered, that was still far preferable to deportation and death.

Ample room for camps was available in North Africa. In the United States, the immigration quotas were almost untouched; in addition, a government committed to rescue would have provided several camps besides Fort Ontario. A generous response by the United States would have put strong pressure on the Latin American nations, Canada, the British dominions, and Palestine. Instead, other countries used American stinginess as an excuse for not accepting Jews. For instance, in Jerusalem on his 1942 trip around the world, Wendell Willkie confronted the British leadership with the need to admit large numbers of Jews into Palestine. The British high commissioner replied that since the United States was not taking Jews in even up to the quota limits, Americans were hardly in a position to criticize.

6. Shipping was needed to transfer Jews from neutral countries to outside havens. Abundant evidence (summarized later in this chapter) proves that it could have been provided without interfering with the war effort.

The preceding steps, vigorously pursued, might have saved scores or even hundreds of thousands. Instead, important opportunities were lost by default. Early in 1943, the United States turned its back on the Rumanian proposal to release 70,000 Jews. It was a pivotal failure; seizure of that chance might have led to other overtures by Axis satellites.

At the same time, Switzerland was willing to accept thousands of children from France if it had assurance of their postwar removal. After refusing for more than a year, the State Department furnished the guarantee. But by then the main opportunity had passed. During the summer of 1943, the way opened for evacuating 500 children from the Balkans. But a boat had to be obtained within a month. The State Department responded with bureaucratic delays. Allied actions, instead of encouraging neutral countries to welcome fleeing Jews, influenced them to do the opposite. For instance, it took more than a year to move a few hundred refugees out of Spain to the long-promised camp in North Africa. With a determined American effort, these failures, and others, could have been successes.

7. A campaign to stimulate and assist escapes would have led to a sizable outflow of Jews. Once the neutral nations had agreed to open their borders, that information could have been publicized throughout Europe by radio, airdropped leaflets, and underground communications channels. Local currencies could have been purchased in occupied countries, often with blocked foreign accounts. These funds could have financed escape systems, false documentation, and bribery of lower-level officials. Underground movements were willing to cooperate. (The WRB, in fact, carried out such operations on a small scale.) Even without help, and despite closed borders, tens of thousands of Jews attempted to escape to Switzerland, Spain, Palestine, and other places. Thousands succeeded. With assistance, and assurance of acceptance into neutral nations, those thousands could have been scores of thousands.

8. Much larger sums of money should have been transferred to Europe. After the WRB was formed, the earlier, tiny trickle of funds from the United States was increased. But the amounts were still inadequate. Besides facilitating escapes, money would have helped in hiding Jews, supplying food and other essentials, strengthening Jewish undergrounds, and gaining the assistance of non-Jewish forces.

9. Much more effort should have gone into finding ways to send in food and medical supplies. The American government should have approached the problem far sooner than it did. And it should have put heavy pressure on the International Red Cross and British blockade authorities on this issue.

10. Drawing on its great prestige and influence, the United States could have applied much more pressure than it did on neutral governments, the Vatican, and the International Red Cross to induce them to take earlier and more vigorous action. By expanding their diplomatic missions in Axis countries, they would have increased the numbers of outside observers on the scene and perhaps inhibited actions against Jews. More impor-

tant, the measures taken by Raoul Wallenberg[1] in Budapest should have been implemented by all neutral diplomatic missions and repeated in city after city throughout Axis Europe. And they should have begun long before the summer of 1944.

The United States could also have pressed its two great allies to help. The Soviet Union turned away all requests for cooperation, including those from the WRB. An American government that was serious about rescue might have extracted some assistance from the Russians.

Britain, though more responsive, still compiled an abysmal record. Until 1944, Roosevelt and the State Department let the British lead in setting policy regarding European Jews. Even when the United States finally took the initiative, Roosevelt did not press for British cooperation. British officials resented the WRB, dismissed it as an election-year tactic, and tried to obstruct its work. The situation did not have to develop that way. An American president strongly committed to rescue could have insisted on a more helpful British response.

11. Some military assistance was possible. The Air Force could have eliminated the Auschwitz killing installations. Some bombing of deportation railroads was feasible. The military could have aided in other ways without impeding the war effort. It was, in fact, legally required to do so by the executive order that established the WRB.

12. Much more publicity about the extermination of the Jews should have been disseminated through Europe. Allied radio could have beamed the information for weeks at a time, on all possible wavelengths, as the Germans did regarding the alleged Russian massacre of Polish officers at the Katyn forest. This might have influenced three groups: the Christian populations, the Nazis, and the Jews. Western leaders and, especially, the Pope could have appealed to Christians not to cooperate in any way with the anti-Jewish programs, and to hide and to aid Jews whenever possible.

Roosevelt, Churchill, and the Pope might have made clear to the Nazis their full awareness of the mass-murder program

---

[1]A Swedish diplomat who saved thousands of Hungarian Jews by furnishing them with Swedish protection papers. — Ed.

and their severe condemnation of it. If, in addition, Roosevelt and Churchill had threatened punishment for these crimes and offered asylum to the Jews, the Nazis at least would have ceased to believe that the West did not care what they were doing to the Jews. That might possibly have slowed the killing. And it might have hastened the decision of the SS, ultimately taken in late 1944, to end the extermination. Even if top Nazis had brushed the threats aside, their subordinates might have been given pause.

The European Jews themselves should have been repeatedly warned of what was happening and told what the deportation trains really meant. (With good reason, the Nazis employed numerous precautions and ruses to keep this information from their victims.) Decades later, Rudolf Vrba, one of the escapees who exposed Auschwitz to the outside world, remained angry that the Jews had not been alerted. "Would anybody get me alive to Auschwitz if I had this information?" he demanded. "Would thousands and thousands of able-bodied Jewish men send their children, wives, mothers to Auschwitz from all over Europe, if they knew?" Roosevelt, Churchill, other Western leaders, and major Jewish spokesmen should have warned Jews over and over against the steps that led to deportation and urged them to try to hide or flee or resist. To help implement these actions, the Allies could have smuggled in cadres of specially trained Jewish agents.

None of these proposals guaranteed results. But all deserved serious consideration, and those that offered any chance of success should have been tried. There was a moral imperative to attempt everything possible that would not hurt the war effort. If that had been done, even if few or no lives had been saved, the moral obligation would have been fulfilled. But the outcome would not have been anything like that barren. The War Refugee Board, a very tardy, inadequately supported, partial commitment, saved several tens of thousands. A timely American rescue effort that had the wholehearted support of the government would have achieved much more.

A commitment of that caliber did not materialize. Instead, the Roosevelt administration turned aside most rescue proposals. In the process, government officials developed four main rationalizations for inaction. The most frequent excuse, the unavailability of shipping, was a fraud. When the Allies wanted to find ships for nonmilitary projects, they located them. In 1943, American naval vessels carried 1,400 non-Jewish Polish refugees from India to the American West Coast. The State and War departments arranged to move 2,000 Spanish Loyalist refugees to Mexico using military shipping. In March 1944, blaming the shipping shortage, the British backed out of an agreement to transport 630 Jewish refugees from Spain to the Fedala camp, near Casablanca. Yet at the same time, they were providing troopships to move non-Jewish refugees by the thousands from Yugoslavia to southern Italy and on to camps in Egypt.

When it was a matter of transporting Jews, ships could almost never be found. This was not because shipping was unavailable but because the Allies were unwilling to take the Jews in. In November 1943, Breckinridge Long told the House Foreign Affairs Committee that lack of transportation was the reason the State Department was issuing so few visas. "In December 1941," he explained, "most neutral shipping disappeared from the seas. . . . There just is not any transportation." In reality, ample shipping existed. Neutral vessels crossed the Atlantic throughout the war. Three Portuguese liners, with a combined capacity of 2,000 passengers, sailed regularly between Lisbon and U.S. ports. Each ship made the trip about every six weeks. Most of the time, because of the tight American visa policy, they carried only small fractions of their potential loads. Two dozen other Portuguese and Spanish passenger ships crossed the Atlantic less frequently but were available for fuller service. In addition, several score neutral cargo vessels could have been obtained and refitted to transport refugees.

American troopships and lend-lease and other cargo vessels could also have carried thousands of refugees across the Atlantic, clearing neutral European countries of fugitives and opening the way for a continuing exodus from Axis territory. War and State department correspondence shows that returning military transports could have performed this mission without hampering the war effort. In fact, U.S. Army authorities in North Africa offered in 1943 to take refugees to the United States on returning military ships. But the State and War departments blocked the plan.

In spring 1944, Roosevelt himself informed Pehle[2] that the Navy could bring refugees to the United States on returning troopships. The War Shipping Administration believed that Liberty ships could also have transported refugees effectively. While the State Department was claiming that transportation for refugees was unavailable, Liberty ships were having difficulty finding ballast for the return trips from North Africa.

The United States and Britain leased Swedish ships to carry food from the Western Hemisphere to Greece. Sweden readily furnished replacements and additions to this fleet. Despite repeated pleas, however, the two great Allies never managed to provide a single boat to ferry Jews from the Balkans to Turkey or to shuttle Jews across the Mediterranean to safety. Yet the War Department admitted to the War Refugee Board in spring 1944 that it had "ample shipping" available for evacuating refugees; the problem, it agreed, was to find places where they could go.

Another stock excuse for inaction was the claim that Axis governments planted agents among the refugees. Although this possibility needed to be watched carefully, the problem was vastly overemphasized and could have been handled through reasonable security screening. It was significant that Army intelligence found not one suspicious person when it checked the 982 refugees who arrived at Fort Ontario. Nevertheless, potential subversion was continually used as a reason for keeping immigration to the United States very tightly restricted. Turkey, Latin American nations, Britain, and other countries used the same exaggerated argument. It played an important part in blocking the channels of rescue.

A third rationalization for failing to aid European Jews took the high ground of nondiscrimination. It asserted that helping Jews would improperly single out one group for assistance when many peoples were suffering under Nazi brutality. Equating the genocide of the Jews with the oppression imposed on other Europeans was, in the words of one of the world's foremost churchmen, Willem Visser 't Hooft, "a dangerous half-truth which could only serve to distract attention from the fact that no other race was faced with the situation of having every one of its members . . . threatened by death in the gas chambers."

---

[2]John W. Pehle was the first director of the War Refugee Board. — Ed.

The Roosevelt administration, the British government, and the Intergovernmental Committee on Refugees regularly refused to acknowledge that the Jews faced a special situation. One reason for this was to avoid responsibility for taking special steps to save them. Such steps, if successful, would have confronted the Allies with the difficult problem of finding places to put the rescued Jews.

Another reason was the fear that special action for the Jews would stir up anti-Semitism. Some asserted that such action would even invite charges that the war was being fought for the Jews. Emanuel Celler[3] declared years later that Roosevelt did nearly nothing for rescue because he was afraid of the label "Jew Deal"; he feared the political effects of the accusation that he was pro-Jewish. The Jews, according to artist Arthur Szyk, were a skeleton in the democracies' political closet, a matter they would rather not mention. "They treat us as a pornographical subject," he wrote, "you cannot discuss it in polite society."[4]

The fourth well-worn excuse for rejecting rescue proposals was the claim that they would detract from the military effort and thus prolong the war. This argument, entirely valid with regard to projects that actually would have hurt the war effort, was used almost automatically to justify inaction. Virtually none of the rescue proposals involved enough infringement on the war effort to lengthen the conflict at all or to increase the number of casualties, military or civilian.

Actually, the war effort was bent from time to time to meet pressing humanitarian needs. In most of these instances, it was non-Jews who were helped. During 1942, 1943, and 1944, the Allies evacuated large numbers of non-Jewish Yugoslavs, Poles, and Greeks to safety in the Middle East, Africa, and elsewhere. Difficulties that constantly ruled out the rescue of Jews dissolved. Transportation somehow materialized to move 100,000 people to dozens of refugee camps that sprang into existence. The British furnished transport, supplies, much of the camp staffing, and many of the campsites. The United States contributed lend-lease materials and covered the bulk of the funding through UNRRA. Most of these refugees had

---

[3]Longtime Democratic U.S. Congressman from Brooklyn, N.Y. — Ed.

[4]The White House even avoided mentioning Jews in a brief presidential message commemorating the first anniversary of the Warsaw ghetto uprising.

been in desperate straits. None, though, were the objects of systematic annihilation.

Between November 1943 and September 1944, 36,000 Yugoslavs escaped to southern Italy. Most crossed the Adriatic by boat, thousands on British naval craft. Some even came out in American troop planes. The aircraft, sent mainly to evacuate wounded partisans, in many cases returned with civilians, including hundreds of orphaned babies. Using troopships, the British moved most of the Yugoslavs from Italy to camps in Egypt.

About 120,000 Poles, mostly men of military age and their dependents, came out of Russia during 1942 and passed into British-controlled camps in Iran. They were part of the remnant of a million and a half Poles the Soviets had deported to Siberia after the seizure of eastern Poland in September 1939. The Soviets released these thousands to join the British armed forces. Two-thirds of them did; the other 40,000 became refugees. Iran did not want them, supplying them was difficult, and conditions at the camps were bad. Most were moved out, mainly on British troopships, between August 1942 and August 1943. Ultimately, about 35,000 went to camps in Africa, India, Mexico, and the Middle East. The greatest numbers were placed in British colonies in East Africa, where camps were made available by shifting thousands of prisoners of war to the United States.

Despite the demands of war, the United States, with British support, extended significant help to the Greek people. Food for Greece moved freely through the blockade, and ships to carry it were located without trouble. American lend-lease funds paid for the project.

The Allies also helped thousands of Greeks to flee Nazi control and provided sanctuary for them in the Middle East and Africa. By 1944, 25,000 Greeks had been evacuated. The largest numbers, reported at between 9,000 and 12,000, were taken to Palestine — most to a former army installation at Nuseirat, near Gaza. Palestine also sheltered 1,800 of the non-Jewish Polish refugees. While the British, intent on keeping the small White Paper quota from being filled, turned back endangered Jews, they generously welcomed these other victims of the storm.

In all, Britain and the United States rescued 100,000 Yugoslav, Polish, and Greek refugees from disastrous conditions. Most of them traveled by military transport to camps where the Allies maintained them at considerable cost in funds, supplies, and even military staff. In contrast, the United States (with minimal cooperation from the British) evacuated fewer than 2,000 Jews to the three camps open to *them.* . . .

It was not a lack of workable plans that stood in the way of saving many thousands more European Jews. Nor was it insufficient shipping, the threat of infiltration by subversive agents, or the possibility that rescue projects would hamper the war effort. The real obstacle was the absence of a strong desire to rescue Jews. A month before the Bermuda Conference, the Committee for a Jewish Army declared:

> We, on our part, refuse to resign ourselves to the idea that our brains are powerless to find any solution. . . . In order to visualize the possibility of such a solution, imagine that the British people and the American nation had millions of residents in Europe. . . . Let us imagine that Hitler would staff a process of annihilation and would slaughter not two million Englishmen or Americans, not hundreds of thousands, but, let us say, only tens of thousands. . . . It is clear that the governments of Great Britain [and] the United States would certainly find ways and means to act instantly and to act effectively.

But the European Jews were not Americans and they were not English. It was their particular misfortune not only to be foreigners but also to be Jews.

Yehuda Bauer

Negotiating for Jewish Lives

Prior to the outbreak of war, the . . . Nazis were pursuing two parallel policies: forced emigration, which became shortly thereafter planned expulsion, and emigration by ransom, which is what the Rublee-Schacht agreement, in effect, amounted to. In 1939–41 emigration was still permitted in most of the Nazi domain. Between the beginning of planned mass murder in June 1941, in the conquered Soviet areas, and the cessation of legal Jewish emigration in October 1941, the two policies were pursued simultaneously: murder in the East, emigration (though partial) elsewhere.

Slovakia

In 1940, some 90,000 Jews lived in Slovakia, where a puppet fascist government, led by a Catholic priest, Father Jozef Tiso, fulfilled all Nazi wishes. Deportations to Poland began in March 1942 with the arrest and transport of 16-year-old girls to Auschwitz. The Tiso government eagerly adopted this atrocity, which was organized by Dieter Wisliceny, the Gestapo expert on Jewish affairs attached to the German embassy at Bratislava. For each Jew deported to Poland, the Tiso government paid the Nazis 500 RM.

A Judenrat imposed on the Jewish community was led by Arpad Sebestyen, who was loathed for his sheer inefficiency and abject slavishness toward authority. However, an illegal leadership group, called the "working group," was formed; it was led by a young, orthodox, anti-Zionist, religious fanatic, Rabbi Michael Dov-Ber Weissmandel, and his relative, a Zionist-secularist woman, Gizi Fleischmann, who was active in philanthropic causes and a leader of the local JDC[1] group.

Reprinted from Yehuda Bauer, A *History of the Holocaust*, © 1988, by permission of Grolier Publishing Co., Inc.

[1] Joint Distribution Committee, an American Jewish aid agency. — Ed.

Although they did not know that deportation[s] meant death, Weissmandel and Fleischmann desperately tried to stop them. They approached Wisliceny with an offer of money through the intermediary of a Jewish traitor who collaborated with the Nazis, Karl Hochberg. Weissmandel told Hochberg in June 1942 that he represented a world association of rabbis and could therefore pay in foreign currency. Wisliceny rose to the bait: If half the bribe of $50,000 was paid within two weeks, the deportations would cease for seven weeks; if the other half was then paid, deportations would cease completely. The Slovaks would have to be bribed separately. The "working group" collected $25,000 locally from Jewish businessmen who had held on to prewar dollars. The deportations stopped. But the second half of the bribe could not be collected — the JDC was not able to transfer cash from Switzerland, and Hungary's Jews refused to help. In September three Slovakian transports were sent to Poland. Finally, orthodox circles in Hungary collected the remaining sum. A fourth transport was sent to Poland after the second $25,000 was paid but after that no more deportations took place for two years.

Although Weissmandel and Fleischmann assumed that the deportations ceased because the bribe had been paid, historians later explained the situation by various other factors, such as the Nazi preoccupation at that time with their Russian offensive and the deportations from the Warsaw ghetto, which took place between July 22 and September 12. On June 26, Wisliceny and the German ambassador, Hans Ludin, met with the Slovak prime minister. In a report on that meeting and in a separate report to his Foreign Office, Ludin said that the deportations were stopped because of church pressure and the corruption of Slovak officials who had exempted 35,000 Jews for economic reasons.

Ludin's statements, however, were untruthful. Nothing like 35,000 Jews had been exempted. By June, nearly 50,000 Jews had been deported, and another 8,000 went in the September transports; of the remaining 40,000, only a few thousand at most were lucky enough to receive Slovak exemptions for economic reasons. The church intervened in March. The request by Slovak officials in May 1942 to see the paradise the Germans were building for the exiled Jews in Poland, caused perhaps by some stirrings of conscience, was denied in the usual Nazi style.

It seems that Ludin's reasons for stopping the deportations were a cover-up, that Weissmandel and Fleischmann were right after all. After the war Wisliceny said that he gave the money to Eichmann, who must have reported to Himmler. The bait was obviously not the paltry sum of money but the prospect of contacts with Weissmandel's "world association of rabbis" and their vast influence on America. After the war, Weissmandel put it this way: "Apart from the money, they wanted in this way to get in touch with Jews in the U.S., for some political reason that was more important to them than the extermination of Jews." What was that political reason?

In November 1942 Weissmandel wrote a letter on prewar Swiss paper using an old Underwood typewriter. He signed the letter "Ferdinand Roth," representative of World Jewry. In the letter, he asked the price the Nazis had set for stopping all deportations throughout Europe. When Wisliceny took the letter to Berlin, the Nazis again appeared to rise to the bait. After protracted negotiations, Wisliceny offered, in the name of his SS chiefs, to stop deportations from Western Europe and the Balkans for $2 million. Further negotiations on Poland and the actual Reich area might follow. By getting the money from abroad, the Nazis thus hoped to establish contact with "World Jewry." However, most Jewish aid organizations in the free world — the JDC, the World Jewish Congress, and others — rejected the Europa Plan, as it came to be called, as a blatant Nazi attempt to extort money; they did not believe deportations would cease. The Allies, of course, would not permit ransom monies to be transferred legally, and no such sums could be smuggled out of Switzerland — the only possible venue — illegally. Only the Jewish Agency and the Histadruth, the workers' trade-union organization in Palestine, managed, somewhat belatedly, to send £50,000 ($200,000) semi-legally to Palestinian Jewish emissaries in Istanbul. More time would pass until ways were found to smuggle such sums into Slovakia from Turkey. In the meantime, in August 1943, Wisliceny told Fleischmann that the negotiations were in abeyance, but that the Nazis might well renew them.

Hungary

The Zionist Va'adah[2] in Budapest was aware of the Europa Plan negotiations in Slovakia. Komoly and Kasztner, the heads of the

---

[2]Zionist Aid and Rescue Committee in Hungary. — Ed.

Va'adah, also decided to negotiate — Komoly would try to reach the Hungarian government and the underground; Kasztner would try to continue where the Europa Plan had left off; Brand[3] would establish escape routes to Slovakia and Rumania. An orthodox group and the Zionist youth movements, led by Rafi Benshalom (Friedl), engineered the flight of a few thousand people to both countries. Komoly's negotiations were fruitless. Kasztner met with Wisliceny and offered the equivalent of $2 million (as in the Europa Plan negotiations) for the ransom of Hungarian Jewry. Although the Nazis accepted the offer and promised that deportations would not occur, they actually viewed the $2 million as an "installment" on the road to "real" negotiations.

However, preliminary contacts ended abruptly on April 25, 1944, when Eichmann himself ordered Brand to appear before him. He offered to release one million Jews (i.e., not only the Jews of Hungary) in return for war materiel and other goods. In subsequent meetings the ransom became more specific: 10,000 trucks and quantities of tea, coffee, sugar, and soap. The trucks would not be used against the West but against the Soviets — a clumsy Nazi attempt to split the Allies. To negotiate via the Jewish Agency for Palestine with the Western Allies to get the goods, Brand would be sent to wherever he chose — he chose Istanbul. He would have a limited, though undefined, amount of time to get results. If the goods did not arrive, the Jews would be killed. When the Allies agreed to the plan, the first group of Jews would be released. On May 19 Brand arrived in Istanbul.

The Va'adah was unhappy with the choice of Brand for the mission. Why was Brand chosen, and not Kasztner? Joel Brand had been educated in Germany, had been a communist opponent of the Nazis, was arrested by them in 1933 and released in 1934, when he went to Budapest and joined the Zionist movement. Resourceful, brave and intelligent, Brand was also a heavy drinker and an adventurer with contacts in the Hungarian secret service.

However, a second figure was involved in the mission: Andor (Bandi) Grosz. Grosz, a convert, was a smuggler and a cheat. He had joined the German military secret service (the Abwehr), which was directed by the conservative anti-Hitlerite Admiral Wilhelm

---

[3]Joel Brand, a Hungarian Zionist and member of the Va'adah. — Ed.

Canaris, to escape punishment in Hungarian courts of law. In 1943 Grosz managed to be sent to Istanbul, where he worked for the Hungarian counterespionage unit as well as the American OSS and the British Intelligence Service. The Va'adah also contacted Grosz, and he became a courier, transmitting letters to and from Istanbul and Hungary. In February 1944 when Himmler's SD finally managed to dissolve the Abwehr, the SD itself became Germany's espionage and counterespionage agency. But the fight between the Abwehr and the SS (the parent body of the SD) had so disorganized the German services that by 1944 the only effective German contact with Western intelligence agencies was the quadruple agent, Bandi Grosz.

The leader of the SD, Walter Schellenberg, and his boss, Heinrich Himmler, were in early 1944 looking for a way to contact the Western Allies. The war was lost unless Germany could be saved by a separate peace with the Anglo-Americans. Himmler also knew that a strong, conservative opposition was bent on trying to eliminate Hitler. If they succeeded, Himmler's SS, rather than the disunited and inefficient rightists, would gain control of Germany. In the meantime, Abwehr contacts could be used to establish a dialogue with the West. But Brand was not the best choice for establishing contacts. It was Grosz who was entrusted with the offer to the Americans of a meeting with German military intelligence officers in a neutral country to discuss the possibility of a separate peace. On May 19 Grosz accompanied Brand to Istanbul — or, perhaps, Brand accompanied him.

Grosz contacted Allied intelligence. Brand, who had only a vague notion of Grosz's assignment, impressed on the Jewish Agency that the lives of a million people hung in the balance. He knew that the Hungarian deportations had started on May 14. The director of the Jewish Agency's political department, Moshe Sharett (who later became Israel's foreign minister and second prime minister), was refused permission by the Turks to come to Istanbul to meet with Brand. The Turks wanted Brand to leave Turkey, but Brand desperately tried to avoid returning to Hungary where he would be killed unless he had something to show for his efforts. After at first refusing to accept him, the British finally agreed to receive him, and he left Istanbul for British-held territory on June 6. Grosz had already done so on June 1.

In Cairo, Brand and Grosz were interrogated, and the purpose of their missions became clear. The Allies of course rejected any idea of separate peace negotiations with the SS. The British refused to negotiate via Brand, although they saw him as an honorable representative of the Jews and released him after a few months. The Americans, mainly the WRB, viewed the offer of the emissaries as a tool to be used to gain time. The Russians refused to permit any effort to be made to save the lives of people under Nazi rule.

It appears that the SS offer was serious. Because the Nazis believed the Jews controlled the West, they could be used as hostages. Their ransom might bring not only valuable war materials to a besieged Germany (this was the story Himmler "sold" to Hitler; Himmler's Nazi competitors knew nothing about Grosz) but might well move the Allies toward negotiating with the SS. . . .

The failure of the Brand mission did not dissuade the Nazis from using the Jews as a pawn to entice the Allies into negotiations. The Nazis contacted Jewish individuals and groups in Istanbul and Lisbon with offers to negotiate. Although the British refused, the WRB agreed to negotiate, intending to drag on discussions in the hope of saving lives until victory came. The person chosen to handle the negotiations was a Swiss citizen, Saly Mayer, the JDC representative in Switzerland. The instructions from Washington, which were transmitted by Roswell D. McClelland at Berne on August 21, 1944, stated that the United States "cannot enter into or authorize ransom transactions of the nature indicated by German authorities. If it was felt that a meeting between Saly Mayer and the German authorities would result in gaining time, the War Refugee Board has no objections to such a meeting." Mayer could not offer goods or money, nor could he speak in the name of the JDC.

Colonel Kurt Becher, a confidant of Himmler's in Hungary, was assigned to negotiate by the SS. The Jews of Budapest, whose deportation had been "postponed," were the first subjects of negotiation. In addition, a transport of 1,684 Jews organized by Kasztner in June 1944, which included not only his family and friends but representatives of all levels of Hungarian Jewry, was part of the bargaining package. After agreeing to send these people to a neutral country in exchange for a high ransom, the Nazis sent them instead to Bergen-Belsen, where people who might be exchanged for Germans abroad were imprisoned. The release of some members of that group was a precondition of the first Mayer-Becher meeting, which took place on the border bridge at St. Margarethen, between Switzerland and Germany, on August 21. On that day 318 Hungarian Jews arrived in Switzerland from Bergen-Belsen.

The Mayer-Becher negotiations continued until February 1945. Mayer managed to shift the discussion from goods and trucks to ransom money. He far exceeded the terms of his brief. A conservative, deeply religious, eccentric Jewish industrialist and philanthropist with a rather misanthropic bent, Mayer talked money to the Nazis, though he was expressly forbidden to do so. He ignored the Swiss government's warning on August 8 that Jews who escaped as a result of a ransom deal would be refused entry into Switzerland. And he actually bought Swiss tractors and shipped them to Germany to give the Nazis a reason to continue the negotiations.

On August 25 Himmler ordered that the deportations from Budapest be stopped — a "goodwill" token to keep the negotiations going. In December the other members of the Kasztner transport from Bergen-Belsen arrived. In the meantime, Mayer was trying to persuade the Nazis to permit the Red Cross to take over all "civilian" internment camps, Jewish and non-Jewish (i.e., slave labor, concentration, and death camps). The Red Cross would be using Allied monies and this would, in effect, constitute payment to the Nazis. But the Nazis wanted to contact the American government, an intention of which Mayer was well aware. On November 5 Mayer pulled off a major coup: He arranged a meeting between the Nazi Becher and the American diplomat McClelland in Zurich, at which he demanded that the Nazis stop all killings, release the orphans, and agree to the intervention of the Red Cross. Though the SS accepted Mayer's Red Cross idea only in part, and kept harping on the subject of ransom, Mayer did succeed in saving some lives. To have the clout that would allow the talks to continue, Mayer persuaded the Americans to transfer $5 million of JDC money to Switzerland to show the Nazis that he could deliver the goods (the money was so tied up, however, that he could not have used it).

In an effort to reach the Americans, the Nazis tried other approaches. Himmler met with a formerly pro-Nazi Swiss politician, Jean-Marie Musy, and sent emissaries who then contacted the WRB representative in Sweden, Iver Olsen. To Musy, Himmler released 1,200 Jewish inmates from Theresienstadt.

On January 15, 1945, a desperate Himmler asked his aide: "Who is it that the American government is really in contact with. Is it a Rabbi-Jew or is it the Jioint [sic]?" (The JDC was known in Europe as the Joint.) . . .

During the last weeks of the Reich, Himmler continued to negotiate. . . . Contrary to the wishes of the extreme SS faction — Ernst Kaltenbrunner, head of the security services, Eichmann, and others — Himmler wanted to keep some Jews alive to serve as hostages. Occasionally, his associates intervened to prevent the mass murders that the extreme faction demanded. In that sense, the negotiations pursued since 1942 served until the end — Ravensbrück, Bergen-Belsen, Buchenwald, and other camps were abandoned to the Allies without fighting.

Was Rescue by Negotiation Possible?

Throughout their rule, the Nazis advocated two alternative solutions, sometimes one to the exclusion of the other, sometimes both simultaneously: expulsion or sale of Jews, and mass murder. Because the Nazis saw the Jews as non-human, they could be sold — in exchange for peace with the West, for instance, to save the tottering Nazi empire. That seems to be the thread running through the story starting with Weissmandel's deal with Wisliceny in Slovakia in June, 1942, and ending with the Mayer-Becher talks in early 1945. In other words, although the possibility of murder was inherent in Nazi ideology, there were, apparently, alternatives. To realize these alternatives, the West needed different priorities: The preservation of human lives required a higher priority than military considerations. By negotiation, by bombing, and other means, some Jews — and others — could have been saved.

Walter Laqueur

The Failure to Comprehend

[T]here is one main pitfall in a work of this kind: the temptations of hindsight. Nothing is easier than to apportion praise and blame, writing many years after the events: some historians find the temptation irresistible. But the "final solution" more perhaps than any other subject should be approached in a spirit of caution and even humility. It is very easy to claim that everyone should have known what would happen once Fascism came to power. But such an approach is ahistorical. Nazism was an unprecedented phenomenon. In Fascist Italy, with all its evils, it is also true that during the twenty years of its existence some twenty enemies of the state (or of Mussolini) were actually executed, and of those some had, in fact, engaged in terrorist action. There was no precedent in recent European history for the murderous character of German National Socialism and for this reason most contemporaries were caught unprepared.

To understand this reluctance not only in Britain and the United States but also inside Germany and even among the Jews themselves to give credence to the news about the mass murder, one ought to consider the historical impact of the atrocity propaganda in the First World War. While this had not, of course, been the first war in which allegations had been made of widespread massacres and unspeakable cruelty, such propaganda campaigns had never before been conducted systematically on such a large scale. Both sides engaged in such propaganda, but the British and French with much greater effect than the Germans who felt aggrieved that they were losing the battle of words even though they had made a valiant effort to charge their enemies (and especially the Cossacks in East Prussia) with every possible crime.

Western allegations of German atrocities began with the violation of Belgian neutrality by the Germans in August 1914. The Germans, it was said, had ravished women and even young children, impaled and crucified men, cut off tongues and breasts, gouged eyes and burned down whole villages. These reports were not only carried in sensationalist newspapers but also endorsed by leading writers. . . .

Some readers probably remembered these stories when in June 1942 the Daily Telegraph was the first to report that 700,000 Jews had been gassed. For when the First World War had ended it soon appeared that many of these reports had either been invented — and some of the inventors admitted this much — or grossly exaggerated. The invasion of Belgium had indeed been a war crime, many Belgian civilians had been executed by the Germans on charges of armed resistance which were frequently unproven and there was a considerable amount of wanton destruction. But neither had the Allies always been wholly innocent and, in any case, it was a far cry from these acts to the allegations previously made with regard to German outrages. In the mid-twenties, Austen Chamberlain, the Foreign Secretary, admitted in Parliament that the story of the corpse factory had been without foundation. And as late as February 1938, on the eve of another war, Harold Nicolson said, also in the House of Commons, that "we had lied damnably," that the lies had done Britain tremendous harm and that he hoped that he would not see such propaganda again. Thus, when in late 1941 and 1942 information was again received about mass murder, about the use of poison gas and the manufacture of soap from corpses, the general inclination was to disbelieve it, frequently with reference to "lessons" from the First World War: no one wanted to be misled for the second time within one generation. Two vital circumstances were ignored: above all the fact that Nazi Germany of 1942 was a political regime very different from the Emperor's Reich of 1914, and secondly that even in the First World War, albeit in different conditions, large-scale killings had taken place in distant parts — the Armenian massacres. The atrocity propaganda of the First World War acted as a deterrent; it was not the only psychological obstacle making the acceptance of the horrible news so difficult, but certainly a very important one. Even what happened before 1939 in Germany and Austria could not be reasonably considered at the time the logical prelude to genocide. Hence the reluctance of the Jews both inside Europe and outside to believe the information about the "final solution." Accusations have been levelled against the Poles, the Western Allies and the Soviet leaders, against the Vatican and the Red Cross and almost everyone else for having betrayed the Jews. This study concerns itself not with the question of rescue but with the transmission of information. For all these countries and organizations the Jewish catastrophe was a marginal issue. This is particularly true for the main strategists of the war against Nazi Germany. Their paramount aim was to win the war against Hitler. Everything else was a matter of little interest and low priority. Winning the war in 1942 was bound to be more than a part-time preoccupation for the outcome was as yet by no means certain.

But *tout comprendre* is not necesssarily *tout pardonner*. When all allowances have been made, when all mitigating circumstances have been accorded, it is still true that few come out of the story unblemished. It was a story of failure to comprehend, among Jewish leaders and communities inside Europe and outside, a story of failure among non-Jews in high positions in neutral and Allied countries who did not care, or did not want to know or even suppressed the information.

It will be asked whether it really would have mattered if the world had accepted the facts of the mass murder earlier than it did. No one knows. Quite likely it would not have made much difference. The Jews inside Europe could not have escaped their fate, those outside were too weak to help, and the neutrals and the Allies might not have done more than they did in any case, which, as is known, was very little indeed.

But there is no certainty. It is unlikely that many of those killed in 1942 could have been saved. Militarily, Germany was still very strong, its hold on its allies and satellites unbroken. There were, however, ways and means to rescue some even then. They might or might not have succeeded, but they were not even tried. It was a double failure, first of comprehension and later of seizing the opportunities which still existed. . . .

The evidence gathered so far shows that news of the "final solution" had been received in 1942 all over Europe, even though all the details were not known. If so, why were the signals so frequently misunderstood and the message rejected?

1. The fact that Hitler had given an explicit order to kill all Jews was not known for a long time. His decision was taken soon after he had made up his mind to invade Russia. Victor Brack, who worked at the time in Hitler's Chancellery, said in evidence at Nuremberg that it was no secret in higher party circles by March 1941 that the Jews were to be exterminated. But "higher party circles" may have meant at the time no more than a dozen people. In March 1941, even Eichmann did not know, for the preparations for the deportations and the camps had not yet been made. First instructions to this effect were given in Goering's letter to Heydrich of 31 July 1941. The fact that an order had been given by Hitler became known outside Germany only in July 1942 and even then in a distorted form: Hitler (it was then claimed) had ordered that no Jew should be left in Germany by the end of 1942. But there is no evidence that such a time limit had ever been set. It would not have been difficult, for instance, to deport all Jews from Berlin in 1942, but in fact the city was declared empty of Jews by Goebbels only in August 1943. Witnesses claimed to have seen the order, but it is doubtful whether there ever was a written order. This has given rise to endless speculation and inspired a whole "revisionist" literature — quite needlessly, because Hitler, whatever his other vices, was not a bureaucrat. He was not in the habit of giving written orders on all occasions: there were no written orders for the murderous "purge" of June 1934, for the killing of gypsies, the so-called euthanasia action (T4) and on other such occasions. The more abominable the crime, the less likely that there would be a written "Führer order." If Himmler, Heydrich or even Eichmann said that there was such an order, no one would question or insist on seeing it.

2. The order had practical consequences, it affected the lives or, to be precise, the deaths of millions of people. For this reason details about the "final solution" seeped out virtually as soon as the mass slaughter started.

   The systematic massacres of the *Einsatzgruppen* in Eastern Galicia, White Russia, the Ukraine and the Baltic countries became known in Germany almost immediately. True, the scene of the slaughter was distant and it took place in territories in which at the time civilians and foreigners were not freely permitted to travel. But many thousands of German officers and soldiers witnessed these scenes and later reported them ·and the same is true of Italian, Hungarian and Romanian military personnel. The German Foreign Ministry was officially informed about the details of the massacres; there was much less secrecy about the *Einsatzgruppen* than later on about the extermination camps. The Soviet Government must have learned about the massacres within a few days; after several weeks the news became known in Western capitals too, well before the Wannsee Conference. The slaughter at Kiev (Babi Yar) took place on 29-30 September 1941. Foreign journalists knew about it within a few days; within less than two months it had been reported in the Western press. The massacres in Transniestria[1] became known almost immediately. Chelmno, the first extermination camp, was opened on 8 December 1941; the news was received in Warsaw within less than four weeks and published soon afterwards in the underground press. The existence and the function of Belzec and Treblinka were known in Warsaw among Jews and non-Jews within two weeks after the gas chambers had started operating. The news about the suicide of Czerniakow, the head of the Warsaw *Judenrat*, reached the Jewish press abroad within a short time. The deportations from Warsaw were known in London after four days. There were some exceptions: the true character of Auschwitz did not become known among Jews and Poles alike for several months after the camp had been turned into an extermination centre. At the time in Poland it was believed that there were only two types of camps, labour camps and extermination camps, and the fact that Auschwitz was a "mixed camp" seems to have baffled many.

3. If so much was known so quickly among the Jews of Eastern Europe and if the information was circulated through illegal newspapers and by other means — there were wireless sets in all major ghettos — why was it not believed? In the beginning Russian and Polish Jewry were genuinely unprepared, and the reasons have been stated: Soviet Jews had been kept uninformed about Nazi intentions and practices, Polish Jews believed that

[1]The area between Dniester and Bug Rivers where about 100,000 Jews were massacred in the summer of 1941 by Romanian troops and German *Einsatzgruppen*. — Ed.

the massacres would be limited to the former Soviet territories. At first there was the tendency to interpret these events in the light of the past: persecution and pogroms. The Jewish leaders in Warsaw who learned about events in Lithuania and Latvia in early 1942 should have realized that these were not "pogroms" in the traditional sense, spontaneous mob actions, nor excesses committed by local commanders. There are few arbitrary actions in a totalitarian regime. The *Einsatzgruppen* acted methodically and in cold blood. The majority of Jewish leaders in Eastern Europe did not yet realize that this was the beginning of a systematic campaign of destruction. The whole scheme was beyond human imagination; they thought the Nazis incapable of the murder of millions. Communication between some of the ghettos was irregular; Lodz ghetto, the second largest, was more or less isolated. But rumours, on the other hand, still travelled fast. If the information about the "final solution" had been believed it would have reached every corner of Poland within a few days. But it was not believed and when the "deportations" from Polish ghettos began in March 1942 it was still generally thought that the Jews would be transported to places further East.

The illegal newspapers and other sources conveyed disquieting news, and the possibility that many would perish was mentioned. But the information was contradictory. Most people did not read the underground press and there were no certainties. Perhaps the Nazis did after all need a large part of the Jewish population as a labour force for the war economy; perhaps the war would soon be over; perhaps a miracle of some sort or another would happen. Rumours are rife in desperate situations and so is the belief in miracles.

After July 1942 (the deportations from Warsaw) it is more and more difficult to understand that there still was widespread confusion about the Nazi designs among Jews in Poland, and that the rumours were not recognized for what they were — certainties. Any rational analysis of the situation would have shown that the Nazi aim was the destruction of all Jews. But the psychological pressures militated against rational analysis and created an atmosphere in which wishful thinking seemed to offer the only antidote to utter despair.

4. Of all the other Jewish communities only the Slovaks seem to have realized at an early date some of the dangers facing them. (So did the Romanians but their position was altogether different.) But even they failed to understand until late 1943 that the Nazis aimed at killing all Jews. The other communities (including German, Dutch, Danish, French, Greek Jews, etc.) seem to have lived in near ignorance almost to the very end. These communities were isolated, the means of information at their disposal limited. But with all this, most Jews in Europe, and many non-Jews, had at the very least heard rumours about some horrible events in Eastern Europe and some had heard more than rumours. These rumours reached them in dozens of different ways. But they were either not believed or it was assumed that "it cannot happen here." Only a relatively small minority tried to hide or escape, aware that deportation meant death. Nazi disinformation contributed to the confusion among the Jews. But the Nazi lies were usually quite threadbare and they cannot be considered the main source of the disorientation.

5. Jewish leaders and the public abroad (Britain, America and Palestine) found it exceedingly difficult in their great majority to accept the ample evidence about the "final solution" and did so only with considerable delay. They too thought in categories of persecution and pogroms at a time when a clear pattern had already emerged which pointed in a different direction. It was a failure of intelligence and imagination caused on one hand by a misjudgment of the murderous nature of Nazism, and on the other hand by a false optimism. Other factors may have played a certain role: the feeling of impotence ("we can do very little, so let us hope for the best"), the military dangers facing the Jewish community in Palestine in 1942. If the evidence was played down by many Jewish leaders and the Jewish press, it was not out of the desire to keep the community in a state of ignorance, but because there were genuine doubts. As the worst fears were confirmed, there was confusion among the leaders as to what course of action to choose. This was true especially in the US and caused further delay in making the news public. In Jerusalem the turning point came with the arrival of a group of Palestinian citizens who had been repatriated from Europe in November 1942. The leaders of the Jewish Agency, who had

been unwilling to accept the written evidence gathered by experienced observers, were ready to believe the accounts delivered by chance arrivals in face-to-face meetings.

6. The Polish underground played a pivotal role in the transmission of the news to the West. It had a fairly good intelligence-gathering network and also the means to convey the information abroad through short-wave radio and couriers. Most of the information about the Nazi policy of extermination reached Jewish circles abroad through the Polish underground. The Poles had few illusions about the intentions of the Nazis and their reports gave an unvarnished picture of the situation. They have been accused of playing down the Jewish catastrophe in order not to distract world opinion from the suffering of the Polish people, and of having temporarily discontinued the transmission to the West of news about the killing of the Jews. The Polish underground, needless to say, was mainly preoccupied with the fate of the Polish people, not with that of a minority. But it did not, on the whole, suppress the news about the mass killings in its bulletins and the information transmitted abroad. There was one exception — the period in late July, August and early September 1942 (the deportations from Warsaw), when the London Government-in-exile, either on its own initiative or following the advice of the British Foreign Office, did not immediately publicize the news received from Warsaw. The evidence is conflicting: the information was certainly played down for some time but there was no total blackout. There was delay in London but no more than the delay among the Jewish leaders who also disbelieved the information when they first received it. It cannot be proved whether or not the London Polish Government-in-exile did show the members of the National Council all the material received. But Zygielbojm and Schwarzbart certainly had access to all essential information. The Polish Government was the first to alarm the Allied governments and world public opinion but it was accused of exaggeration, as were the Jews at a later date. From this time up to the end of the war the number of victims given in the official declarations of the Allied governments was consistently too low. Even after it had been accepted in London and Washington that the information about the mass slaughter

was correct, the British and US governments showed much concern that it should not be given too much publicity.

7. Millions of Germans knew by late 1942 that the Jews had disappeared. Rumours about their fate reached Germany mainly through officers and soldiers returning from the eastern front but also through other channels. There were clear indications in the wartime speeches of the Nazi leaders that something more drastic than resettlement had happened. Knowledge about the exact manner in which they had been killed was restricted to a very few. It is, in fact, quite likely that while many Germans thought that the Jews were no longer alive, they did not necessarily believe that they were dead. Such belief, needless to say, is logically inconsistent, but a great many logical inconsistencies are accepted in wartime. Very few people had an interest in the fate of the Jews. Most individuals faced a great many more important problems. It was an unpleasant topic, speculations were unprofitable, discussions of the fate of the Jews were discouraged. Consideration of this question was pushed aside, blotted out for the duration.

8. Neutrals and international organizations such as the Vatican and the Red Cross knew the truth at an early stage. Not perhaps the whole truth, but enough to understand that few, if any, Jews would survive the war. The Vatican had an unrivalled net of informants all over Europe. It tried to intervene on some occasions on behalf of the Jews but had no wish to give publicity to the issue. For this would have exposed it to German attacks on one hand and pressure to do more from the Jews and the Allies. Jews, after all, were not Catholics. In normal times their persecution would have evoked expressions of genuine regret. But these were not normal times and since the Holy See could do little — or thought it could do little — even for the faithful Poles, it thought it could do even less for the Jews. This fear of the consequences of helping the Jews influenced its whole policy. The position of the International Red Cross was, broadly speaking, similar. It had, of course, fewer sources of information than the Catholic Church and less influence. But it also magnified its own weakness. It was less exposed, in fact, to retaliatory action than it thought, and while its protests might well have been to

no avail, it could have made known directly and indirectly the facts it knew. Some of its directors did so.

The neutral governments received much information about the "final solution" through many channels. There was no censorship in Sweden (except self-censorship) and in 1942 Swiss press censorship did not prevent publication of news about the fate of the Jews. Not all Swiss newspapers showed an equal measure of understanding and compassion, and the Swedish press had instructions not to report "atrocities," but their readers could have had few doubts about the true state of affairs by late 1942.

9. Neither the United States Government, nor Britain, nor Stalin showed any pronounced interest in the fate of the Jews. They were kept informed through Jewish organizations and through their own channels. From an early date the Soviet press published much general information about Nazi atrocities in the occupied areas but only rarely revealed that Jews were singled out for extermination. To this day the Soviet Communist Party line has not changed in this respect: it has not admitted that any mistakes were made, that the Jewish population was quite unprepared for the *Einsatzgruppen*. It is not conceded even now that if specific warnings had been given by the Soviet media in 1941 (which were informed about events behind the German lines) lives might have been saved. As far as the Soviet publications are concerned the Government and the Communist Party acted correctly — Soviet citizens of Jewish origin did not fare differently from the rest under Nazi rule, and if they did, it is thought inadvisable to mention this. The only mildly critical voices that have been heard can be found in a few literary works describing the events of 1941–2. Some Western observers have argued that the (infrequent) early Soviet news about anti-Jewish massacres committed were sometimes dismissed as "Communist propaganda" in the West and that for this reason the Soviet leaders decided no longer to emphasize the specific anti-Jewish character of the extermination campaign. This explanation is not at all convincing because Soviet policy at home was hardly influenced by the *Catholic Times*, and it should be stressed that domestically even less publicity than abroad was given to the Jewish victims from the very beginning.

In London and Washington the facts about the "final solution" were known from an early date and reached the chiefs of intelligence, the secretaries of foreign affairs and defence. But the facts were not considered to be of great interest or importance and at least some of the officials did not believe them, or at least thought them exaggerated. There was no deliberate attempt to stop the flow of information on the mass killings (except for a while on the part of officials in the State Department), but mainly lack of interest and disbelief. This disbelief can be explained against the background of Anglo-American lack of knowledge of European affairs in general and Nazism in particular. Although it was generally accepted that the Nazis behaved in a less gentlemanly way than the German armies in 1914-18, the idea of genocide nevertheless seemed far fetched. Neither the *Luftwaffe* nor the German navy nor the Afrika Korps had committed such acts of atrocities, and these were the only sections of the German armed forces which Allied soldiers encountered prior to 1944. The Gestapo was known from not very credible B-grade movies. Barbaric fanaticism was unacceptable to people thinking on pragmatic lines, who believed that slave labour rather than annihilation was the fate of the Jews in Europe. The evil nature of Nazism was beyond their comprehension.

But even if the realities of the "final solution" had been accepted in London and Washington the issue would still have figured very low on the scale of Allied priorities. 1942 was a critical year in the course of the war, strategists and bureaucrats were not to be deflected in the pursuit of victory by considerations not directly connected with the war effort. Thus too much publicity about the mass murder seemed undesirable, for it was bound to generate demands to help the Jews and this was thought to be detrimental to the war effort. Even in later years when victory was already assured there was little willingness to help. Churchill showed more interest in the Jewish tragedy than Roosevelt and also more compassion but even he was not willing to devote much thought to the subject. Public opinion in Britain, the United States and elsewhere was kept informed through the press from an early date about the progress of the "final solution." But the impact of the news was small or at most shortlived. The fact that millions were killed was more or less meaningless. People could identify perhaps with the fate of a single individual or a family but not with the fate of millions. The statistics of murder were either disbelieved or dismissed from consciousness. Hence the surprise and shock at the end of the war when the reports about a "transit camp" such as Bergen-Belsen came in: "No one had known, no one had been prepared for this."

Thus the news about the murder of many millions of Jews was not accepted for a long time and even when it had been accepted the full implications were not understood. Among Jews this frequently caused a trauma in later years which in extreme cases led to the belief that every danger facing Jews, individually or as a group, had to be interpreted in terms of a new holocaust. Such a distortion of reality is psychologically understandable, which does not make it any less dangerous as a potentially disastrous political guideline. The impact among non-Jews has been small. There have been, after all, many intelligence failures throughout history. Optimists could still argue that one failure should not inspire pessimism and strengthen the argument for worst case analysis. As the long term (1910–50) British diplomat rightly said, his record as an inveterate optimist has been far more impressive than that of the professional Cassandras forever harping on the danger of war. He had been wrong only twice. . . .

It has been said that in wartime there are no "strategic warnings," no unambiguous signals, no absolute certainties. Not only the signals have to be considered but also the background noise, the interference, the deception. If even Barbarossa and Pearl Harbor came as a surprise, despite the fact that the eyes of the whole world were scanning the horizons for such signals — and despite the fact that there was much evidence and many warnings to this effect — is it not natural that European Jewry was taken unaware? But there was one fundamental difference: Barbarossa and Pearl Harbor were surprise attacks, whereas the "final solution" proceeded in stages over a long period. Some have claimed in retrospect that *Mein Kampf* and Hitler's speeches should have dispelled any doubts about the Nazis' ultimate murderous intentions. But this is wrong. The "solution of the Jewish question" could equally have meant ghettoization or expulsion to some far-away place such as Madagascar. It was only after the invasion of the Soviet Union that there was reason to believe that large parts of European Jewry would not survive the war. At first there were only isolated rumours, then the rumours thickened and eventually they became certainties. A moderately well informed Jewish resident of Warsaw should have drawn the correct conclusions by May 1942 and some of them did. But the time and the place were hardly conducive to detached, objective analysis; the disintegration of rational intelligence is one of the recurrent themes of all those who have written about that period on the basis of inside knowledge.

Democratic societies demonstrated on this occasion as on many others, before and after, that they are incapable of understanding political regimes of a different character. Not every modern dictatorship is Hitlerian in character and engages in genocide but every one has the potential to do so. Democratic societies are accustomed to think in liberal, pragmatic categories; conflicts are believed to be based on misunderstandings and can be solved with a minimum of good will; extremism is a temporary aberration, so is irrational behaviour in general, such as intolerance, cruelty, etc. The effort to overcome such basic psychological handicaps is immense. It will be undertaken only in the light of immediate (and painful) experience. Each new generation faces this challenge again for experience cannot be inherited.

The reaction of East European Jewry can only be understood out of their specific situation in 1942. But there are situations which cannot be recreated, however sophisticated the techniques of simulation, however great the capacity for empathy and imagination. Generalizations about human behaviour in the face of disaster are of limited value: each disaster is different. Some of those who lived through the catastrophe have tried in later years to find explanations. But while their accounts are of great interest, they are no longer *a priori* reliable witnesses. Their explanations are rooted in a different situation and this is bound to lead to a rationalization of irrational behaviour. The "final solution" proceeded in stages, chronologically and geographically. This should have acted as a deterrent, but it did not, on the whole, have this effect. There were no certainties, only rumours, no full picture, only fragments. Was it a case of a "people without understanding," which had eyes and ears but saw not and heard not? The people saw and heard but what it perceived was not always clear, and when at last the message was unambiguous it left no room for hope and was therefore unacceptable. It is a syndrome observed by biblical prophets and modern political leaders alike, that it is natural for man to indulge in the illusions of hope and to shut his eyes against a painful truth.

But it is not natural for man to submit passively to a horrible fate, not to try to escape, however great the odds against success, not to resist, even if there is no prospect of victory. True, there are explanations even for paralysis, but later generations can no longer accept them — hence the abiding mystery. Total hopelessness (the psychologists say) results in inaction; when there is no exit, such as in a mine or a submarine disaster, this leads to resignation.

The reaction of Dutch or Hungarian Jews can be compared to that of people facing a flood and who in contradiction of all experience believe that they will not be affected but are individually or as a group invulnerable. Some social psychologists will argue that such a denial of a threat betrays a fear of not being able to cope with it. But if such an explanation was true for some it certainly did not apply to others. They genuinely did not know what was in store for them. Danish Jews were perfectly able to escape to Sweden and if they did so only at the very last moment the reason was that they genuinely believed that they would not be deported. Equally, to give another example, the Jews living in Rhodes could have fled without difficulty to Turkey and would have done so had they known their fate in Auschwitz. But they did not know. Other Jewish communities were indeed trapped but their situation was still not identical with that of the victims of a mine disaster. Comparisons are only of limited help for understanding human behaviour in unique situations. In many cases the inactivity of Jews, individuals and groups, was not the result of paralysis but on the contrary of unwarranted optimism. . . .

One of the questions initially asked was whether it would have made any difference if the information about the mass murder had been believed right from the beginning. It seems quite likely that relatively few people might have been saved as a result and even this is not absolutely certain. But this is hardly the right way of posing the question, for the misjudgment of Hitler and Nazism did not begin in June 1941 nor did it end in December 1942. The ideal time to stop Hitler was not when he was at the height of his strength. If the democracies had shown greater foresight, solidarity and resolution, Nazism could have been stopped at the beginning of its campaign of aggression. No power could have saved the majority of the Jews of the Reich and of Eastern Europe in the summer of 1942. Some more would have tried to escape their fate if the information had been made widely known. Some could have been saved if Hitler's satellites had been threatened and if the peoples of Europe had been called to extend help to the Jews. After the winter of 1942 the situation rapidly changed: the satellite leaders and even some of the German officials were no longer eager to be accessories to mass murder. Some, at least, would have responded to Allied pressure, but such pressure was never exerted. Many Jews could certainly have been saved in 1944 by bombing the railway lines leading to the extermination centres, and of course, the centres themselves. This could have been done without deflecting any major resources from the general war effort. It has been argued that the Jews could not have escaped in any case but this is not correct: the Russians were no longer far away, the German forces in Poland were concentrated in some of the bigger towns, and even there their sway ran only in daytime — they no longer had the manpower to round up escaped Jews. In short, hundreds of thousands could have been saved. But this discussion belongs to a later period. The failure to read correctly the signs in 1941–2 was only one link in a chain of failures. There was not one reason for this overall failure but many different ones: paralyzing fear on one hand and, on the contrary, reckless optimism on the other; disbelief stemming from a lack of experience or imagination or genuine ignorance or a mixture of some or all of these things. In some cases the motives were creditable, in others damnable. In some instances moral categories are simply not applicable, and there were also cases which defy understanding to this day.

Suggestions for Additional Reading

Only a few of the most important studies of the Holocaust can be included here. This brief bibliography is restricted to literature available in English and does not include any of the works excerpted in this volume.

Reliable general surveys and analyses of the Holocaust may be found in:

Lucy S. Dawidowicz, *The War Against the Jews* (New York: 1975).

Martin Gilbert, *The Holocaust: A History of the Jews in Europe During the Second World War* (London: 1986).

Michael R. Marrus, *The Holocaust in History* (Hanover, N.H., and London: 1987).

Leni Yahil, *The Holocaust: The Fate of European Jewry, 1932–1945* (New York and Oxford: 1991).

Useful collections of documents related to the Holocaust are:

Lucy S. Dawidowicz, ed., *A Holocaust Reader* (New York: 1976).

Raul Hilberg, ed., *Documents of Destruction: Germany and Jewry, 1933–1945* (Chicago: 1971).

Richard S. Levy, *Anti-Semitism in the Modern World: An Anthology of Texts* (Lexington, Mass., and Toronto: 1991).

John Mendelsohn, ed., *The Holocaust: Selected Documents in Eighteen Volumes* (New York: 1982).

On the Jews and antisemitism before the Holocaust, see:

Jacob Katz, *From Prejudice to Destruction: Anti-Semitism, 1700–1933* (Cambridge, Mass.: 1980).

Steven T. Katz, *The Holocaust in Historical Context* (New York: 1994).

Richard S. Levy, *The Downfall of the Anti-Semitic Political Parties in Imperial Germany* (New Haven, Conn., and London: 1975).

Ezra Mendelsohn, *The Jews of East Central Europe Between the Two World Wars* (Bloomington, Ind.: 1983).

George Mosse, *Toward the Final Solution: A History of European Racism* (London: 1978).

Donald L. Niewyk, *The Jews in Weimar Germany* (Baton Rouge, La., and London: 1980).

Bruce F. Pauley, *From Prejudice to Persecution: A History of Austrian Anti-Semitism* (Chapel Hill, N.C.: 1992).

Leon Poliakov, *A History of Anti-Semitism*, 4 vols. (New York: 1965–1986).

Peter G. J. Pulzer, *The Rise of Political Anti-Semitism in Germany and Austria* (New York: 1964).

Karl Schleunes, *The Twisted Road to Auschwitz: Nazi Policies Toward the Jews, 1933–1939* (Urbana, Ill.: 1970).

The most useful books on Hitler and the Nazi state are:

Karl Dietrich Bracher, *The German Dictatorship: The Origins, Structure and Effects of National Socialism* (New York: 1970).

Christopher R. Browning, *The Final Solution and the German Foreign Office* (New York: 1978).

Alan Bullock, *Hitler: A Study in Tyranny* (New York and Evanston, Ill.: 1962).

Philippe Burrin, *Hitler and the Jews: The Genesis of the Holocaust* (London: 1994).

Joachim C. Fest, *Hitler* (New York: 1974).

Henry Friedlander, *The Origins of Nazi Genocide: From Euthanasia to the Final Solution* (Chapel Hill, N.C.: 1995).

Heinz Höhne, *The Order of the Death's Head: The Story of Hitler's SS* (London: 1972).

Eberhard Jäckel, *Hitler's Weltanschauung: A Blueprint for Power* (Middletown: 1972); and *Hitler in History* (Hanover, N.H.: 1984).

Robert Koehl, *The Black Corps: The Structure and Power Struggles of the Nazi SS* (Madison, Wis.: 1983).

On the Holocaust experience, a few of the most important firsthand accounts by victims are:

Moshe Garbarz, *A Survivor* (Detroit: 1992).

Raul Hilberg et al., eds., *The Warsaw Diary of Adam Czerniakow* (New York: 1979).

Judith Isaacson, *Seed of Sarah* (Urbana, Ill.: 1990).

Gerda Klein, *All But My Life* (New York: 1971).
Primo Levi, *Survival in Auschwitz* (New York: 1969).
Frida Michelson, *I Survived Rumbuli* (New York: 1979).
Filip Mueller, *Eyewitness Auschwitz* (New York: 1979).
Emmanuel Ringelblum, *Notes from the Warsaw Ghetto* (New York: 1974).
Elie Wiesel, *Night* (New York: 1970).

Scholars' efforts to understand the Holocaust experience may be found in:

Yitzhak Arad, *Ghetto in Flames: The Struggle and Destruction of the Jews in Vilna in the Holocaust* (Jerusalem: 1980).
Hannah Arendt, *Eichmann in Jerusalem* (New York: 1963).
Yisrael Gutman and Michael Berenbaum, eds., *Anatomy of the Auschwitz Death Camp* (Bloomington, Ind.: 1994).
George M. Kren and Leon Rappoport, *The Holocaust and the Crisis of Human Behavior* (New York: 1980).
Isaiah Trunk, *Jewish Responses to Nazi Persecution* (New York: 1982).

On Jewish resistance, one may consult:

Reuben Ainsztein, *Jewish Resistance in Nazi-Occupied Eastern Europe* (New York: 1974).
Yehuda Bauer, *They Chose Life: Jewish Resistance in the Holocaust* (New York: 1973).
Yisrael Gutman, *The Jews of Warsaw, 1939–1943: Ghetto, Underground, Revolt* (Bloomington, Ind.: 1983).
Shmuel Krakowski, *The War of the Doomed: Jewish Armed Resistance in Poland, 1942–1944* (New York: 1984).
Annie Latour, *Jewish Resistance in France* (New York: 1981).
Dov Levin, *Fighting Back: Lithuanian Jewry's Armed Resistance to the Nazis, 1941–1944* (New York: 1985).
Yuri Suhl, ed., *They Fought Back: The Story of the Jewish Resistance in Nazi Europe* (New York: 1975).
Nechama Tec, *The Bielski Partisans* (New York: 1993).

Gentile reactions to the Holocaust are considered in:

David Bankier, *The Germans and the Final Solution* (Oxford: 1992).

Randolph L. Braham, *The Politics of Genocide: The Holocaust in Hungary* (New York: 1981).

Frederick Chary, *The Bulgarian Jews and the Final Solution, 1940–1944* (Pittsburgh, Pa.: 1972).

Helen Fein, *Accounting for Genocide: National Responses and Jewish Victimization During the Holocaust* (New York: 1979).

Sarah Gordon, *Hitler, Germans, and the "Jewish Question"* (Princeton, N.J.: 1984).

Michael R. Marrus and Robert O. Paxton, *Vichy France and the Jews* (New York: 1981).

Meier Michaelis, *Mussolini and the Jews: German-Italian Relations and the Jewish Question in Italy, 1922–1945* (Oxford: 1978).

Jacob Presser, *The Destruction of the Dutch Jews* (New York: 1969).

Emmanuel Ringelblum, *Polish-Jewish Relations During the Second World War* (New York: 1976).

Nechama Tec, *When Light Pierced the Darkness: Christian Rescue of Jews in Nazi Occupied Poland* (New York: 1986).

Leni Yahil, *The Rescue of Danish Jewry* (Philadelphia, Pa.: 1969).

Susan Zuccotti, *The Italians and the Holocaust: Persecution, Rescue, and Survival* (New York: 1987).

On issues surrounding the rescue of the Jews by outside forces, see:

Irving Abella and Harold Troper, *None Is Too Many: Canada and the Jews of Europe, 1933–1948* (Toronto: 1982).

Yehuda Bauer, *Jews for Sale? Nazi-Jewish Negotiations, 1933–1945* (New Haven, Conn.: 1994).

Saul Friedlander, *Pius XII and the Third Reich: A Documentation* (New York: 1966).

Martin Gilbert, *Auschwitz and the Allies* (New York: 1981).

John F. Morley, *Vatican Diplomacy and the Holocaust, 1939–1943* (New York: 1980).

Monty N. Penkower, *The Jews Were Expendable: Free World Diplomacy and the Holocaust* (Urbana, Ill.: 1983).

Bernard Wasserstein, *Britain and the Jews of Europe, 1939–1945* (London: 1979).

Alex Weissberg, *Desperate Mission: Joel Brand's Story* (New York: 1958).